My Stars Are Still Shining

My Stars Are Still Shining

A MEMOIR

Amina Warsuma

Shining stars lead me to and from the incidents that have happened in my life. I wish to share what I have learned from my experiences and hope to enlightened the world by them. My stars are still shining and leading me to new adventures and experiences that I may one day add to this memoir.

ISBN - 10: 0692864423
ISBN-13: 9780692864425 (Custom Universal)

To Jayson. You are my number one son.

Contents

CHAPTER 1

Babies in Harlem

I HAVE OFTEN WONDERED HOW people enter other people's lives and become a significant part of their senior years. I'm not talking about family or grandchildren. I'm talking about strangers. This memoir is about my life and how I happened to come into the lives of Miss June, who was sixty-nine, and her daughter Billie, who was fifty-one when I came into their lives. There is a beginning, a middle, and an end of our relationship. I must start from the beginning of their lives, because never in a thousand years could they imagine meeting me.

My mother, Virginia, hadn't been born when Miss June and Billie lived in Mobile, Alabama, without an inkling of New York or what the future held in store for them. I give an account of what transpired and led up to their migration to Harlem, forsaking their past life to become settled into being Harlemites. Thirty-four years later, out of the blue, Miss June and Billie discovered me as an infant. I was floating down the river of life, and they fetched me out, not realizing they both would be entwined in my life forever.

On January 10, 1885, Elizabeth June Keller was born and grew up in Mobile, Alabama. She lived with her mother and father and her eighteen siblings. Elizabeth was the oldest and had to babysit her brothers and sisters. While her parents went to work, Miss June was not able to attend school because of her responsibilities. She resented the restrictions imposed upon her, and she became an angry bully, attacking the kids who passed her house on their way to school. Miss June took their lunches. Some of the kids fought her back, except those she beat up.

When Miss June turned eighteen, she was excited to get out of the house before her siblings came home from school each afternoon. While shopping in town for her siblings, she met a white sheriff named Bill Hasty, and there was an instant attraction. Sheriff Hasty looked like he could have been on the TV western *Bonanza*. He had a big body like Hoss Cartwright and a handsome face like Ben Cartwright.

Miss June was five foot seven and half Muskogean Indian. They were relatives of the Choctaw tribe, which was forced to leave Mobile, Alabama, and move to a reservation in the 1800s. She had beautiful, dark, reddish-brown skin and a thin, shapely figure. That appealed to Sheriff Hasty, along with her calm temperament. White men in the South didn't like emotional black women. That was a white lady's job—to be emotional and demand more than her man was willing to give. He approached her. He had money, position, and power. And he liked her. She wasn't fazed by his parents' rejection of her. He and Elizabeth June were lovers.

She became pregnant, and at eighteen, she gave birth to her daughter, Willie Mae Hasty, on February 26, 1903. Willie Mae was the child of Sheriff Hasty. He called his daughter Billie for short and called her mother Miss June. After Miss June became a new mother, the time came for her to have her own house. Sheriff Hasty rented a small house in the black section of Mobile, and Miss June and Billie moved in. She bought comfortable, quality furniture at a low price from a black carpenter who lived in her neighborhood.

The sheriff paid for everything and provided generously for Miss June and Billie.

Sheriff Hasty didn't have a wife at the time; he had two brothers, two sisters, parents, and grandparents. In the 1900s, they all lived in a big house in the white section of Mobile. White men slept with black women all the time in the South. It was the norm, and if a white man raped a black woman or girl, nobody cared it was the norm. When Sheriff Hasty started sleeping with Miss June, his family didn't care. By no means did they accept her. Billie could pass for a white child, and Sheriff Hasty and his family wanted to raise her. Miss June refused to let them; she believed her daughter should be with her mother. Sheriff Hasty didn't force her to give up Billie.

He allowed Billie to visit him and his family. As a child and young girl, she blended in with Sheriff Hasty's family. Billie looked exactly like him. She had a beautiful milky-white face, a big body, and jet-black hair.

When she got angry, the skin tone on her face turned red, and you could see traces of Muskogean Indian. Growing up between 1903 and 1924, Billie had two families. She graduated from high school, which is a plus to her character.

At that time in America, Miss June couldn't marry Sheriff Hasty because it was illegal for blacks to marry whites. Although he cared deeply for Miss June, his family pressured him to get married to a white woman. As time passed, Sheriff Hasty married a white woman, and Miss June chose not to experience childbirth again. She never forgot how physically painful it was to give birth to Billie.

It didn't look right for Miss June to be unmarried with a child, so she married a black man named Mr. Denny Harris. He made sure everyone addressed him as Mr. Harris. He moved in with Miss June and Billie. Mr. Harris had a good job working in the lumberyard, cutting wood for house construction. He had a heavy workload; he left early in the morning and returned late at night. One day he didn't come back. Miss June filed a missing persons report. Nonetheless, Mr. Harris had vanished, never to be seen again. No one ever searched for him or had hopes of seeing him again.

In the South, it was a known fact that a certain number of black men disappeared, as if they never existed. Many did not have a birth certificate, because they were born in a shack and not in a hospital. Miss June kept her married name: Mrs. Elizabeth June Harris. It looked respectable, and it gave her the image that someone thought she was good enough to marry. Many black men and women got fed up with a life of drudgery, hard work, and no respect. It wasn't easy for a woman to walk out on her family. Is it considered mama's baby and papa are maybe? That's an old saying that the people of the South used it means that it was mama's baby and maybe papa's There wasn't DNA testing to prove a man was the father of a child. A man could easily deny the child. Without a word, the black male would walk out on their families, jobs, and towns. They ran off, searching for a glimmer of freedom and their pot of gold at the end of the rainbow.

Although Billie could pass for a white woman, she identified herself as black. At twenty-two years old, Billie married a black man named Mr. Earl West. Earl held a good-paying position as a chauffeur for a wealthy white family in Mobile. Billie and Earl saw each other on her way to visit Sheriff Hasty since she always walked by the wealthy family's house to visit her father. Earl sat in the family's limousine and discreetly admired Billie from afar. Even with his courageous, handsome, masculine persona, he didn't dare speak or flirt with Billie.

Earl perceived Billie to be a white woman, and he knew a black man would be hanged from the highest tree if he were caught flirting with a white female. Cornell and a group of attractive mulatto women all spent time together. Cornell befriended Billie, in the South individuals, who are similar are grouped together. Depending on what color your skin tone appeared to be. Cornell gave house parties on weekends, and Billie had an open invitation. One night Earl and Billie attended a party at Cornell's home. Cornell formally introduced Earl to Billie, and they liked each other right from the start. Cornell's house had a trail of beautiful, well-dressed girls and men lined up along the walls of the living room and outside on the porch. Some of the men and girls were dancing with each other in the middle of the living-room floor. Gentlemen were sitting at the dining-room table drinking liquor and eating with the girls.

Cornell's parties became a release from the daily stresses and strains of hardworking Southern life. Cornell loved being the ultimate hostess. She had the good fortune to have an array of scantily clad, beautiful, mulatto, brown- and dark-skinned girls all around her. Where there were girls, the men came flocking at her feet like bees to honey. They spent whatever money they had to stay in her good grace. One wrong word from Cornell, and the men were inevitably cut off from the honeycomb of girls. Out of all the girls at the party, Earl accompanied Billie throughout the night. Earl asked Billie to go out on dates with him, and she agreed. In those days, you either clicked or you didn't with a man.

There were too many women who were marriage material for a man to choose from. Earl needed a wife, and Billie gained a husband. Cornell liked to party and waste time. She couldn't envision Earl changing Billie's life and be seriously married to her. After Earl and Billie married, he moved her out of Miss June's house. The newlyweds acquired their own comfortably furnished residence on the same street as Miss June's house. Billie couldn't imagine living far away from her mother. Billie and Earl stayed married for three years. Billie eased into the role of a stay-at-home wife while her husband worked every day. Billie partied all day with her friends Cornell, Marion, Katherine, and Money.

Cornell could pass for a white woman. She was single, while the rest of the ladies were married and had dark-brown skin. There were rumors she was a lesbian. She looked and dressed like a beautiful 1920s silent movie star. Cornell had long, wavy brown hair that cascaded down her back. She had an impressive figure compared to Billie, who was fat but blessed with a beautiful face.

Marion moved to Chicago, and Katherine and Money moved to Harlem. Cornell and a group of beautiful mulatto girlfriends stayed in Mobile. While Earl went to work, they all drank, smoked cigarettes, and played the Victrola at his house.

Cornell got paid to take beauty burlesque nude pictures. She and her girlfriends were all unmarried, and men showered them with money and gifts. Every weekend at Cornell's house, she had a party and charged an entry fee. Cornell and her gang of girls loved money, vice, and pleasure. As the leader of her pack, Cornell influenced Billie's behavior. Billie's husband would come home to find dinner unprepared and the house messed up. He never said a word to Billie about her responsibilities as a wife. He kept getting up to go to work and being a good husband. After a while, his silence made her feel guilty. Billie loved her husband, and she realized that her drinking and partying every day wasn't right.

Intuitively she knew if she didn't change, one day she could wake up single. Billie quit drinking and having parties at the house. She became a responsible wife. While Cornell continued to have parties at her abode, Billie started being the good wife and stopped attending the parties. She stayed home and took care of her husband.

As time marched on, Cornell decided that the grass seemed greener in Harlem. She packed her things and moved to New York. Billie had her husband and Miss June to keep her company.

Cornell, Marion, Katherine, and Money wrote letters that told stories of the sights and sounds of Chicago and Harlem, with streets paved with gold, great prosperity, and freedom. They all prospered, which motivated Billie to start sewing and become a seamstress. She acquired a job during the day, working in an alterations shop in Mobile. Miss June had moved back in with her parents after her husband disappeared. She still had brothers and sisters to take care of who were in junior high and high school. Miss June helped her mother and father, who worked hard cleaning rich white people's houses.

Sheriff Hasty and Miss June rekindled their affair. Sheriff Hasty's marriage didn't bother Miss June. It made no difference whether he remained single or married. In the eyes of the world, she would forever be his mistress. Sheriff Hasty's mother praised Miss June for having the beauty of a rare brown rose flower; too bad she wasn't the right color. In the South, white women didn't care if their husbands were sleeping with black women. Sheriff Hasty's family had forbidden Miss June to visit the house or participate in family events or outings. They welcomed Billie with open, loving arms. If Miss June could pass for white, she would be accepted. A shadow of dejection and conflict fell upon Billie.

Because her father's family discriminated against her mother, the South had its reality. If you were white, you are right. If you are, yellow you were mellow if you're brown stick around, if you were black stay back. Miss June seldom ventured out in the world. She had to stay home and take care of her siblings, and she never directly dealt with discrimination. She had Billie, and without hesitation, Sheriff Hasty took care of them both. When Billie married Earl West, she couldn't bring him to Sheriff Hasty's family's house either. As a result, Billie, her husband, and Miss June became a close-knit family; they stuck together.

One day they all were at a carnival in Mobile, and a drunken black man pulled out his gun. He started shooting up in the air and waving the gun. A stray bullet hit Billie's husband in the heart, and he died on the spot. After the funeral, in August 1928 Miss June and Billie were bored with their life in Mobile. They both craved novelty, excitement, and something new. They were two single women, mother and daughter, who were eighteen years apart: Miss June, forty-three, and Billie, twenty-five. They decided to move up north to start a new life with new opportunities. Billie and Miss June loved each other; wherever Miss June went, Billie followed.

Marion and her husband, Nubby, got settled in Chicago in the Roaring Twenties. Chicago was a gangster town, and money flowed. Nubby got that name because he lost his hands while he played on a railroad track in Mobile. A train ran over his hands, so the doctors amputated them. Marion wrote Billie letters about Chicago, the gangs, and speakeasy clubs. Chicago had the reputation of being a windy city and an action town.

Money married a man named Burt, whom she met at a party in Mobile. He was forty-eight years older than Money. When they arrived in Harlem, she became pregnant and gave birth to a baby boy.

Money and her child settled in Harlem, and they were well taken care of by her husband. Money's husband had a good-paying position as a merchant seaman. His ship traveled all over the world, while she stayed home and raised their child. Cornell resided in a well-furnished abode and worked at the Cotton Club and speakeasies in Harlem. She received payment to party and indulge in all kinds of vices with the club patrons.

Katherine also settled in Harlem. She wrote Billie and told her that Harlem appeared glamorous; it looked like the place to be. Katherine told Billie that the FBI had called her and accused her of selling dope. She replied that she had sold pussy before, but she had never sold dope.

On that response, they hung up the phone. Billie found it humorous. If Katherine were in Mobile, she would have been arrested based on accusations, not facts. Katherine had buffet after-hour parties in her apartment where everyone wore beautiful clothes and jewelry. In the mid-1920s, many Harlemites were changed by a real life and comfortable living. No one believed the Harlem Renaissance (New Negro Movement) could last. Finally, there existed a happy place where black people could come and develop. It featured jazz, art, dance, theater, and literature. Black people continued the exodus from all over the country and the Caribbean to migrate to Harlem.

Jazz contributed to integration more than anything else. Music brought blacks and whites together in harmony. Broadway had glittering lights, dance halls, and rich, generous white people who were hiring blacks to work for them. Deciding between Harlem and Chicago, Billie and Miss June chose Harlem. It remained strange that Miss June's retribution for being a bully didn't affect Billie. She never got beat up, because if you were white or looked white, you were protected from all kinds of abuse. Miss June had a deep-seated anger and karma that foreshadowed her to New York.

Miss June and her daughter arrived in Harlem in January 1929 and settled at 219 West 121st Street. Billie moved down the street to 201 West 121st Street. Billie's building stretched around the corner to Seventh Avenue. Billie's bedroom window looked out onto Seventh Avenue. Miss June had three bedrooms and a dining room; Billie had four bedrooms. Miss June and Billie rented out their spare rooms, and they were never without a lodger.

Frank and Birdie, Miss June's brother and his wife from Mobile, moved to 121st Street and Eighth Avenue. Other people from the South were coming and going.

For Miss June, 1929 was a significant year. Her menstruation stopped. With all the excitement in her new life, she hadn't suffered from the effects of menopause yet. She met a handsome black man by the name of Joe, who was a demon in disguise. She didn't go slowly with Joe to get to know him. Miss June had not moved slowly with Sheriff Hasty or Mr. Harris. She habitually jumped in feet first for fear of another woman taking the opportunity. Joe and Miss June became a couple fast. Joe liked to gamble, and he won a lot of money. He continued to save his money, because Joe had a dream that one day he would open a bar in Harlem. Miss June's men had two things in common: money and ambition.

Sheriff Hasty inhered the characteristic of being responsible, reliable, and dependable. Mr. Harris had never been at home because of his heavy work schedule. He worked hard, brought back the money, and paid the bills. Joe desired to earn money, and he appeared to be a different type of lover and a good man for Miss June. She and Joe partied with a group of her friends. They loved drinking, dancing, and enjoying the good times—until the good times turned dark.

Miss June's boyfriend loved to fight and argue. Joe hit her, and she hit him back; they fought like two men. He punched her in the stomach and breast.

Miss June had been fighting most of her life. She fought back, and she beat him. He couldn't beat her, a woman, which made him furious. Miss June behaved like a Hollywood star—she was perpetually the life of the party—and Joe was determined to prove that no woman was going to beat him. Because the apartments were large and rooms were rented out, the landlord didn't make a profit; the tenants did. The owner didn't care as long as he received his rent on time. Neither Miss June nor Billie ever paid rent; their lodgers did. They were friends of people from the South, trying to save up money to get their place. Once they got settled and life became good, they moved out, and someone else moved in.

Occupying an apartment became a big responsibility because of the furniture, the rental lease, and the expense of moving. Once people moved into a neighborhood, they stayed put. Lodgers who rented a room had only their clothes and personal items—no furniture. It allowed them with ease to pick up and move from place to place. They got a chance to live in different parts of Harlem and were free to travel.

On December 31, 1929, Miss June and Joe had been arguing, and she didn't wish to spend New Year's Eve with him. Her brother Frank, his wife, Birdie, and two other friends from the South invited her out.

They were all dressed up and went to a party in Harlem, on 123rd Street between Seventh and Eighth Avenue. The brownstone building was crowded with well-dressed people. They all welcomed Miss June and her brother and friends. A tidy man of color escorted them to a buffet table filled with black eye peas, rice, corn bread, smoked pork neck bones, fried chicken, liquor, whiskey, and champagne. No one knew anyone, but everyone reached out and connected with one another.

Miss June embraced the love and anonymity from the white man's peering eyes. In Mobile, Sheriff Hasty knew all the black people's names and where they lived. His deputies were always watching over the black population's shoulders. Harlem made Mobile's slave oppression a thing of the past. They all partied, drank, and talked, even though nobody could remember anyone's name.

They had a great time and left at three in the morning. Earlier, there had been a snowstorm, and a thick, white blanket of snow covered the sidewalks and streets. The cars had disappeared under the piles of snow, and people were drunk. No cars or buses were driving on the streets. The New York subway trains ran all night despite the storm.

Because they weren't far from home, they decided to walk. Everyone was inebriated as the group walked in the cold. However, they felt no pain. They had only the streetlights to guide them home through the dark, deserted streets. From several blocks away, they could hear the sounds of drunken partygoers. "Happy New Year," the partygoers yelled and blew their New Year's Eve horns.

As they stumbled on the corner of 121st Street and Seventh Avenue, there suddenly appeared six black drag queens. Walking in front of Miss June and the others, the men were all decked out in dresses, furs, wigs, makeup, feathers, and rubber booties, which protected their big low-heeled shoes from the snow. They minded their own business. All the drag queens were high from drinking, and they were shouting, yelling, and laughing like wannabe women. You could see they were men in drag.

Migrants from the South were like babies in Harlem. Frank started calling them the F word, and his companions were laughing at them. The drag queens turned around and beat up Miss June, Frank, Birdie, and two friends. The drag queens kicked their butts, knocked them down in the snow, and hit their heads. Still, they managed to get up off the snowy ground and run. As the drag queens chased them down the street, they kicked them in their asses. The partygoers barely escaped, and they ran into Miss June's building.

Miss June fumbled, then found her keys in her purse, and opened the door. They all charged into the apartment, and then she quickly locked the door.

No one dared to look out the window, because Miss June lived on the first floor. Everyone feared that the drag queens were going to throw bricks at the window. The drag queens never chased them into the building, because most people had guns, lye, or acid in their apartments.

Everybody went to sleep and woke up later that New Year's Day. They were feeling sore from the beating. Miss June laughed at how the drag queens whipped them and kicked all their butts. They all swore that they would never laugh at a drag queen again or use the F word.

Being from Mobile, Alabama, they didn't see such outright bold behaviors or the colorful characters they saw in New York City. It looked all fascinating, glittering, and thrilling with cutting-edge fashion. After 1930 arrived, Miss June continued to see Joe. It remained a compelling relationship, one she couldn't let go of, yet one she couldn't have. Alcohol and menopause played an important part in the dynamics of their relationship.

Miss June partied because her lodgers paid the rent, and she unfailingly had money, liquor, and food. She did not get an education. Her only job was to run her house. Most of her lodgers were friends of friends from the South, and they partied with her. The occupants cleaned their rooms; she only had to clean the bedroom, bathroom, kitchen, and living room. She mopped the kitchen and waxed the floors. Miss June was responsible for paying the rent and utilities, and she kept the profit.

Television did not exist before the 1950s, however they had the radio, movies, books, and newspapers. Miss June and Joe had a lot of time on their hands to get into arguments. Joe wanted to be the center of attention. He wanted Miss June to focus all her attention on him. Miss June was famous, and she told jokes and stories. Later Miss June said, "Your mother, Virginia, told me she needed a man. She looked like a big black gorilla in heat. I would fuck John George River dry." Miss June laughed. Joe did not like that type of dry wit, humor, and independence.

With Miss June's ability to make people laugh, a crowd ceaselessly rallied around her. She was not an affectionate or submissive type of woman. She never said, "Oh honey, oh baby, I need you. I am lonely. Baby, please treat me right," and plead with Joe to behave civilly.

She didn't know how to defuse his anger or how not to make him angry. If Joe had a weak woman, he could emotionally abuse her—if not physically—to get attention and free sex. Miss June didn't pacify or sugarcoat Joe's bad behavior. His abuse had become a habit to get attention. Joe couldn't emotionally manipulate or scare her, because she wasn't emotional. Miss June had a coolness to her temperament that suppressed the anger from her past life in Mobile.

Everyone worked outside the home during the day except Miss June. Friends and lodgers were regularly in the apartment after six o'clock. On weekends, they incessantly drank and partied. Joe needed a woman who catered to him.

Miss June needed a man to provide for her as Sheriff Hasty did. He treated her well and took care of her. Even though segregation and violent racism loomed in the South, Miss June had her pride, and Joe didn't like that. He wanted to see a woman down, begging to be with him, and Miss June didn't cater or come down for him. Joe drank and picked fights with Miss June, and she beat him again and again. During all those fights, Miss June's body sustained a lot of punching. Joe punched her body as if it were a punching bag.

She never learned to be a professional boxer, and the kids in Mobile, Alabama, barely got the chance to punch her.

Miss June won the fight. One day Joe and a group of Miss June's friends were in her living room. She had a bowl of apples on the coffee table with a knife. Miss June picked up the knife and an apple. She peeled the apple and ate a slice of the apple. Miss June enjoyed eating apples; they were her comfort fruit. Joe couldn't stand to see her calmness, so he decided to pick a fight with her. He called her all kinds of bitches and motherfuckers, and he lunged at her. She had the knife in her hand and pointed it toward Joe. He landed on the knife, and it went straight into his heart. He fell to the floor. They called the police although Joe was dead when they arrived.

A policeman took Miss June into custody. Her friends testified that Joe had hit her first on many occasions and in their presence. They said he continuously picked fights with her, and he domestically abused her. Love has a dark side, and Miss June had become a victim of it. She had suffered for her love life. Mr. Harris, the epitome of a good man, had disappeared from her life. She couldn't marry Sheriff Hasty or live with him, nor could she live in peace with Joe. Miss June declared that it had been an accident and that she didn't mean to kill Joe. He fell on the knife, and the murder was committed in self-defense.

When the court found her not guilty, she was set free. The judge dismissed the case, and Miss June returned home.

In 1932, Miss June was forty-seven. It was another significant year for her. She had started bleeding. She went to the doctor, and he diagnosed her with cancer of the uterus. The hospital admitted Miss June for radiation treatment. They say bad luck comes in threes, and this was the straw that broke the camel's back. The nurse left the radiation on her for too long, and it burned her bladder. After that, she had to wear diapers, because she couldn't hold her urine. In those days, they didn't have Depends or diaper panties for adults.

Then, on top of that, she had gallstones that she passed painfully during the night. Many cloth diapers had to be washed and dried. I assumed that all the punching in her stomach and breasts caused cancer. She couldn't have foreseen that Joe was to be the last lover in her life. Joe was dead by her hand, and Miss June was plagued and cursed with sickness for the rest of her life. Though she had comfortable amenities and lots of visitors, being confined to her home imprisoned her. She could not enjoy Manhattan anymore. The whole island of Manhattan, a city that never slept, stayed alive twenty-four/seven.

There were dance halls, after-hours clubs, the Cotton Club, and others. The Great Depression had an impact on Harlem. Thanks to the churches of God and the devil of vice, the Harlemites were caught in between and survived. Life was good times, politics, and survival. If you had your rent paid, food on the table, and a little money in your pocket, you were OK. You were poor at the same time; you just didn't know what being poor meant.

Harlem represented security and a safe place to be for blacks; they had unity, protection, and freedom unlike in the South. They were glamorous and enjoyed their newfound freedom. Harlem was such a charming place, despite the landlords not making repairs and charging high rents.

When the Harlemites picketed the landlords to lower the rents, they complied. They were still negligent with repairs or slow in making them. The people with pride kept their apartments beautiful and clean. Men carried their weight and threw money at their women.

Women in Harlem were glamorous and ambitious, and they worked for money and security. No moochers were tolerated; no one wanted to be out on the street. They had a sense of responsibility and pride about themselves. Everything had to be perfect—the house spotlessly clean, with everything in its place. Clothing had to be fashionable, coordinated, ironed, starched, and pressed, with matching colors. Black people were going forward in a positive, uplifting way.

From 1929 into the 1930s, Billie worked as a dance hall matron in a dance hall on Broadway. Her job duties were to make sure the white girls had their panties on before they went out on the dance floor to dance with the white paying gentlemen.

When the Depression hit hard, Billie and Miss June gave rent-pay house parties. These types of parties went on in Harlem quite a lot. One weekend, everyone came to Miss June's and Billie's house and paid a dollar. The next week, they'd go to someone else's house and pay a buck. The more people, the more profit. If two hundred people came to their house, they had a $200 profit. The rent was $21 a month, and everyone paid that or less in Harlem. All the whites moved to the suburbs or downtown.

Billie and Miss June played the Harlem numbers. Billie hit big for $10,000, and that was a lot of money in the Depression. Billie was psychic, and she'd win at the numbers all the time. Billie bought a large three-foot, steel, combination safe that hid her money. Beneath her clothing-filled closet, she concealed the safe. Miss June steadily hit small-time five dollars or ten dollars a day.

That is how these women survived during the thirties; they never starved. The rich people were jumping out of their windows, and those who had lost their jobs were down in the Bowery in soup lines. A lot of gangsters made money in Prohibition from the 1920s to 1933. When the stock market crashed in 1929, a lot of the speakeasy clubs survived in Chicago and New York. Adults drank liquor instead of eating food. Alcohol, cigarettes, and coffee were big sellers. A cup of coffee and a cigarette for breakfast made people feel full and decreased their urge to eat. Also, cigarettes with alcohol suppressed the appetite. It worked during the 1930s when food was scarce.

Miss June and Billie unceasingly stocked their kitchen cabinets with extra canned food. Billie continually surrounded herself with beautiful, stylish, and ambitious people. A couple of her close friends from Mobile, such as Katherine and Money, weren't beauties like Cornell and her crowd of mulatto women. They had ambition, and they were from Mobile, so she kept in touch with them. Billie at first partied with Cornell, who deeply embedded herself into the vices of Harlem. Billie again distanced herself from Cornell, who drank and smoked cigarettes excessively. Eventually, Cornell died from a heart attack in the 1930s.

During the Depression, Billie met an incredibly handsome, light-skinned man with jet-black wavy hair. He was tall, charming, and as handsome as Errol Flynn, if not more so. His name was Manuel Henderson, and he dressed casually, sometimes in khaki-colored suits. Light colors looked good on him. Manuel worked at a favorite bar in Harlem as a bartender. He made excellent tips. Billie went for looks every time. Her men had to be good looking, dressed neatly if not extremely well, and have an engaging temperament. Billie believed that beauty, ambition, and a honey-coated personality opened doors. She always said you catch more flies with honey than with shit.

Billie and Manuel fell in love and married. Women snatched up men fast; being by yourself was not profitable for a black man or a black woman. Having a large circle of friends and neighbors helped you a great deal. Black people had to stick together. Manuel and Billie stayed married for twenty-four years. During those years, he and Billie had arguments and fistfights; despite that, they stayed together.

Manuel even cheated on her with another woman. One day Manuel worked an early shift, and that afternoon Billie came to visit him. It wasn't a fancy bar, and it meshed with Manuel's casual attire. The walls were brown, with a long, black bar in front of a mirrored wall. It was a man's bar, and women flocked there. Manuel could see the bar patrons in the rear of him when he looked into the mirror at the liquor stand. An attractive, casually dressed woman was sitting in the bar. Billie had seen her sitting in the bar a couple of times.

"Who is that woman?" she asked Manuel.

"Oh, that's Moses's old lady," he replied.

Billie had a premonition that this woman was having an affair with Manuel. She left the bar, went home, and forgot about the woman. After the bar had closed, and she and Manuel were in bed asleep, the phone started ringing around four, five, and six o'clock in the morning.

Billie answered the phone, and the caller hung up. Intuitively she knew it was this woman from the bar. Manuel slept like a baby, especially if he worked the night shift. As soon as his head hit the bed, he fell asleep. If he worked the day shift, the phone rang after midnight. Manuel never answered the phone, and Billie never told him about the hang-up calls. Finally, the woman called at two o'clock, and Billie answered the phone. She asked to speak to Manuel.

"He's asleep, and it's two in the morning," Billie informed her.

"Tell him Sylvia called." Sylvia hung up the phone. Billie let two days go by before she confronted Sylvia. On the third day, a hard rain poured upon Harlem. Billie had finished with all her domestic chores early that morning. Despite the nasty weather, she decided to go to the bar. It was on the corner of 125th Street and Eighth Avenue, right across the street from the subway train station. At certain times of the day, a rush of people patronized the bar—after lunch, during happy hour, and then when the night crowd came.

When Billie entered the watering hole, a smell of beer penetrated the air. There was a steady yet slow flow of people. Sylvia sat at the end of the counter and watched Manuel clean the shot glasses. Billie sat down across from Sylvia and talked to Manuel for a moment.

All the while, she kept her eye on Sylvia. After a couple of seconds, Sylvia got up from her seat and exited the bar. Billie got up from her seat and told Manuel that she had to go home and prepare dinner; she said she wanted to stop in and see him for a moment.

Billie exited the bar and trailed Sylvia to the 125th Street subway station. As Sylvia descended the subway stairs, Billie confronted her about calling and having an affair with Manuel.

"You better not call my house anymore and harass me. And leave my husband alone," Billie said to her.

"Don't tell me what to do. I am a grown woman. I do as I please," Sylvia responded. When Billie got mad, she turned red in the face. She became like ten thousand enraged, caged apes on Sylvia. Even though the rain flooded the streets and continued to pour down upon them, Billie had closed her umbrella and used it to beat Sylvia on the subway stairs.

Sylvia started hitting Billie back, and a crowd formed around them at the top of the staircase. The wife and the one who wanted to be the wife were battling it out. Sylvia lost the fight. In anger, Billie behaved and looked like a white bull in a china shop—a far cry from the belle of the ball, which was the image she had cultivated and pretended to be on so many occasions. Sylvia ran down the subway stairs and escaped Billie's wrath. Billie's motto was, "I may not be able to beat you. However, I'll bet you a funky mule everyone will know you've been in a fight."

It spread like wildfire throughout the neighborhood that Billie beat up Sylvia. Before Manuel could get off his shift from work, everyone had heard the news. Billie went home, fixed herself up, and prepared dinner as if nothing had happened.

When Manuel got home, he confronted Billie and said, "I heard you were out there fighting. What were you doing out in the street fighting?" Manuel looked for bruises on Billie.

"I wasn't fighting. I whipped Moses's old lady's ass," Billie replied. Manuel never said another word. Sylvia was so afraid of Billie that she never came back to the bar, and the affair ended. Women who were brave enough to disrespect Billie occasionally threw themselves at Manuel. Manuel's and Billie's arguments and fights were about him flirting and not being able to say no.

After twenty-four years of marriage, Manuel got sick and died of liver cancer on November 21, 1953. Billie stayed by his bedside. I had been born the day before. I've heard in astrology circles about a death in the family within either a year before or a year after the birth of a Scorpio. And when a Scorpio dies, there will be a birth in the family within the year before or the year after. It happens at least 95 percent of the time. I invariably thought it was uncanny that seven months after Manuel died, I entered Billie's and Miss June's lives.

Billie matured from being fat into a heavyset, attractive, madam-looking woman.

She habitually kept a lit, unfiltered Chesterfield cigarette in the side of her mouth. She always wore fashionable black glasses, red lipstick, and fingernail polish, and she regularly went to the hairdresser.

She thought of herself as a natural beauty when she awoke in the morning. "You have to go to bed late and wake up early to be smarter than me," Billie said to me. Billie had great pride in her cleverness and her ability to keep what she knew to herself. Every two weeks she went to the hairdresser. Occur by Avon is the strong perfume scent she wore. Being a seamstress, she made her clothes fashionable. Billie appeared to be classy, and she had an aggressive, pleasant attitude. Billie advised me that I should try to elevate myself.

Sometimes Billie seemed compassionate, with a touch of emotional intelligence. I often wondered how she became the opposite of Miss June, who cursed like a sailor. Daughters usually take after their mothers in some way, especially when they have a close relationship. Billie never used profanity. Although she and Miss June were both responsible, reliable women, Miss June had a glass head she never hid her thoughts Miss June always spoke her mind. Her tongue wagged amusingly.

You never knew what Billie was thinking underneath her smile; she kept many things to herself. Billie modeled herself after her fathers' sisters, his mother, and Cornell. As it came to pass, Billie distanced herself from all of them except Money and Katherine, who remained her Mobile, Alabama, friends. They were not able to compete with Billie because of their black skin color.

Billie wore conservative, fashionable suit dresses that hugged her large figure and confidently displayed her cleavage. You couldn't read Billie; she had everything together about herself and surroundings. Back then people talked about you if they could read you. They'd say she's messy, sloppy, or trashy, or she can't keep her cool. You couldn't say any of those things about Billie. She had her circle of friends and her church activities.

She projected an air of control that warranted your respect, because you were afraid not to. Women who were jealous of her never dared to confront her.

Billie met an attractive man named Jim, who came to her house and spent half the night. I didn't know he was married. Occasionally

Billie ran into his wife in passing on the street. Jim's wife tried to be friendly and talk to Billie.

"How are you?" she said with a smile on her face. She liked Billie and wanted to extend the conversation.

"I'm OK," Billie replied with a smile and cut the conversation short. Billie kept walking as if she had somewhere important to go. Maybe Jim's wife knew, and she wanted Billie to confront her. Billie was borrowing her husband to fill her lonely nights and days. She didn't wish to break up his marriage. Billie had compassion for Jim's wife's feelings. She wasn't trying to be up in her face or have an association with her. Billie told me this after fifteen years of being in a secret affair with Jim. Billie's loneliness got the better of her after Manuel died, and the incident happened. On the contrary, she knew that adultery was wrong.

Billie kept many secrets. Her secrets eventually dissolved Miss June's and my relationship.

Miss June and Billie became a part of my life in the year 1954 in the month of June. My mother, Virginia, left my father, Ali, when I was three months old and moved in with her mother, Mrs. Walden. She left me alone at seven months old to go out at night. She and her mother had an argument about her leaving me alone. Her mother asked her to move, because she wouldn't be responsible for an infant left alone at night.

My mom brought me to Harlem in 1954. I was seven months old when she rented a room from Mrs. Johnson at 219 West 121st Street, Apartment 1E, in New York. For some reason, I never knew her first name, or maybe I forgot it. Mrs. Johnson had a yellow skin tone and wavy black hair. She came up from South Carolina to Harlem. Mrs. Johnson worked for rich white people as a housekeeper and a cook. She owned her house down South and the land her family passed down to her. Mrs. Johnson saved her money and used it for the upkeep on her house down South. She made good money, so she could afford her apartment in Harlem. She didn't have constant lodgers like Miss June and Billie did, nor did she super organize her apartment like Billie did. Mrs. Johnson worked hard and stayed to herself.

Later on, she acquired a white cat named Mickey. Mrs. Johnson had diabetes and gave herself insulin shots every day. She baked cakes and ate them despite her diabetes. Mrs. Johnson owned a big TV that sat in the middle of the living room, which was in the front of the apartment—unlike Miss June's living room, which was in the back of the apartment. In many apartments, you don't have a choice as to where to put the living room. These buildings were designed to give the tenant a choice. Mrs. Johnson kept her television turned to channel 2, CBS, all day, and she loved to watch *Perry Mason* on her days off.

My mother, Virginia, was an educated, highly skilled woman. She had to work, and there wasn't anyone to babysit me except an old lady who lived across the hall from Mrs. Johnson in Apartment 1W. Little did I know that Mrs. Elizabeth June Harris aka Miss June would become a major grandma figure in my life—along with her mulatto daughter, Willie Mae Henderson, aka Billie.

Miss June was the perfect candidate for the job. My mother took full advantage of the situation and of Miss June's love for me. She left me there and moved downtown to Eighty-First Street.

Miss June had been a shut-in since 1932. She and her daughter survived the Depression and World War II. Miss June washed her clothes and diapers by hand on a glass washboard in the kitchen sink. She then line-dried them outside the kitchen window in the backyard. Back then the kitchen sink had two sinks, one large and one small. We washed our dishes in the small sink and our clothes in the large sink. In spite of her illness, Miss June kept the large apartment clean and neat, along with her body.

You could sometimes smell the urine-soaked diaper on her if she drank too many liquids. Billie told me that in 1953, at sixty-eight, Miss June did her best to stay on top of her illness. She didn't get a washing machine until ten or twelve years later, and someone gave her that. I remember how much noise it made when it entered into the spin cycle.

In 1955, Miss June had a dog named Pal, a German shepherd. I was around two or three years old, and I'd ride on Pal's back—down the long, dark, green hall that extended to the living room, which had a window with a fire escape terrace that we opened in the summer. The living room led to a small hall with a dining room on the left side, and straight ahead you walked into the large kitchen. A bright yellow lead paint covered the walls.

Miss June used the enclosed dining room as a storage room she called the little room. She kept locked inside the small room bedsprings, mattresses, and furniture from the 1920s. Along the long hall, the spine of the apartment, most were designed like a railroad, with two bedrooms and a bathroom in the middle and the entrance door to the apartment.

Straight ahead of the apartment's entrance door was Miss June's master bedroom, with a large window that looked out onto the street. Under the hall light stood a small table with a black rotary-dial telephone on top of it. Miss June placed the table in the middle of the hallway by the bathroom door. If the phone rang and she came out of the bathroom or from the kitchen, she could answer the phone there or take it in the bathroom. She also had a phone in her bedroom.

That hallway phone table frustrated me. I'd slide off Pal's back and push my stroller down the hall. I'd continue to get the wheels caught on the phone table's leg. I used to struggle to free the stroller and try to get it past the phone table to the door of Miss June's bedroom. Pal could get up onto the windowsill and sit, and I'd be right beside him. Pal was a big old, fine, proud-looking German shepherd. Pal and I looked out onto the street at the people as they passed. Looking out the window had the same view as a 3-D color movie screen that stayed fascinating. The sight of individuals who regularly walked back and forth through the block continuously filled our daily lives with life.

Even in the winter, we didn't open the window. We sat on the windowsill and looked out as far as our eyes and necks could stretch to see the people. We watched until we could no longer see them as they walked out of the window frame. Right under the window was a basement with a four-foot-high fence. That protected the people on the street from falling into the basement as they leaned over it to talk to Miss June. Several people sat or leaned up against the porch on the left side of Miss June's window to speak with her. She rested her elbows on a pillow as she looked out the window.

There were plants on each side of the large windowsill. Sometimes they smelled from the horse manure she put in the soil. It worked, because her plants grew tall and beautiful. Miss June looked out the window for an hour or two and talked to everyone who passed by. Neighbors on the block liked her, and when Miss June got tired, she sat in a chair by the window and peeled her apples for a homemade apple pie. After Miss June had snapped the ends of her string beans before cooking them, we ate fresh vegetables.

Miss June, being from Alabama, ate soul food: grits, salt pork, bacon and sausage, cornbread, and buttermilk biscuits with gravy for breakfast; and fried pork chops, pork neck bones, smothered chicken gizzards, fried chicken, greens, and macaroni for lunch and dinner.

We had a beautiful antique, blue-and-white gas stove from the 1900s, with two porcelain door handles for the top and bottom ovens on the right side of the stove, along with four small porcelain pilot handles to release the gas on the stove. The stove sat on four legs raised above the floor. I remember bumping into the porcelain pilot handles and accidentally turning on the gas. The gas spewed out of the pilots so strong, you could smell it in a matter of seconds. Those stoves were dangerous and started many fires, leaving several people homeless in Harlem. Luckily Miss June cooked and handled the oven with caution.

With all the money she made throughout the years, Miss June kept that antique stove. Despite the fact that she had a do-it-herself attitude, services were provided, such as the deliveries from the milkman. He came at six o'clock in the morning and put fresh milk and orange juice at our door.

On Saturdays, the soda man delivered a case of big orange, grape, and ginger ale soda bottles and seltzer water with the powerful silver spray pump on its bottles like in the old 1920 movies. Then she got surplus food from welfare that consisted of cheese, powdered milk and eggs, and canned beef with globs of fat on it.

Since the kitchen faucet didn't have a washer on it, Miss June tied a white diaper rag around it to strain the water. That rag turned rusty from the drinking water. I couldn't understand why the landlord refused to send a plumber to put a washer on the faucet. I drank cold milk instead of water, and Miss June didn't eat like a sick person. The food we ate didn't have fiber in it. Later on, the medical community discovered that a lack of fiber in diets caused cancer. I got sick and went into the hospital. I remember being one year old, and I stayed in Sydenham Hospital for constant constipation.

Before the doctors could treat me, they had to have my mother's signature. Miss June couldn't go downtown to see my mom, so Billie went. Billie knocked on her door. When it opened, a large, black African man named Arthur stood there. Billie asked if my mother was there. He answered no, unaware that Billie could see Virginia hiding behind the door. Billie said to tell her Amina was in Sydenham Hospital, and the doctors couldn't treat her without her mother's consent. If she was not at that hospital in one hour, Billie said she was going to call the police.

By the time Billie got back uptown, my mother was at the hospital signing the papers for the doctors to treat me. I stayed in the hospital for a week, and they cleaned out my bowels and fed me food with fiber.

My mother had a secretarial job, and although she didn't make as much as the white executive secretaries, she had a good salary that afforded her a luxurious wardrobe and an apartment on Eighty-First Street in downtown Manhattan.

My mother's window had a glorious view of Central Park West. The building's entrance was inside the block, a couple of blocks up the street from Hayden Planetarium. That property was prime real estate; if you lived across the street from Central Park West, then you were hip. Whether you lived on Fifth or Eighth Avenue, the tenants had a view. That was significant value in New York real estate. In the 1950s, being a secretary became a way for a woman to earn money in the corporate world.

Men dominated the business community. They owned the businesses and were the ones who hired the workers. Rarely did you see a woman with her own business without a husband. Secretarial jobs were tedious and detailed; they were the only way a woman could flourish in the corporate workplace. She had to have top-notch secretarial skills. New Yorkers analyzed how you spoke, where you lived, and what you wore. If you were black, they wanted to know what you did for a living.

Most blacks who lived in Harlem were successful professionals, and others were good blue-collar workers. They shared Harlem with the handymen and the poor welfare recipient. There were black doctors, lawyers, teachers, businesspeople, nurses, and housekeepers who wanted to live among their people, without the watchful eye of the white man.

After World War II had ended, the economy boomed with prosperity. In the 1950s, if you were a dark-skinned black woman living at a Manhattan downtown prestigious address and not in Harlem, you had to have a high-paying legal job. White people who lived in the neighborhood watched my mother coming and going and saw her associates. Virginia associated with highly educated Africans who spoke several languages. Whites were intrigued by Africans, whereas blacks had repelled them in the 1940s and 1950s when blacks didn't wish to be called Negro. They wanted to be called colored and assimilated into the American fabric and system, which is a white man's system.

Blacks connected with Africa through music—jazz, soul, then pop, and through dance.

I remember if a black person called another black person black, in an argument. This individual was offended and ready to engage in a fight. You could call the person the N word. Still, you couldn't call the person black. As they say, birds of a feather flock together. Virginia hung out with Africans and became more like them. Her wardrobe started reflecting the African culture. My mother sometimes wore

African clothes, and the black people laughed at her when she visited Harlem—until James Brown came out with the song "Say It Loud—I'm Black, and I'm Proud."

Slowly I started seeing a shift in the black consciousness within the forty years. If you spoke well, you were considered an Oreo. Now that view is outmoded, because we have a black US president, President Obama. His father is from Kenya, Africa.

I remember watching Oprah's show in the eighties, even though she proudly recognized herself as black on national TV. Blacks said she resembled a token. Oprah replied, "Yes, I am a paid token." My mother was the opposite. She cared about what people said. She wanted to have the freedom and life that the wealthy white women had. For her, it became a constant struggle. She had to be tied down as a secretary or a mother. She never really cared about money; she cared about freedom more than me or anything else in this world. She resented what people said and when they reacted in an opposing way. She resented the mold that society attached to her.

As I reflect back, it seemed like she had slavery days on her mind. She wanted to exercise her right to be free at any cost. Later on in her life, it became a catalyst for a shocking life transformation.

When Virginia's life changed to a somewhat stable life that propelled me into a whole new world that I never hoped for or dreamed about in my entire existence. I had to make the transition from an unstable childhood filled with neglect. To create my success because I never had the stability that is what prepared me in my late teens for a dramatic life-altering change. That made me a successful adult in the game of chance.

Between the ages of one and three, I continued to be shuttled back and forth between Miss June's and my mother's apartment on Eighty-First Street. I used to walk in my mother's high heels. She had dresses that were fashionable and a shape like Marilyn Monroe to go with her fabulous wardrobe. When she wanted to be with her boyfriend, Arthur, she dropped me off at Miss June's house. Arthur traveled back and forth from Africa to America. When he arrived in New York, he stayed with my mother, and she didn't want me around.

Arthur paid her rent, because he maintained a profitable importing and exporting business of African goods. He made lots of money. Arthur traveled all over the world and stayed in America three to six months out of a year. My mother had her cake, and she ate it too. If Virginia had an inch, she took a mile; with Arthur, she had a freewheeling relationship. That benefited her and accommodated her freedom.

Eventually, Arthur wanted to marry my mother and move her to Africa. He desired her to travel and be with him full time; she wanted her freedom. She began applying for higher-paying jobs, and she still wanted to maintain her freedom. I started living with my mother full time, and Arthur visited her infrequently. He never spent the night when I was there. I know when I went to sleep that she went out at night to be with him.

I'm assuming he was aware she left me alone in the apartment. That didn't suit his image of an African woman. If she had married him, he had enough money to afford a babysitter, or she had to stay home with me. Either way, his ideal of a wife and his needs conflicted with her quest to be free. When we moved to Yonkers, I never saw Arthur again.

CHAPTER 2

My First Taste of Wealth

U PON TURNING THREE YEARS OLD, I still lived with my mother on Eighty-First Street. The United Nations had an American ambassador of Sudan and a diplomat ambassador from Sudan. My mother acquired a job with the United Nations as an executive secretary to Sudan's ambassador. The American ambassador to Sudan had a white secretary. The representative from Sudan had brown skin and wavy hair, and his wife had light skin and straight black hair. He had a different perspective, because Sudan had all shades of black people.

Many years later I read that only light-skinned Sudanese were hired to work in the Sudanese government. He appeared to be wealthy—or maybe the luxuries were the perks that came along with his job. He had a beautiful wife and two kids along with a two-story mansion in Yonkers, New York.

He had a Polish housekeeper and a cook and a private nanny for his kids. He gave my mother the status she had been struggling for in the corporate world. He didn't wear African clothes; instead, he wore expensive, tailored British suits. He had a driver who drove a large black limousine. I considered this man to be the epitome of style. He moved my mother and me into his lovely home, which had four bedrooms and four bathrooms, a large dark-blue kitchen, a dining room, and a living room.

My mother and I stayed in the huge triangle-shaped attic on the top floor. A window divided our beds, which were twelve feet apart. Our white beds were pushed up against the slanted walls. We had a large white closet, a dresser, and a chest of drawers. Lilac-painted walls matched the lilac carpet. Beautiful white ruffled bedding covered our beds. The room looked like it came out of a fairy tale. It was an extra child's room, for his nieces and nephews when they came to visit from Sudan. Now they had to share his kid's room; he had given their room to my mother and me.

I saw Virginia only at night; during the day she became so involved with living her new life, she forgot about me. She'd get into the limousine with him and his wife, and they'd drive off to the United Nations in Manhattan. It was summer, and I did not attend nursery school. The Polish cook and I were left alone in the mansion. A governess would take his kids to the city on outings.

The kids were eight and nine years old, a boy and girl. They didn't play with me, nor did they speak English well. I spent my time in the kitchen with the Polish cook. She babysat me while she prepared the meals for the family. She spoke English with an accent, and she dressed in a white-and-gray uniform with a white cap tied around her head. She looked like a washerwoman. I'd sit in the corner on the floor, playing with my toys.

The kitchen was huge, and she prepared food on a long, blue marble table in the center of the room. It matched the white sink, stove, and refrigerator. The kitchen had dark-blue walls and a blue-and-white linoleum floor. The floor looked like saltwater taffy candy with the white in the middle and the dark-blue circles that thinly spiraled around the white. I loved to play on that floor.

I played for hours while the cook prepared the meals. I sat in a high chair at the table, watching her make the food. Once she made

Polish meatballs in the shape of fingers, and she gave me a taste of the raw meat. She seasoned it well, and salmonella wasn't as rampant as it is now. When the ambassador celebrated the Fourth of July, he had a daytime party on the patio. It had a large green door covering the swimming pool that he never filled with water. All the rich kids in the neighborhood were swimming and enjoying their pools.

Even though New York had a heat wave that summer, neither he nor his children bothered with swimming. They were used to the hot desert weather in Sudan, and swimming pools were not part of their homes' architecture.

His wife, kids, my mother, and other guests attended the Fourth of July party. The cook brought out all the food and put it on a long, green, wooden table with bench seats. My mom didn't give me a lot of attention; she became busy entertaining the guests. I ran about the lawn freely, lying in the grass. The other kids played with one another, and I prevailed in my loneliness.

Night fell upon the mansion, and all the guests left. My mother gave me a bath and put me to bed. That's when Virginia went out. I don't know if she went to meet Arthur or her friends. Years later, I found out this was a habit of hers, and it had been going on for quite some time.

For one year and a couple of months, I lived the wealthy life. I had loads of toys and expensive, fashionable clothes at the mansion.

My mother put me in a nursery in Yonkers. The school had a private minibus that picked me up from the house at eight in the morning and returned me at six. My mother rode in the limousine to work even when the ambassador and his wife and kids were in Sudan. My mother still worked at the UN, managing his office.

Late one night in August, as I recall, when I was around four years old, going on five, a storm with lightning and thunder woke me. My eyes looked around the room and stopped on the moonlight that gleamed through the attic window directly over my mother's empty bed.

I got out of my bed and stood by the window. I looked out to see if I could see my mom. A forest of trees blocked my view as they continued to twist and curve in the wind. The rain fell on their thick leaves and tapped hard on my windowpane. Tall, thick trees lined the street, and beautiful flowers surrounded the mansion. On the warm spring or hot, muggy summer days, a beam of sunlight streamed in and out of the penumbra that cooled the sidewalks.

I couldn't remember ever seeing a thunderstorm in the middle of the night. As I looked out the window, something beckoned me to go out and find my mother. I put on my dark-pink, rose-colored rubber raincoat and my hat and boots. I grabbed my clear umbrella with a dark pink rose on it. I exited the attic and followed the night-lights along the steps that guided me down the stairs. My mission was to find my mother.

I made my way to the front door. With my little hands, I opened the door and went out into the pouring rain. A single street lamp glowed dimly in the gloom of the dark, deserted sidewalk. Later on, I saw the drawing of the little girl on the Morton salt box. She appeared to be walking in the rain with a dark background, dressed exactly like me.

It made me think back to that night. I had an unlikely source of courage; I embraced the soft summer rain because it felt good and exciting. As I peered up at the dark sky, the rain felt like drops of stars tapping on my umbrella and raincoat. No strong wind pushed me forward or swept me off the ground. I walked to the boulevard in the steady shower of rain. Cars were going in both directions, and I didn't dare cross the street.

I stood there on the corner and watched the cars go by, hoping my mother was in one. Something told me to stay there on the corner and not to cross the street. I stood there for an hour. I watched and listened to the sights and sounds of the rain splashing from the cars' tires as they drove past me. A police car turned the corner and stopped. Two white police officers got out of the car and approached me.

One of them said, "Little girl, where is your mother?"

I replied, "I'm looking for my mommy."

"What is your name?"

"Amina."

"Come with me, and we will find her." He escorted me to the police car, and I got in. He closed the door, and off we went to the Yonkers police station. I remember a beehive of activity spread through the graveyard shift at the Yonkers police station. They were working, organizing their paperwork, and putting things in order. I didn't see any arrests that night; we lived in a quiet neighborhood. Our generous community had a plethora of police officers, and they found things to keep themselves busy. I had no identification on me; therefore, the police called every house in the neighborhood.

They finally called the ambassador's house, and he answered the phone. He confirmed that he had a little colored girl living in his house by the name of Amina. He went upstairs to the attic, but neither I nor my mother was there. He told the police to hold me there and that my mom would arrive to pick me up. Virginia must have come home and discovered my empty bed. The ambassador told her that the police picked me up on the street and detained me.

Thirty minutes later, she came walking into the police station, and they released me into her custody. A few days later, the police visited the ambassador, and they reported my mother to him. Since I was a child of a former employee of his, they wanted to let him know that because of her negligence, I could have been killed. Social child welfare and the state could take a child away from a negligent parent if a report is filed.

Because we lived in the ambassador's house, he felt responsible in some way. He did not want to take that risk of having something like that on his record. He had responsibilities of his own. He lived on the other side of the mansion, and my mother and I lived on the kitchen side. In the middle of the night, he liked to eat a snack, and on his way to the kitchen, he caught my mother coming home.

Several times before, when I had been asleep and Virginia had gone out, he had found her coming home after midnight. He warned her about leaving me alone and said not to do it again. Knowing my mother and her rebellious behavior, she continued to do it with impunity. This time the police caught her.

Now we were being evicted from Yonkers. I guess if I were a teen, I would have thought about all the perks of residing in a wealthy community that the ambassador bestowed upon me. I was living in a mansion, but I didn't have Mommy around. I was four years old and looking for my mother I'm glad she didn't blame me nor did she reveal her anger that her plans were foiled. I lost my parent, and she lost her good job because of her irresponsible behavior, and she did not care.

My mother looked at her behavior as her secret; she loved to sneak out at night and leave me alone. I think as much as the ambassador liked my mother, he saw beneath her mask and realized she didn't care about anything except her freedom. In the 1950s, women were viewed as spouses, mothers, and homemakers. If you were not good at these three positions, you were judged harshly as a woman.

My mother didn't fit into that mold, and her rebellious streak seeped out in this form of a secret nightlife. Running the streets, hanging out with her man and friends, and living a single, free life compelled her to be a neglectful mother who didn't care.

Being in her thirties, she had a difficult time acquiring a babysitter. At that time, no one accepted the image of a single black mother running the streets every night, no matter how much Virginia paid them. She didn't have the money to put me in boarding school, and I don't think they had one for black children. That is why she lived a double life in secret. I learned from my mother's covert activities. Eventually, what someone does in the dark comes to light. I tried to have an image and life I could live.

I found myself living a double life and not knowing what kind of life I wanted to live. I left my fate in the hands of the universe. I became a cat with nine lives. Curiosity killed the cat, and satisfaction brought him back. My mother never stayed on the track of being a mother. That's not what she represented, and her ego didn't allow her to give me up for adoption. My first taste of wealth made me realize that this was a life I could have, and I never forgot it. What was going to happen next? Where were we going? What were we going to do?

CHAPTER 3

My Introduction to Music

MY MOTHER AND I GOT lucky, and we landed at Mrs. Martine's brownstone house in Brooklyn. She was a tall, light-skinned black woman with wavy, reddish-brown hair. Mrs. Martine spoke in a high-pitched, soft, mousy voice. She had a real heart and soul. Her husband had died and left her the brownstone. It was three stories high, and she gave us the small ground-floor apartment. Our apartment had fluorescent lights that lit up the gray-blue walls. Mrs. Martine kept it clean, and again my bed had been placed against the window.

Our apartment didn't have a lock on the door. Mrs. Martine hadn't planned to rent the apartment, and she refused to put a lock on the door. She wanted an open house so she could come and go as she pleased. My mother turned the radio on when she ventured out at night, leaving me in bed asleep. I'd awaken in the middle of the evening to the songs playing on the radio.

Among several songs that played on the radio, "Charlie Brown" was the one that played the most. Sung by the Coasters, "Charlie Brown" became a hit song as it rose on the charts. It played four or five times every night on the radio. I was four going on five, and I remembered the lyrics. Of all the songs that played on the radio, "Charlie Brown" grabbed my attention. I could also hear the cars drive by on the street. My mother left the window open a little to let air into the apartment. That's the rule in New York; a window had to be cracked year round because of the gas stoves in the kitchens.

"Charlie Brown" played for a month on the radio. As I listened, I learned, and I never forgot the message: Charlie Brown was a prankster in school, and he finally got caught.

That song resonated with my mother because she got exposed by Mrs. Martine. She came into our apartment a couple of nights and saw that my mom wasn't there after midnight. She saw that I was alone in the bed, listening to the radio. The radio played, not only to keep me company, but also to deter strangers from coming to the window and in case Mrs. Martine came into the apartment. They would assume an adult was home and awake. That is the only reason my mother left the radio playing all night. Mrs. Martine confronted Virginia, and they got into an argument.

Mrs. Martine asked her to move; she wasn't going to be responsible if something happened to me in the apartment at night.

During that time, only rich white people had nannies living in with them, which allowed them to travel, run the streets, and attend numerous parties. They didn't have to come home for days or months; all they had to do was call—that's if they felt like it. As long as their bills and salaries got paid, nobody cared. The nanny cared for the child or children. The wealthy white woman had no questions asked, no persecution, scolding, or consequences. The Queen of England spent only ten minutes a day with her children. In *Gone with the Wind*, Rhett Butler scolded Scarlett for leaving their child alone at night.

A black woman with a child who continued to live a single life became unsung. A black mother could live a nonrestrictive life if she had many children, because the older kids took care of the younger ones.

They raised themselves in her home; there were no adults around to complain or report the mother to child services.

After she left Eighty-First Street in Manhattan, my mother couldn't keep an apartment of her own. Mrs. Martine wasn't a pushover like my mom thought. She owned property, and that represented success in the fifties. If you were black and owned property like a brownstone, as Mrs. Martine did, you were considered accomplished. Now we had been evicted again from another well-to-do place. I have the memory of "Charlie Brown," the words to the song singing in my ear. That is when my love for music began.

CHAPTER 4

From Pillar to Post

WITH TWO SUITCASES FILLED WITH clothes, my mother and I rode the train from affluent Brooklyn to the rundown part of the Bronx. I hadn't been back to the Bronx since I was born in Morrisania Hospital on November 20, 1953. A moonlit night appeared in the Bronx sky when we got off the El train, as my mother and I walked down the steps and across the street. We entered a building and walked up three flights of stairs. We came to a dark-brown door, and my mother knocked. A shabby-looking, older black woman in rags opened the door. Standing there with a smile on her face, she invited us in. Once inside the apartment, we were standing in the living room, positioned in the middle of the railroad-style apartment.

In the 1900s, most apartment buildings in New York were designed like a railroad track. They had a long hall that to me looked like a spine running through the flats. Rooms were situated either on the left or the right side of the corridor or in the middle of the track. The apartments with the rooms in the midst of the flat were cheaper to rent, because the rooms had no doors. Tenants or visitors who entered the rooms or resided in them could walk straight through each chamber that traveled from the front to the back of the apartment.

Tenants with a lot of kids rented this style of apartment because they could always see what their children were doing in their rooms.

These non private rooms were difficult to rent out to lodgers because of the lack of privacy. Families or seniors occupied these tenements. The toilet room is the only room that had a lock on its door. The kitchen contained the stove, cabinets, refrigerator, and two sinks for dishes and washing clothes. A large bathtub sometimes had a shower with the curtain rod circling it. Most of the time, the large tub sat right in the middle of the kitchen floor, with the stove in the background.

The kitchen could be situated in the back or the front of the apartment; all the same, they were in the classified ads in the papers as railroad apartments.

This woman's bathtub sat in the middle of her kitchen in the back of her apartment. In the front was the bedroom to the right, and to the left, straight ahead, were several other bedrooms. I looked both ways, and I saw hoards of furniture, bags of clothes, and lamps. I saw piles of junk from the twenties, thirties, and forties—decades of stuff that the smiling woman had never thrown out.

Today we would call her a hoarder. Although she had swept the floor, she wasn't aware that the floor needed mopping. Nor had she washed or taken a bath in a week. A foul smell that emanated from the apartment assaulted our nostrils. As she drew near to us, the odor became stronger.

With a happy face, she showed my mother and me to the front bedroom. We entered the bedroom, and we saw bags and suitcases of junk filling one side of the room. She had made a narrow clear path between the bed and the garbage. She had the bed positioned next to the window; that layout must have been the style at that time. It changed when people started shooting at the window and killing people in their beds.

My mother opened the window to let a little air into the room. She pulled back the bedspread and sheets. They were not dirty, and nor had they been slept on by anyone. The woman slept in the back room because of the noise from the El train. Every ten minutes a train loudly passed by the window.

In New York, the brick buildings didn't shake when the El train rambled across the tracks. In the fifties, most El trains were in the slum areas of New York. Most apartments were in the front, and if you lived on the third or fifth floor, all you could see was the El train passing by your window.

My mother slowly and carefully escorted me to the toilet room. The apartment had a narrow space carved out to walk to the bathroom. I looked at the junk piled up to the ceiling on both sides of the walls. It seemed fragile as an avalanche that had become used to the loud, rumbling sound of a railroad train traveling through a winter wonderland. The darkened hallway dimmed my vision so that I could only see the narrow path before me. I thought I'd better not bump into anything. I became overwhelmed by fear, because I didn't want the junk to come tumbling down upon me.

My mother and I approached the toilet room door. I tried to relax, and I felt safe when we entered the little toilet room. Much to my mom's surprise, the woman had toilet paper. Virginia put some on the toilet seat and let me go to the bathroom. There was a little sink in the room, and I washed my hands. She took toilet paper, wet it, and wiped my face with it. My fear had subsided. I tried not to forget how we walked to the bathroom. My mother took my hand, and I held on tightly. We exited the bathroom and walked into the dimly lit apartment to the bedroom up front. My mom put me on the bed with my clothes on and covered me with the blanket.

Virginia told the woman she would be back and exited the apartment. That night I lay there alone, and the woman never came into the room. I could hear the El train all night like a thundering earthquake. The El slammed and banged across the tracks as it passed the window.

I looked at all the junk in the room as I lay in the bed. The thought of my mother not ever coming back scared me out of my wits. How could she abandon me in that filthy apartment with this woman who kept smiling? Despite the roaring noise from the train and the overwhelming junk in the poorly lit room, I managed to fall asleep. My mother came back early the next morning, when I was half-asleep. She had a taxicab waiting downstairs. She had no time to bid the woman a long good-bye.

Because I heard the El train all night and worried that my mother would not come back, I couldn't wake up and enjoy the moment of seeing her return. She quickly picked me up, and we exited the apartment and building. As soon as she removed me from that filthy apartment, a breath of fresh air flowed freely into my lungs. My mind went blank, and I fell into a deep sleep. Virginia put me into the taxi, and I continued to sleep. The taxicab drove off and across the Bronx Bridge into Manhattan.

CHAPTER 5

My First Responsibility

WHEN I AWOKE, I FOUND myself in Mama Do Johnson's large apartment in Harlem, not far from Miss June's house. Her husband, Mr. Johnson, came from Africa. She had three kids with dark-brown skin, one girl and two boys. They were six, seven, and eight years old. She gave me the playroom to sleep in, and once again, my bed was next to the window. I didn't see my mother anywhere. Mama Do Johnson treated me well, yet her kids abused me. I recall being in the playroom, playing with toys. Mama Do Johnson had many toys. There were toy soldiers and cars for the boys to play with, blocks with ABCs and numbers on them, and dolls.

It happened to be raining outside, and the kids and I were playing on the floor in the toy room. I was playing with a soldier figure and the blocks. Mr. Johnson had a green army belt with a gold-color metal buckle on it. One of the boys had it in his hand. I was so involved with the toys that I didn't see him raise the belt up at me. He swung the belt at me and hit me in my head with the belt buckle. I remember crying and seeing blood dripping down my forehead onto the floor.

Mama Do Johnson came into the room and asked, "What happened?"

"He did it," the little girl yelled.

"He hit her in the head with the belt," the other boy and the girl said at the same time and pointed to the kid.

Mama Do Johnson took me into the bathroom and cleaned me up. The cut was on my scalp above my forehead; I had a bump and small cut. Luckily, I didn't need stitches. Mama Do Johnson took her belt and beat her son. Her kids never hit me again; however, they continued to abuse me.

I didn't attend school. Instead, I stayed home with Mama Do Johnson while her children were in school. I don't remember ever going outside. At night, I'd lie in my bed and listen to the cars drive by on the streets. While the sounds of the city swirled around in my ears, my heart continued to wish for my mother to come and get me. Mama Do Johnson let me sit in the kitchen with her and eat my breakfast, lunch, and dinner.

I never ate with her and her family. Mama Do Johnson washed me up and put me into bed before she served dinner to her husband and kids. One day I was asleep in the chair, and the little girl stood over me. I felt her drop something in my right ear. I didn't know what it was, and my ears hurt for a few days. I didn't tell Mama Do Johnson, because I didn't know what she had done. All I knew is at certain times of the day I had a sharp pain in my ear, and then it stopped.

Mama Do Johnson had retro chairs covered with green-and-red plastic, the ones you see in a 1950s diner. The kids picked at the chairs, and one of the green chairs had a hole in it. Even with the plastic torn off the chair, the kids still used to sit on it. The sharp pain kept shooting through my ear, so I shook my head, and I felt something rattle around in my ear. I decided to lean my head to the right side and hit my head with my small hand. Out popped a piece of green, balled-up plastic from the chair. The little girl had rolled it up in her hand and dropped it in my ear while I slept. She was a mean little girl, and she never helped her mother.

I became Mama Do Johnson's little helper. I prayed every night for my mom to come and get me. Mama Do Johnson's kids were so mean to me that I didn't play with them. A feeling of delight came over me when they left the house and went to school. At the same time, I felt lonely.

One day a young, light-skinned, pretty, well-dressed woman named Eva came to see Mama Do Johnson. She had her baby in her arms, and his nickname was Pudding. He looked like light toffee pudding. He had black, wavy hair. Pudding resembled a beautiful baby doll, and I fell in love with him. My lonely days were over. Mama Do Johnson put Pudding in the middle of her bed. I didn't leave his side. I sang to him, kissed him, and hugged him.

Pudding was my first responsibility. I babysat him while Mama Do Johnson did the housecleaning, laundry, and cooking. She could leave me with Pudding and know he would be safe. I was four going on five years old. Mama Do Johnson went to the grocery store several times and left me with Pudding.

When she came back, Pudding and I were in her room where she left us. I felt like Pudding's protector. I did everything except change his diaper and fix his milk. Mama Do Johnson did that, and I held his bottle and fed him. Pudding had a young mother in her mid twenties. Eva worked in a secretarial job. She would bring Pudding every morning at eight and pick him up at six o'clock.

Eva was invariably well dressed in business suits, jewelry, and high heels and carried a matching handbag. She wore makeup and lipstick, and her nails were short, polished, and manicured. She had her hair cut short and curly, which complemented the shape of her face. Eva had the image of being organized, attractive, classy, and responsible.

I never saw her husband. I never thought for a moment why she couldn't be my mother. I loved my mom so much that I became blinded by my loyalty to her. I also felt that it was no one else's responsibility to be my mother; it was hers alone. Not for a second did I become jealous of Pudding. I loved him too much to be jealous. When Eva brought him to Mama Do Johnson's, I became as happy as a lark. Every day he was my only joy and responsibility.

I didn't see Pudding on weekends; I wished I did. Eventually my dream came true, and unexpectedly Eva started bringing him on some Saturdays. Pudding's mother looked neat in her dungarees and sweaters.

She paid Mama Do Johnson weekly for babysitting Pudding, except I was the one babysitting him. One Saturday, Pudding's mother brought him to Mama Do Johnson's and left. Mama Do Johnson's kids were home; I didn't play with them. Pudding was all I needed. I received unconditional love from that baby. The other children were mean, jealous, and unloving. We all were in Mama Do Johnson's room. She told me she was going to the store and left me to watch Pudding, and then she left. The kids, Pudding, and I were in the room alone. Pudding lay in the middle of the bed as usual.

When the kids started one by one approaching the bed and slapping Pudding on his hands, I yelled, "Leave him alone."

Every time I tried to stop one of the kids from hitting Pudding, one of the others ran and hit him. They laughed and kept taking turns hitting him. Pudding belted out a screaming cry. Mama Do Johnson came back, hearing Pudding screaming at the top of his lungs. She rushed into the room, terrified. Pudding, being seven or eight months old, never cried. He was a happy, calm baby full of love, and caring for him was easy.

Mama Do Johnson didn't work hard for her money. I never forgot the look on her face when she entered the room. She knew she had no business going to the grocery store and leaving Pudding.

Mama Do Johnson had left Pudding and I alone many times before, and nothing had happened.

"What's the matter with Pudding?" she asked, raising her voice.

"She hit him," the kids said right away, pointing at me. Mama Do Johnson looked at me.

"No, I didn't. Your kids hit Pudding," I said.

"She hit him—yes, she did," the kids yelled.

"No, I didn't."

Mama Do Johnson thought for a second. "I know Amina wouldn't hurt Pudding. She loves Pudding," Mama Do Johnson said. She took her thick belt out of the closet and whipped all three of the kids, chasing them to the front of the apartment. As they felt the lash of her belt, the kids screamed in pain as Pudding had.

She had the appearance of a heavyset, big, strong, tough black woman. Her husband was a big, black African man, whom I hardly saw; he worked a lot of hours. He left before I woke up, and Mama Do Johnson put me to bed when he got home for dinner. I saw him on weekends for a moment, and then he was gone. Mama Do Johnson had to keep the apartment together and take care of the kids and me. When her husband came home, she had to take care of him. Pudding was an extra responsibility that she gave to me.

When she beat her kids, she beat them, so they didn't do it again. Her children continuously had severe behavior issues, and they didn't give her any peace. Mama Do Johnson had no delusions about her kids. She knew they were mean. She made her children go into their rooms, and she closed their doors. Later that day, Pudding's mother came to pick him up. The backs of Pudding's hands were red and bruised. I don't know how Mama Do Johnson explained it to Pudding's mother, Eva.

After that day, I never saw Pudding again. Eva never left him with Mama Do Johnson again. I withdrew into my lonely world. I lay in bed, and tears trickled down my face.

I wished my mother would come and get me. It seemed as though she vanished out of my sight. Although my mom never came to visit, she had the decency to tell Miss June where Mama Do Johnson lived. Miss June got in a taxicab and visited me. For the first time since I had been staying with her, Mama Do Johnson took me downstairs and outside to greet Miss June. She was a shut-in, doomed to a life of disease and pain, and she couldn't walk up five flights of stairs. Her love for me seemed to be greater than her illness. It made her reach deep down inside herself and do things she couldn't do.

There she sat proudly in the taxicab when I came out of the building. She got out of the cab and stood in front of the door. I ran with open arms to her and wrapped my arms around her waist. Miss June couldn't pick me up and called me by the nickname she gave me: Meeda.

"Hi, Miss June."

"Meeda, how are you doing? Are you OK?"

"Miss June, I miss you."

"I have to go home now. I wanted to see you."

"OK, Miss June."

She didn't kiss me good-bye, call me baby, honey, or sweetheart. Miss June wasn't affectionate, though her actions spoke louder than her words and displayed her deep love for me. She escorted me to the sidewalk, and Mama Do Johnson grabbed my hand. Miss June got back into the taxi.

"Good-bye, Miss June." She waved good-bye, and the taxi drove off. That was a good day for me. I didn't cry or have time to think about my mother. Surprisingly the fear and worry that had besieged me in the past vanquished. Somehow I knew that someday I'd be living with Miss June again. A surge of confidence overwhelmed me that made me feel that Miss June would be a never-ending force in my life. No matter how much time we were apart, a bond existed between Miss June and me. She did more for me than my mother ever did regarding reliability.

Virginia had affection, and she would hug and kiss me. Miss. June had a sense of humor, and she laughed more with me and at me. She had a calm and unemotional temperament with everyone. Miss June met her problems head-on, while my mother ran away from hers. I was so happy to see her that I didn't think about Pal who had died or my situation.

I went back upstairs with Mama Do Johnson. I didn't tell Mama Do Johnson or Miss June that I missed my mother. I secretly wished I could go back and live with Miss June. When winter arrived, I couldn't open the window to hear the sounds of the city cars at night. To me, it resembled living in prison on the fifth floor. Mama Do Johnson's apartment was in the back of the building. When I looked out my window, I saw the back of another building.

Down below was a backyard. Looking at it from a child's eyes, it seemed to be a block long, with buildings on each side. Clotheslines connected two buildings opposite each other. Tenants hand-washed their clothes and hung them on the lines to dry. On the ground were piles of garbage and bricks, rubbish, junk, stray dogs, cats, and rats. Little spaces of clear pavement, thousands of small rocks, and broken glass covered the rest of the backyard. Sometimes kids went back there out of curiosity to play, and they walked on the rubbish.

Once winter had befallen Harlem, I didn't hear any kids or cars. Snow covered the ground. New York had become a silent city as the temperatures dropped into the teens. No one ever told me what month it was.

As I slept through the night, I remember it being cold. I had pants over my pajamas and a wool hat on my head. My little winter coat was used as an extra blanket on top of my blanket. It was common in Harlem for boilers to break and for superintendents not to send up the heat to the rooms. The landlord got it fixed, because he didn't want to buy a new boiler.

Since the boilers were from the 1800s, they continued to break—especially on the coldest nights or days of the year. Mama Do Johnson's apartment was no exception. When I awoke, a haze of smoke hovered over me in my room. I got out of bed and slipped into my shoes, dazed and confused. I didn't stop to fasten them. I put my coat on, and I walked out into the hallway. A fire blazed out of the kitchen doorway. I could see ahead to Mama Do Johnson's empty bedroom.

"Mama Do Johnson. Mama Do Johnson," I called out. I got no answer as I passed the empty kids' room. I realized I was alone in the apartment. They all had rushed out of the apartment and forgotten me. The toy room was the last room next to the exit door, which had a long, iron, police lock bar on it. There is a trick to opening a police bar–locked door from the inside. I didn't know how to open it. I had only been outside once during my stay at Mama Do Johnson's apartment. Something said don't go to the door to and try to open it.

Next to my room was the bathroom, then the kids' rooms, the kitchen, living room, and the master bedroom. The flames from the fire roared from the kitchen. I passed the kitchen and continued to walk forward to Mama Do Johnson's room.

When you entered the front door, all the rooms were on the right side of the apartment wall. The living room and Mama Do Johnson's rooms were straight ahead. I didn't panic or scream. It seemed like my instincts were leading me to Mama Do Johnson's room. The smoke filled the apartment. Ahead of me were a haze and the smell of smoke. As I walked closer to Mama Do Johnson's room, a young, handsome, tall, blond fireman appeared out of nowhere.

He extended his hand to me. "Give me your hand," he said. I gave him my hand, and he held it.

"What is your name?"

"My name is Amina."

"I am going to carry you on my back downstairs to safety. When I stoop down, I want you to get on my back, grab hold of my neck, and don't let go."

"OK."

I got on his back and wrapped my arms around his neck and my little legs halfway around his rib cage. The whole back apartment, including my room, blew up in flames. The blaze blocked the front door. The window in Mama Do Johnson's room was open, and the fireman came into the apartment through her window. With me on his back, holding on for dear life, he climbed out of the window. There wasn't a fire escape. He had an extended ladder on the side of the window.

"Hold on tight," he said to me. He reached over and stepped on the ladder. I looked down, and there were five flights to the ground. Mama Do Johnson and her three kids, along with the tenants, were standing below, looking up at me. I could see a blanket of ice and snow below covering the rubbish in the backyard. Thank God the wind did not blow on this bright, icy, sunny morning, which prevented the fire from spreading. It was cold.

Even though I didn't have any socks on, the fire that had engulfed the apartment and sprayed flames out of the window warmed my body. As the fireman and I descended the ladder, I looked down again. My shoe fell off, and I watched it hit the ground below. Mama Do Johnson grabbed my shoe out of the snow. I clenched my arms tight around the fireman's neck. I didn't let go for fear of falling to my death.

When we reached the bottom of the steps, I touched the ground, and the fireman escorted me to Mama Do Johnson. She bent down, grabbed my foot, and put my shoe on. Being alive made me happy, standing there in the cold with Mama Do Johnson and her kids.

I looked around and saw all the people from the neighborhood and the tenants watching the fire above. That day I realized that the only one who looked out for me was me. Mama Do Johnson and her kids left me asleep and escaped the fire. I felt abandoned; the only real love I received was from myself. I was alone. Mama Do Johnson had her husband and kids. I had pride as a child. I felt ashamed of being homeless again, and the only clothes I had were on my back.

If I had never awoken or had not had the courage to walk to the back of the apartment, I might not have survived. I began to feel the cold travel up my legs.

"We are waiting for the Red Cross to come and take you to a shelter," one of the firemen said. A feeling of gratitude washed over me, and at the same time, I felt stripped bare and full of shame in front of all the people. I had no one at that moment—no home, possessions, money, or mother. Again I had no control over my life. The first five years of my life, the same questions appeared in my mind. Where was I going? What was going to happen to me?

CHAPTER 6
Stability in My Life

I GAVE UP ALL HOPE and resigned myself to be doomed in the land of the homeless forever. Out of nowhere, my mother appeared, and she swept me off to Miss June's. Mama Do Johnson no longer had a house. Suddenly I had a home filled with unaffectionate love. I can only remember that Mama Do Johnson lived on 116th Street between Seventh and Lenox Avenue. She lived five blocks from Miss June.

Although the memories of Mama Do Johnson stayed with me, she faded into my past. I never saw her or her family again. Stability felt like a warm blanket that I had longed for during the cold winter nights. When I lived at Miss June's, I never forgot that feeling of stability.

On the first day my mother and I arrived at Miss June's, my mom had bought me a fancy new outfit: a beautiful light-green nylon dress, socks, black patent leather shoes, and a gray coat. All my clothes were lost in the fire. When I left the Red Cross shelter, this was the only outfit I had. I thought my mother would purchase me a new wardrobe once we got settled at Miss June's.

We were at Miss June's no more than ten minutes when my mother said, "I am going to the store. I'll be right back." She exited Miss June's apartment, and day after day, Miss June and I waited for her to return. Finally, a whole week went by, and my mother didn't come back.

Neither Miss June nor I had an inkling as to when she'd return. Miss June knew Virginia did not become incarcerated. She left no phone number, address, or a friend's number.

My mother disappeared for five years. Again I was left with only the clothes on my back. Much hardship had befallen black men and women of a darker skin tone. Irresponsible, careless, disappearing behavior for black people received forgiveness. The black community didn't judge them harshly my mother garnered sympathy instead of persecution for being a negligent mother. From the majority or black people others didn't take on her responsibility. Being black, you couldn't hide. You couldn't say you were Jewish, German, or European.

You were black no matter what language you spoke. I wore the same dress for a week. Miss June didn't have any money to buy me clothes. She appealed to Mrs. Hunter, who had nine children, some girls and some boys. Her husband worked as a super for Mr. Delany, a light-skinned West Indian man. He owned twin buildings, 219 and 221. She had many clothes that were hand-me-downs. All sudden, I had a box full of clothes. The winter and spring passed, and summer arrived.

CHAPTER 7

Being a Brat Has Its Consequences

SUMMER WENT ALONG FINE. THE city had planted trees along the block, and they bloomed, providing some shade from the blazing heat. As kids, we would sit under a tree and play. One sunny day I met a lovely little girl named Anne. She didn't live on the block; she was visiting someone in my building. She had a light-skinned complexion with wavy, sandy-blond hair and piercing, green, cat-shaped eyes. She was with another little girl named Sara, who lived on the block several doors down from my building.

We were sitting under a tree playing with dolls. Being a little taller than both girls, I must have looked like a giant to them. However, I approached them. I remember Anne playing with me first, and then she and Sara were playing together, and not with me. I felt left out. Because of Anne's beauty, everyone treated Anne like a little princess. I had no intention of hurting her; I'd never had a fight in my life or ever hit anyone.

My attitude became possessive. What was Anne doing playing with Sara? They were sitting on the ground under the shade of the tree talking. Sara jumped up, got in my face, and said to leave her friend alone. She attacked me. She turned into a wildcat on me, scratching my face and punching me, and I didn't hit her back. I stood there in shock and screamed and cried. No one came to my rescue or broke up the fight before Sara had severely beaten me up.

This fight scene played out to the end. It was traumatic for me, because I had never been attacked or beaten, not even by my mother at that time. Sara grabbed my thumb and bit a hole in my thumb. As my thumb was in her mouth, her teeth clenched down hard, and I screamed and cried.

Miss June heard the screams and looked out the window. She yelled, "Fight back! Fight back!"

I stood there and let little Sara beat me up. I have never been so vulnerable and afraid. Miss June finally came out of the building with a belt in her hand. She crossed the street and watched as I got torn to pieces. Miss June finally broke up the fight and beat me with the belt for not fighting back. She held my hand as we crossed the street, and she hit me with the belt.

When we entered the house, Miss June struck me a few more times with the belt. Then she took me into the bathroom and washed my face. I had scratches on my face. When I went outside again, little Sara didn't bother me. Anne went back to wherever she lived. The kids on the block teased me, saying that little Sara beat me up. I never forgot that attack; it did something to my psyche.

After that day, I learned to fight back. No mercy was ever shown to me, not even from Miss June. That is when I realized I lived in a ghetto. I couldn't be afraid of anyone, even though I remained afraid of little Sara.

Fear came in twos. After little Sara, there was Dee Dee, a dark-skinned girl who terrified me. I became best friends with two sisters who lived in the next building, Lola and Corin. Lola was older than I and not afraid of anything. Dee Dee feared Lola. I told Lola that Dee Dee scared me, and Lola wrestled Dee Dee to the ground.

"See, how easy it is? I can take her any day. There is nothing to be afraid of," she said. I learned to survive in the ghetto. I made friends with the girls who were tough and fearless and who could fight.

I don't remember ever getting into a fight with light-skinned black girls. They were treated special, like princesses. The light-skinned girls who lived on the block had pretty clothes and lots of toys, and they acted softer and more feminine. I remember one, named Diana, who moved in building 217 on the block. She was a true tomboy. I took to her right away. She could run fast, and she knew a little judo; she gave me a judo throw, and I hit the ground. She laughed all the time. She had a little brother, and they both wrestled together all the time.

Diana and I ran, and she toughened me up. I became athletic, and running came in handy later on. To beat me up, you had to catch me. A year later Diana's mother suddenly moved, and I never saw Diana or her brother again.

CHAPTER 8

Attending a Ghetto School

FALL ARRIVED, AND I STARTED school. I registered at PS 81, located on 120th Street, one block from where I lived. One block down on 121st Street was PS 144, which my friends Lola and Corin attended. I never understood why I didn't go to PS 144. It looked like a new school building.

Lola's and Corin's parents worked, along with a Chinese girl named Nancy. Her parents had a Chinese laundry on the corner. They didn't live in Harlem. They brought Nancy to work, and she went to school. Nancy taught Corin how to speak and write Chinese. Both schools were in walking distance, with a street crossing guard on Seventh Avenue. That is when I realized that the system separated black kids among the classes in the ghetto; Miss June was on welfare, and the children who were dirt poor went to PS 81.

Any kid whose parents worked or owned a business went to PS 144. PS 81 was an old Gothic-looking school where the school desks were attached to the floor and chair. The top of the desk came open, and you could put your books into it. On the right side of the school desk, it had a hole for an inkwell. At ten o'clock, a waitress rolled a tray of cookies and half pints of milk into the classroom. The snack cost us ten cents. Then at lunch, we had a different soup and sandwich every day. My favorite was pea soup with a hot dog.

I remember being in first grade on picture day. That day my teacher, Mrs. Johnson, took a thick wooden ruler and smacked my hands a couple of times. I was unruly in class, because I had never been hugged or kissed by anyone except my mother. I acted out with a show of bad behavior. I think children need affection from whomever they are living with, whether parents or other caretakers. For the first time in my life, I had stability.

That fall a woman named Mamie moved in with Miss June. Mamie didn't work for Miss June; she was a lodger who paid for her room and board. She had a record player, which she later gave to me. Mamie shopped, cleaned, and cooked for Miss June. She combed and braided my hair every morning and got me ready for school. After Mamie had gotten me dressed and sent me off to school, she went to work around ten in the morning.

Mamie had the most beautiful party dresses and high heels. She straightened her short jet-black hair and snatched it back off her face. Mamie had a matching long, human-hair ponytail piece. She laid it on her lap and combed it straight before attaching it to her hair. Her makeup consisted of face powder, red lipstick, and eyeliner.

Mamie looked like a little brown Barbie doll. On weekends, her boyfriend and a group of friends came by the house to pick her up to go ballroom dancing. Before they all left, they drank whiskey, smoked cigarettes, and danced to the records playing on her record player. With a high and music in their ears, they all left the house merrily on their way to ballroom dancing. Mamie worked hard during the week, and on the weekends, she partied hard.

She did everything for Miss June and a lot for me. Mamie liked to be sort of bitchy with everyone except Miss June. She wanted to appear big because of her small frame. Mamie walked around being bossy, swishing her shoulders back and forth. Nobody dared to correct her when she pronounced Miss June as Miss Jones. It was Miss June's house, and bodacious Mamie acted like it was hers. She loved scrubbing and cleaning that large apartment until it was spotless. It made her feel powerful and needed.

In fun, I would be sassy to her, and she'd snap back at me with her bossy attitude.

"Don't get fresh with me, missy," she retorted. Mamie fell hard for her boyfriends. Despite her loving heart, they dumped her because of her bossy, bitchy attitude. She poured herself into her work, stuffing pickles in jars at a factory. She had to love and nurture someone; that is what she needed.

Everything that Mamie did for Miss June, she did passionately and without payment. Mamie and Miss June were both unaffectionate women who had their hearts broken. They both were atoning and repenting for their past sins. She and Miss June both suffered for love. Mamie loved to be driven, competitive, and bossy. Her responsibilities to us made her forget her painful breakups. You had to look beneath the surface to see that deep down inside, she had a good heart and soul.

On my seventh birthday, Miss June gave me a party. I never had a birthday party again. Every year afterward, I was too afraid to ask why I only received a present, not another party. I never forgot my seventh birthday. That day I wore a new avocado-green chiffon dress. The color matched Miss June's long hallway walls and bedroom.

All the kids on the block attended, and a happy feeling came over me. I didn't think about my mother and why she wasn't there. Mamie baked me a two-layer coconut cake with vanilla icing in the middle, topped with sweet white coconut flakes. There were seven pink birthday candles on top of the cake. The kids and I ran up and down the long hallway from the bedroom to the living room.

I received several gifts from each child who attended my birthday party, and I had so much fun. We laughed, played, and danced to the music on Mamie's record player. Then the candles were lit, and everyone sang "Happy Birthday." I made a wish and blew out the candles. The cake was cut and served with vanilla, chocolate, and strawberry ice cream. That day I wasn't trying to make sense out of my life.

After my mother abandoned me, I accepted the fact that she wasn't going to be there. She had never given me a birthday present or attended any of my birthdays except for the day I came into this world.

It was Saturday, the day after my birthday, and Billie let me spend the night at her house. I remember I used to be so happy to spend the night with her. She cooked dinner, and she had every kitchen appliance in her blue-and-white fluorescent-lit kitchen. She also had a floor-model TV in her well-furnished light-beige living room. Billie lived in the upper-class society in Harlem. At dinnertime, Billie prepared her food like the British, with a little seasoning. Her food was unlike Miss June's soul food cooking, because Billie couldn't eat spicy food. She had gone to Mexico back in the 1930s and had eaten some hot chili that destroyed her stomach.

Billie made the best vanilla-and-lemon pound cake. A gallon of Breyer's vanilla ice cream remained in the fridge for dessert. Her dog, Blackie, sat at the kitchen table, covered in black fur with a white streak down his neck. I didn't know at the time that dogs took on the energy of their owners. Blackie had his moods like Billie. If he went to her bed or was eating, I should not bother him. When we ate dinner, she gave him scraps from the table, and he sat at the table waiting to get a taste of our food.

For breakfast, she gave him toast and a piece of bacon. Blackie ate his canned dog food, and he loved vanilla ice cream. I wondered why Billie kept vanilla ice cream in the fridge. As a kid, I loved chocolate ice cream. I didn't know that dogs couldn't eat chocolate. Everything she ate she shared with Blackie except chicken and meat bones. He didn't digest them well; he had stomach problems like Billie. Blackie was the exception, because dogs love bones to chew on and eat.

Blackie and I sat in the window in Billie's huge master bedroom. We looked out from the second-floor window down onto Seventh Avenue. I missed Pal. I can't remember him being moody. I could growl in his face, and he never took me seriously. He loved kids because Miss June loved children. Blackie was serious like Billie. I growled in his face as we sat in the window. Suddenly he bit my nose hard. I was surprised that his teeth didn't break the skin. I grabbed my nose and held it to stop the throbbing pain.

Billie was in the kitchen, and I didn't want her to know that Blackie bit me. Billie entered the room, and Blackie got scared and ran under the bed. I pretended as if nothing had happened. She didn't notice the bite, which left a dent in my nose. That cut from Blackie's attack is visible to this day. That night Billie gave me a shower in her huge bathroom. Everyone took showers in the cast-iron claw-foot bathtub that was six feet long. You could easily drown in it. After my shower, I got into her king-size bed. The sheets had been washed and ironed by a Chinese laundry on Seventh Avenue. Lying on those crisp sheets, I fell fast asleep. I awoke early Sunday morning, washed up, got dressed, and sat at the kitchen table. I looked forward to having homemade waffles for breakfast.

Billie purchased a beautiful silver waffle iron that she kept clean and shiny. After breakfast, she washed the dishes, dried them, and put them away. I dusted all the figurines on the mirrored shelf cabinet in the living room.

After I had dusted the living-room furniture, I could sit down and watch the floor TV. All the best shows came on Sunday: *Gunsmoke, Bonanza,* and *Walt Disney.* The prime-time channels were 2, 4, and 7. The ghost channels were 5, 9, 11, and 13. All old movies came on 5, horror films on 9 and 11, and 13 had educational shows.

During the week at Miss June's, I watched shows on her small TV: *Romper Room, Diver Dan, Officer Joe Bolton, The Three Stooges, Bozo the Clown,* and *American Bandstand.* Miss June watched the soap operas early in the day: *General Hospital, As the World Turns,* and *The Edge of Night.* Billie walked Blackie at ten thirty, and then she and Blackie visited Miss June at eleven. On weekends when Mamie slept late, Billie combed my hair. I can still smell the Dixie Peach Pomade in my thick, braided hair. She also made sure that I washed up, and I was clean and free of odor.

When I was a child, Billie didn't compete with me, but that changed when I got older. In the black community, competition starts when the daughters or sons come of age. The mindset is to do as I say, not as I do. When the parent is dating, drinking, smoking, and cursing, the child adopts these behaviors too. Then the mother says, "I am the only sinner in this house. If you don't like it, then get out and get your place. I am not going to have you disrespecting my house."

I felt the parent should say that if you are dating, drinking, smoking, and cursing like I am, do it in here where I can see it. That is the ghetto; it pushes the child out into the street with a life choice of win, lose, or draw. Die or change. Many people made a draw in the ghetto. Others got killed or survived and lived from paycheck to paycheck. Money was flowing, and some took their money and went back down South. Others found it hard to save, although they had their daily wants. Some Harlemites never left the ghetto. Their lives had peace and prosperity. They grew old and died.

One evening, four other girls and I were standing on Miss June's stoop. Claud popped up and said, "Let me take a picture of you all." We all posed, and the photograph came out to be a good photo full of young energy. I cut the other girls out of the picture, because it was too long to put in my photo album. He did that from time to time. He'd show up and take a picture of me, Miss June, or Pal and me looking out the window. He roamed around Harlem, and if he saw a good shot on the spur of the moment, he took a photograph.

Claud developed the pictures himself and brought them back to us. I think Miss June paid him something for the pictures. Claud became Billie's boyfriend. A talented photographer, he also played golf. Claud dressed sharply, and he wore his salt-and-pepper hair cut short. That complemented his smooth-shaven milk-chocolate complexion, along with a tall, slender physique and navy-blue eyes.

Claud had a happy full-of-life personality as if he didn't have a care in the world. He came on the scene in 1955 and hung around until about 1966. Billie broke up with him, and he didn't come around anymore to take pictures. I'd see him standing on Seventh Avenue, old and lonely without his camera.

One day, Billie and I were looking out the window. We saw Claud downstairs, standing on the corner.

"Billie, there is Claud! What happened to Claud?" I said.

She didn't answer or yell hello; she ignored him. Claud started looking dehydrated and walking slowly like an old man. During the last eight years, his quick, youthful spirit had disappeared, and eventually Claud died. I never found out what happened between them; she kept it a secret.

I knew he had gotten sick, and he fell fast. I was too young to do anything about it. Billie saw him and looked the other way. That's the way of the blackboard ghetto jungle. Only the strong survive. Once you became an adult—and if you didn't take life seriously—too bad for you. After the Depression, people had suffered, and their hearts were hardened. Especially toward men: they were expected to have and keep a job to pay the bills. Billie was smart. She never paid rent; the lodgers paid her rent, and she worked. I assumed Billie expected Claud to give her a little money, and all he could do was take pictures. He probably wanted her to support him, and she didn't.

She told him the same thing she said to me—that he wasn't going to make it with photography; she said it wasn't a stable job. Although Claud had an education, he loved the freewheeling lifestyle of a photographer and a golf player. Claud died in the sixties. If only he had lived to the seventies, he could have been a successful photographer. He took beautiful natural photographs, and he had real talent.

Golf was a white man's sport. Black people had to play on their courses and couldn't make any money off it. A successful merchandising store opened up on the corner of 121st Street and Seventh Avenue. I walked past it every day on my way home from school. Golf club members were packed inside, buying the merchandise.

For me, elementary school wasn't that bad. We had old books and equipment. When I moved in with my mother, the district closed PS 81 down and made it into an adult education center.

They built a new elementary school across the street from Miss June's on 121st Street between Seventh and Eighth Avenue for all the poor kids. It took the place of PS 81, while the popular kids still attended PS 144. There was segregation within the ghetto community. You weren't brought up to become successful; you were brought up to get a job, not to imagine or have any ambition for anything else.

A majority of black people had a sense of pride about themselves and their family's appearance. It became necessary to have manners, a clean body, combed hair, and matching, wrinkle-free, colorful clothing. Whether they were hand-me-downs or not—as long as you were neat and clean, you were OK. Miss June and Billie did the best they could for me.

CHAPTER 9
Being at the Mercy of Others

LENNARD WAS A BIG FAIR-SKINNED man who visited Miss June. He had a loud, thick, medium-pitched voice. Lennard ran numbers for the Mafia from farther uptown in Harlem. His bookie paid large sums of money; Miss June didn't go out, so he came to her. She gave him her five or ten dollars to put on her number. If she won, Lennard delivered the money personally to her.

Harlemites had to go to the policy store to pick up their money. Individuals crammed into the seedy, smoky place and sat around all day reading their dream books and newspapers. If they hit, they got paid right there on the spot. If they hit big, they had to wait a day for the Mafia to bring the money in suitcases. The Mafia paid. They couldn't afford for someone to say, "I hit the number, and I didn't get paid."

Lennard had a stack of money, and he gave Miss June change for a twenty-dollar bill. For my birthday, he bought me the prettiest dress and gave me nine dollars, and I put it in my little bank. My bank had a shape like the old-lady-in-the-shoe house, and it was the color of maroon and made of plastic. There was a slit in the top where I could put my coins in, and it had an opening button under the shoe that I could twist open and put dollar bills inside. I had my bank for a couple of months; I didn't touch it.

Mamie continued to take care of me and help Miss June. I went to school every day dressed in a clean and neat outfit, my hair combed and braided.

After five years of not seeing my mother, she showed up with a pair of red shoes. They were the ugliest pair of orthopedic shoes I had ever seen. Miss June and Mamie made me wear those shoes, as my mother instructed. At the time, I didn't have bad feet. Even at that early age, I had a fashion sense of what looked good and what didn't.

My mother knocked on Miss June's door in the middle of the night. The door didn't have a knocker; you had to knock on the door with your fist. My mother had a sharp tap that identified her before she announced her name. She had changed her name from Virginia to Amina, the same as mine. She changed it later on so as not to be confused with me. I awoke to the knock on the door. Miss June jumped up out of bed and let her in.

She needed money right away. Her eyes locked on my little shoe bank on the bed stand. My mother grabbed my bank and took out my nine dollars. She quickly put the money in her coat pocket and hugged and kissed me. Virginia told Miss June she had to leave. She walked out the door, and I didn't see her for a year.

Many nights I tried to stay awake to listen for her knock at the door. As the alarm clock ticked, I fell into a deep sleep. Before I knew it, the bell rang, and morning had arrived. I had to get up to go to school. I went to the bathroom and sat on the toilet. My body swayed from side to side as I still slept. Mamie came into the bathroom.

"Come on. Let's get you washed up and ready for school," Mamie said. Day after day my school life continued without the appearance of my mother.

A year had passed. I was eight years old and settled into my life at Miss June's. An old man from India approached my mother with an offer to pay her $10,000 to buy me and take me to India. I'd become his wife once I turned thirteen and started menstruation.

My mother needed money badly and became excited at the prospect of getting all that money. Finally, this was her chance to get out of the daunting responsibilities of being a mother. Not hesitating to think about the old man's offer or even examine it carefully, she rushed to Miss June's house, this time in broad daylight. At that point, Miss June had two other lodgers, Albert and Nan, a couple staying in the first bedroom. Mamie remained in the second bedroom. My mother told Miss June and Mamie about her deal with the old man from India.

I am so sorry to this day that Mamie, Billie, or Miss June didn't reveal this situation to me until many years after the fight. Billie took it upon herself to tell me. Mamie and my mother were in the living room, and they were arguing. Virginia had the advantage, being larger and taller than Mamie. A fight broke out between them. Albert and Nan were standing in the doorway of the living room. They were watching the brawl, and I got in between Albert and Nan. I am small, and I looked at the fight.

"Go ahead, Mommy, get her," I said. Albert looked down at me and didn't say a word. He turned his eyes back to the fight. Miss June came to the living door. Nobody said a word; they watched.

Mamie had short hair without her ponytail switch. My mother pulled her hair and twisted her head; she tried to throw her down onto the living-room floor. Mamie stood her ground and fought Virginia back fiercely. Billie came and broke up the fight. I was a child who missed and loved her mother dearly. Without ever knowing the truth of any situation, I only knew that my mom wasn't around.

When I mentioned it in anger, Miss June and Billie scolded me and said, "That is your mother." They did not say one word to turn me against her. God told me to honor thy mother and father; he didn't say what kind of mother or father. I don't know; why they never reported my mom to child welfare maybe it was because she was black, and they were from Mobile, Alabama, the South. Everyone who lived on the block came from the South.

Black people felt empathy toward one another's hardships and psychological problems in the late fifties and early sixties. The fact was, Mamie fought my mother tooth and nail to prevent her from selling me to that old man. I think Mamie threatened to call the cops on Virginia. She saved me from a pedophile.

One day I came home from school, and Mamie had moved from Miss June's. I never saw her again. I asked Miss June about her. She told me Mamie got her a place somewhere in Brooklyn. She never left an address or sent a Christmas card or called. Some years later I heard she died. Mamie drank whiskey heavily on weekends. I never knew her last name or where she came from or where she was born.

Mamie had suddenly moved in with Miss June. She stayed many years, saved up her money, and suddenly she left. Mamie didn't even say good-bye to me. I wondered if she heard me root for my mother during their fight. I hoped she knew that I didn't know what she and my mom were fighting over. If I had known what my mother's intentions were, Mamie would have had my support 100 percent.

My mother moved in with Miss June when Mamie moved out, and she got a job as a waitress at an Indian restaurant in Harlem. She knew the man who owned the restaurant. He went by the name of Mia. I'd go over there and eat; he had the best curry food. She stayed for a while. When she was home, she slept all day. She worked from four o'clock to midnight. She didn't come back until two or three in the morning.

My mother became a tyrant and a Muslim religious fanatic. I remember she scraped the inside of her ankle while she was waitressing at the restaurant. It became a big, open sore, and it didn't heal. That's an early sign of disease—when you don't heal. In my mother's effort to escape reality, she became obsessed with Allah. She thought about Allah twenty-four/seven. On the other hand, she didn't pray six times a day.

After living with Miss June for a while, she couldn't go to work; her mind wasn't on it. She went to the street corner with a stepladder and spoke on 125th Street. She stayed out all night in front of Chock full o' Nuts, a coffee shop chain of restaurants all over New York.

The Chock full o' Nuts location was right under the Hotel Theresa. Before Fidel Castro came to stay there, blacks hated the system of segregation. The hatred became a platform for the Martin Luther King Jr. riots. I love Chock full o' Nuts coffee. I even worked at one of their locations as a teenager. I had a heroin addiction that I tried to kick cold turkey. My stomach became knotted up in painful cramps. I walked out on the job in the middle of my shift. I lost the job along with the heroin addiction.

At this location, there were nuts, militants, and radicals standing in front of the coffee shop all afternoon until the wee hours of the night. Customers had to pass these fanatics to get into the cafeteria. Laborers who worked at the stores on 125th Street and tourists who stayed at the Hotel Theresa patronized the coffee shop. Billie passed by there on her way to work on 125th Street. Billie's apartment window was right above the store front headquarters of the Black Panthers.

In the early sixties, change and radical beliefs that bucked the system were emerging. The Black Muslims sold papers on the corner. Later on, the voices of Malcolm X and Martin Luther King Jr. spoke loud and clear. Early on, this was a perfect scenario for my mother to be swept away in this life-altering force. She became mentally consumed with her fanaticism. She lost her job at the restaurant; she couldn't be on the corner preaching and then go to work. My mother had no since of time.

I've never known her to wear a watch. When I came of age, Billie gave me a watch. Miss June told her she had to move. In spite of my mother's behavior, she allowed me to stay. Virginia wanted me to live with her, and I refused; my life was in Harlem. I was not a Muslim. I am a Christian, although I attended mosques in the fifties.

My mother made me take Arabic classes at the mosque. Peace-loving, well-to-do Muslims surrounded me. They traveled all over the world to different mosques. They came to America to visit the mosques to pray and celebrate. A myriad came from Egypt, Saudi Arabia, Pakistan, Africa, and Sudan. They were a rainbow of colors; they did not consider themselves white or black. I'd see very dark black men with red hair and blond-haired, blue-eyed, and white-skinned Egyptian women—or the opposite.

If you stated that they were white, they would reply that they were Egyptian. In Egypt, people are not classified by the color of their skin; whether black or white, all Egyptians are equal. They lived a cosmopolitan life and spoke Arabic, English, African, French, and Italian. In Mecca, the holy city, everyone ate and slept in the same room; there was no segregation.

Even though my mother was among them, none of them reached out to help her with her responsibility as a mother. Miss June became the only one she could dump me on. She must have appeared to be a fanatic to them. They did nothing to deter her from coming to the mosque. They didn't argue with her or try to detain her or stop her from ranting on about her obsession for Islam. She prayed when she attended the mosque and never prayed at home.

They were peaceful, loving people who minded their own business. After their stay here in the United States, they went quietly back to their countries. As a Christian, Miss June sent me to Sunday school in my mother's absence. I came of age, enjoying my freedom with the other kids in Harlem who were nine, ten, twelve, and thirteen years old.

We stayed out late at night on the block, and nobody bothered us—not to say that there wasn't danger in the streets. Some blacks who lived in Lenox Terrace were wealthy and bourgeois. Even though they lived in Harlem, I never saw any of their kids on the streets. We were kids of poverty and had lots of freedom.

My mother was determined to get me to move with her, and we got into an argument. She attacked me, hitting me in the head with her fist, and I fought back. Flashing before my eyes were all the times she'd been on the street corner, along with all the years I lived with her and Miss June.

My friends discreetly pulled me into the hallway to tell me about my mother on the street corners. I was embarrassed and ashamed that they all knew I was an abandoned child who wore only hand-me-down clothes like an orphan.

My mother became a mad tyrant filled with anger and hate. She hid her abusive personality beneath the surface. In the fifties, she hid it under a cheerful facade. When we lived on West End Avenue, after my mother got off work, she would pick me up from school. My mother and I went to the movies every night in the fifties. She wanted to escape the reality of her daily life by getting lost in the movies.

How I loved her. So at Miss June's, I tried many nights to stay awake, hoping to hear her knock on the door—so that I could yell to Miss June, that is my mommy.

I remembered those awful beatings she gave me in the middle of the night when I lived with her. How she dragged me by the hair up the steps, beating me for going to the movies with her male friend. Sister Marion was a large woman who married a well to do small Pakistan man we called him Pop. He had a disease he kept a spit can that he spat in by his bed at all times. He and Sister Marion were muslins they had a grown son and daughter. My mother left me with Sister Marion when she lived in Harlem on 110th Street. When Sister Marion moved to West End Avenue, my mother and I moved in with Sister Marion. Sister Marion and Pops bought a house in Brooklyn that is where my mom's abuse of me reared its ugly head. If it weren't for Sister Marion, I'd probably be dead by my mother's hand. All the times I was hungry and left alone while she was supposed to be at work or who knows where, fate had someone there to prevent her from going off the edge.

Time did not have mercy on my mother. I saw her descending into a vagabond lifestyle filled with cruelty, hate, and poverty. All I could think about was breaking free of her, living my life, and taking charge of my life. I had thick shoulder-length hair, and she grabbed my hair and pulled it. I became so tender-headed. I still remember the horror of my screams as I kicked her as hard as I could in the sore on the inside of her ankle.

She let go, and I ran out of Miss June's house. When I returned, she forced me to go with her. She refused to let go of me because all her anger and frustrations were taken out on me. Once I was gone, there was no one for her to beat up. I agreed with her, and I went into the kitchen and got a butcher knife. I had a trench coat on, and I hid the knife inside the belt of my pants and closed my jacket.

When we got into the taxicab, the driver took us over the Harlem River Bridge. I looked out the window of the cab as we were crossing the bridge from Manhattan to the Bronx. I panicked as we got closer to my mother's new abode. I pulled the knife out and attempted to stab her in a fit of rage. She grabbed my hand, sank her teeth into my hand, and the knife fell out of my hand. She punched me in my face, and I hit her back. We were rumbling in the back of the taxicab.

"I'm not staying with you. I will kill you first!" I yelled.

Either the taxicab driver was stunned or he enjoyed watching the fight from his rearview mirror. He didn't say a word, and he kept driving. When we got to her destination, she dumped me at a kind woman's house. As I waited for my mother to come back, I told the woman about my mom. I didn't speak ill of her, although I told the woman all the things she had done to me. I explained my mother's negligence. I told the truth, and I told the story so well and in such a calm manner that I convinced the woman to help me.

She revealed that my mother's welfare checks were coming to her house, because Virginia didn't have the mailbox key to her new apartment. I asked her to give me my mother's county check, and she said she knew of a grocery store that cashed checks.

The woman gave me Virginia's money; she believed everything I said about my mother. No one could make up a story like mine. I cashed the check and went back to Miss June's house to stay. Virginia called Miss June and told her I tried to stab her, and I stole her welfare check. She became afraid that if I didn't stay with Miss June, I'd kill her. My mother, scared straight, told Miss June I could stay with her without any interference from her.

I had a flashback to when I was in preschool, and Miss June had given me bubble baths. She used Tide soap powder detergent to make a bubble bath. I broke out in sores all over my legs and vagina. Instead of taking me to the skin doctor right away, my mother beat me and terrorized me into saying I had been molested by a small boy in the preschool I attended. His mother got on the phone with me and denied that her son had done anything to me.

I had a stuffed tiger teddy doll with a long tail. My mother threw me on the bed, pulled down my pajamas, opened my legs, and she kept poking the tiger's tail in my vagina to simulate the little boy's penis. She interrogated me all night, asking, "Did he stick something like this inside of you?"

I screamed and cried. "No!"

"Yes, he did!" she said as she slapped me. Miss June left the room as my mother interrogated me. Virginia made a big deal out it and blamed everyone. She had to get to the truth of what happened. At the same time, my mom didn't accept the truth I was telling her. She swore this child had molested me, and she made me confess to it. She beat and terrified me. I became tired and scared. I wanted to go to sleep and for her to stop slapping me. She had taken me out of the school.

I don't know what happened to the little boy. I guess his mother took him out of the school. The teacher never stood up and said, "I was watching these kids. They were never out of my sight, and nothing happened." My mother went into a frenzy. It scared Miss June because I was living in her house in her care. I was only five years old, and this angry woman had me pinned to the bed, interrogating me. No one stepped in to back me up.

As I said no, my mother said yes, something did happen. Nothing happened. It was one child's word against another child's word. The sores kept occurring, and huge scabs appeared on my legs. My mother finally took me to the hospital. They took a sample of one that covered the sore on my leg and discovered that Miss June had put detergent in my bath water. Miss June had never gone to school, so she didn't know.

My mother was an educated, mean, and cruel woman who thought the worst. Virginia never called the school or the child's mother to apologize for making me accuse her son of an act he didn't commit.

When I lived with my mom, Virginia, in 1963, the World's Fair opened in Queens, and my mother had a job in the African pavilion. She made sure she worked the night shift from four to midnight, and she got home around two in the morning. She'd wake me up and re-member something I did two weeks ago and start beating me in the middle of the night. How is a nine-year-old child going to remember what she or he did three weeks prior?

No one was there to protect me as my mother sat on my bed fum-ing in anger. If she didn't hit me with her fist in my head, then she'd beat me with a belt.

The extension cord was the worst. I remember how it stung when it slashed across my legs. Scared out of my wits, I padded myself with pillows under the covers, so when my mother woke me up and started to beat me, I'd jump under the covers and shield myself with the pil-lows. She tried to pull the covers off me. In her attempt, she became frustrated by the difficulty of pulling the covers and pillows off me and trying to beat me with the belt or cord at the same time.

I prayed to Jesus Christ many nights, wishing she wouldn't come home and beat me. She never came back in the middle of the night and snatched the covers off me while I slept. That wasn't her modus operandi; she had to wake me up and talk to me first to build up some chump charge against me. She needed an excuse to work herself up into an angry gorilla frenzy.

Like she needed justification for beating me three to four times a week. It became an outlet for the frustrations of her life. The fact was that she had the responsibility of a child. She pretended to be caring for her daughter by herself. My mother was a horrible cook. Nevertheless, she kept a decently clean house. When she was there, she slept during the day. She made me pick the corns off her feet and comb her coarse, short hair. It calmed her nerves, and she fell into a deep sleep.

When fall arrived, she began to disappear. My mother stopped waking me up in the middle of the night. I didn't see her at all. I set the alarm clock to wake me up for school. I started cooking breakfast for myself, and I had lunch in school, my only prepared meal.

When the kids bullied me, I fought back. Every day I had a fight with a bully. When my mother finally came home, I told her I was a victim of bullying. Being a latchkey child was not fun, so she put me in judo class to learn how to protect myself. My mother feared that if something happened to me, then she'd be liable.

When I attended the Japanese Buddhist Academy, I was the only African American child in the judo class. I looked mature for my age because of my tall height. I started making friends with influential, courageous, feminine women who fought back. They were brown and black belts in judo. I sparred with all the Japanese black-belt men, and they threw me all over the mat with no mercy. I was left alone to fight my battles. I didn't back down, and the bullies backed off.

It became known that my mother left me alone in the apartment. Neighbors heard her beating me every other night. I'd scream at the top of my lungs. The landlord complained. Maybe that is why she stopped and disappeared.

I went back to stay with Miss June. I brought all my female judo friends up to Harlem to meet Miss June. The day that my mother released me into Miss June's custody, I felt spiritually independent.

No longer was I at the mercy of others. I could take my life into my hands. If my ship sank, then it was my choice to jump overboard, with the option to sink or swim. Dealing with one crisis after another, I continued to drown in the sea of life.

Fortunately, the universe provided someone from somewhere to throw me a lifesaver of love. They say God takes care of all fools and babies. I agree. He took care of me in my darkest hour. I wasn't ever going to live with my mother again.

My father is Somali from the culture of Puntland, where the ancient Egyptian black pharaoh originated, along with language, formal dress, and the arts. Inscriptions of Queen Hatshepsut of Egypt claim that her perfect mother, Hathor, was from Puntland. Other inscriptions indicate that Egyptians in the Eighteenth Dynasty considered Puntland the origin of their culture. Puntland was not only a significant partner in trade, however; it was also a source of cultural and religious influence and a land the Egyptians viewed as their place of origin, blessed by the gods.

Virginia loved the idea of marrying a Somali man and having his baby. With all the rich history, she didn't want to be a slave or have a child from a man who had slave ancestry. She didn't want to be who she was pretending to be: a wife and mother. I remember being three years old, when my mom and father visited me at Billie's house. Virginia had found out about female genital mutilation. She learned that Somali women did this to Somali girls. Virginia thought that was horrible and if she went to Somalia, this would happen to her and me. A great shame about this horrific ritual done to married and unmarried women had befallen upon her. Plus, women had great freedom if they were nomads, wandering the hot desert. Virginia could not see herself in a desert she didn't know how to cook. How was she going to hunt and kill cattle and prepare her meals? Being a nomad is isolated and self-sufficient.

Staying at home doing domestic chores didn't suit her. My mother knew if she went to Somalia with my father, then she couldn't be free to come and go as she pleased. I'd be at the mercy of whoever she let take care of me. Miss June and America were familiar territories; Somali was another world that my mother wasn't willing to take the risk to get to know.

The Muslim community closely monitors their women. They travel in groups and are not out after dark without their husbands. My mother came and went as she pleased without watchful eyes on her every move. Despite her hateful attitude, America was the most friendly country.

It's hard to become and remain a success when you don't know where you come from or who you are. When the destiny ship comes, you don't get on it, because you don't know where you are going. A lot of black people accepted that their ancestors were slaves and made the best of their lives. Some even became wealthy and famous.

My mother couldn't accept that she had descended from slaves. She continued to chase freedom; she was talented and skilled. There was no reason that she shouldn't have had a prosperous life. My mother said it was the white man or the black people. She blamed everyone, refusing to admit that she should have blamed her free-wheeling attachment to me. Most of her anger was taken out on me. Success comes with responsibility versus freedom. She had a constant struggle in balancing the two concepts.

I knew deep down inside that she couldn't do it long-term. Her mental illness didn't allow her to see the truth or admit that she was the one who was holding herself back. My mother had help; some people loved her child and went above and beyond for her daughter. She was too jealous to realize she had a blessing.

My mother still had the freedom to come and snatch me up whenever she wanted to. There were no legal adoption or guardian documents. They say there is a thin line between genius and mental illness. My mother, Virginia, became like the vagabond in the New York Bowery who had a good education and came from a stable home. Even with a great head start in life, she still ended up in the Bowery.

CHAPTER 10

I Was a Victim of Bullying

I'VE HEARD AND READ ABOUT preventing bullying, and I have even gone to police functions to prevent bullying. Looking at these awareness campaigns brings back memories of my childhood right up to high school and college, where bullies made me their victim.

Being a latchkey child in elementary school is all about survival. I can't remember a year of being in one place when I lived with my mother. Not only did I get bullied, I also saw others get bullied. Between being shuffled from Virginia's to Miss June's, I lived with Sister Marion three times in my life when she lived in Harlem. She moved downtown to West End Avenue and then bought a brownstone in Brooklyn. My mother dumped me on Sister Marion and disappeared. When we lived in Brooklyn, I had to take care of myself.

We lived downstairs, and Sister Marion stayed upstairs. Most of the time, I'd steal food from grocery stores. I didn't see my mother for days, and she had canned food in the cabinet that I couldn't open. I was in the third grade. I walked a couple of blocks to elementary school. I ate lunch in school, and I had no dinner.

A girl bullied me at school and as I walked home after school. When I finally saw my mother, I told her about this girl. My mom found out where she lived, and we went to her house. Her mother had two other kids. She had cooked franks and beans, and the kids were setting the table when we arrived.

I hadn't eaten since lunch, and starvation overwhelmed my stomach. The aroma filled my nostrils. It smelled so good; I craved a taste, knowing I couldn't ask for any food. My mother told the girl's mother that she had been bullying me. The girl's mother didn't scold her in front of us. She said her daughter wouldn't bully me anymore. After that, I went to school, and I remained hungry.

A young woman named Jean lived in a house across the street. I befriended her, and I spent time with her after school and on weekends, and she fed me. Before that, I'd go into grocery stores and steal cupcakes, fruit—whatever I didn't have to open with a can opener or heat up on the stove. Sister Marion talked to my mother about me being hungry.

"There is canned food in the boxes for her," Virginia said.

We didn't have a refrigerator, so she kept canned foods in boxes. Sister Marion had a refrigerator. My mother had not made a deal with her, so it wasn't Sister Marion's responsibility to feed me. She had taken care of me when we lived in Harlem. When I didn't see Jean, I stayed in the house and looked out the back window at the backyard.

One spring day in mid-afternoon, I saw this little black girl. She was around six years old, and she didn't have any clothes on. Five white boys from eight to ten years old were surrounding her and looking at her. She quietly stood there like she didn't realize what was happening to her. One of the boys grabbed her arm and turned her around so the other boys could see her naked body. They hadn't seen a little naked black girl before. It wasn't clear to me whether they were going to assault her sexually.

I didn't let it get that far. The boys were bullying her, and they had made her take off her clothes. I ran upstairs and told Sister Marion.

She and I both rushed downstairs, and we entered the backyard. When those boys saw this large, tall figure dressed as a covered-up Muslim woman, it scared them. They took off running, leaving the little girl standing there naked.

"Child, where is your mother? Where are your clothes? Where do you live?" Sister Marion asked.

Scared and shy, the little girl moved in close to Sister Marion. She put her arms around her waist and laid her head against her apron. Sister Marion became flustered and hugged the little girl. The little girl didn't speak. Sister Marion took the little girl into the house and covered her with a sheet.

She called the cops, and they came and took the little girl away. No one said anything about it ever again. At the time I attended elementary school, adults wouldn't talk to me about an incident like that.

After that terrible beating my mother gave me, Sister Marion finally put my mom out. We moved back to Manhattan, and I attended PS 145. Virginia disappeared. I'd stay after school and play in the gym until five o'clock. On a snowy day, I was in the gym, playing with a ball. I was standing in the center of the gym, not bothering anyone. While all the other kids were running around the gym playing, I was off by myself. A tomboyish Puerto Rican girl approached me. I found out later that she went by the name of Doreen.

All of a sudden, she said, "Meet me outside after school. I want to fight you."

"OK," I said. I didn't run, back down, try to defuse anything, or talk my way out of a fight. I wasn't afraid. When the gym was over, it was five o'clock, and I went outside to go home. The snow was falling heavily on the ground. Doreen and a crowd of kids were standing outside waiting for me. I'd done nothing to this girl. I hadn't ever seen her before that day.

When I stepped out on the sidewalk, she confronted me. She threw the first punch, and we fought. She tried to get me on the ground. I grabbed a car door handle, and in the process, my thumb got sprained. She finally got me on the ground, and she pummeled away, punching me in my face. I blocked her punches to my arms. She finally stopped hitting me. I was already down on the ground, and she'd won the fight.

Doreen and the crowd walked away. I got up out of the snow and ice. I picked up my book bag. My dress had become soaking wet from rolling around in the snow. I brushed the snow off my dress. I had on boots and tights. There wasn't a grown-up in sight. No tears were trickling down my face. I gracefully accepted defeat. I had been beaten so much by my mother that Doreen seemed like a lightweight to me.

When I saw my mom, I told her what happened. She found out where Doreen lived, and we visited her house. Virginia spoke to Doreen's mom. Doreen's mother called Doreen into the living room and scolded her in front of us. Doreen did not bother me again in school. Maybe I could have prevented Doreen from beating me up by running all the way home. Then I thought, why should I run? I was a goody-goody. The bullies were victimizing me. I started picking fights with boys. I was fighting all the time with teachers too. Fighting became a daily routine for me.

Some fights I'd win. Some I'd lose; I didn't care. The pent-up energy of neglect and being alone all the time made me angry, and I needed an outlet for that anger. I moved back to Miss June, who used to fight all the time in her youth. She encouraged me to stand and fight; she said don't run or back down. When I lived with Miss June, I couldn't run and tell Miss June. She would make me stand and fight.

I remember another bad fight I had. I attended summer school across the street from Miss June's house. I was in sixth grade—around ten, going on eleven years of age. I had a white male counselor. He had dark hair, and he wore black eyeglasses. Although he wasn't that tall, he looked like Clark Kent.

There was a chubby black girl with a stinky smell on her body. She never combed her smelly, kinky, poorly braided hair. She became enthralled by the counselor, and they held hands. She had a crush on him, and he didn't push her away. We were both in sixth grade, along with the other girls in the class. It looked awkward. He seemed to like the individual attention she showed him. Since he was a man in his thirties, I would think he'd be attracted to a woman in her twenties. That wasn't the case.

When the class went on field trips, all the girls lined up, held hands, and walked behind him. There were ten of us lined up in twos, so when we got on and off the subway, we'd all be together. She always got in front of all of us, and walked beside the counselor, holding his hand. With her tight pants on or shorts, she swished when she walked as if she were his girlfriend. When we got to our destination, she continued to hold his hand.

They held hands regularly when we went to the zoo, Central Park, Staten Island, Coney Island, or Rockaway Park. While the rest of us girls were talking to one another and enjoying the field trip, I kept seeing them blatantly together, and it annoyed me. The other girls didn't care, and it didn't bother them. They were from the South, so they weren't going to say anything to a white man. It bothered me. She seemed disgusting to me, so I picked at her.

I'd say nasty things to her like, "You stink. Why don't you comb that nappy head of yours?" She'd stand closer to him. He protected her feelings. I was jealous that a well-built, handsome white man—who was too old for her or me—allowed her to give him all this attention, and he was responding positively to it.

I could understand if he liked the girls in building 221 next to my building. They sat out on the stoop all night in the summer and ate Cornstarch. They also dressed like Twiggy in some of the most fabulous fashions that they created and tailored.

They wore cluster curls in their hair and used foundation powder on their faces. They applied eye shadow and thick false eyelashes on their eyes, and they painted their long nails white. They wore big chunky earrings, seventeen-inch miniskirts with white knee-high boots—sexy girls. They were running after the Temptations in the back of the Apollo as groupies. In that scenario, inspiration replaced jealousy; he did not see these girls, even though they sat on the stoop across the street from the school. They slept all day and came out at night after the school closed.

If he had seen them and been with them—they were seventeen, eighteen, and nineteen—that made more sense to me. He was in his thirties. The situation with him and the sixth grader did not feel right to me. This rude behavior, however innocent it may have been, was none of my business. A mutual attraction that was taboo was being carried on in front of my face. I was too young to put my finger on it, and I could not communicate how I felt.

Adults were in the school to assist me. I didn't know how to tell them that there was something wrong. At the time, I didn't know what the word *pedophile* meant; I had never heard of it. He could have said in his defense, "I am a counselor showing affection to this underage girl." It seemed too close for comfort to me, and nobody else said anything.

All the other girls respected authority. Most of the girls in the class were from the South. They were taught not to say anything if a white man said or did anything, no matter how terrible. Go about your business and don't ever confront anyone.

I had a lack of trust and a bit of doubt. Why? Because the authority had left me to fend for myself, and being alone made me independent in thought. There was no Internet so I could Google a question and get the answer. I had to think to get my answers. Whether they were right or wrong, I had to trust my instincts.

One day we were in the gym. She did something, and I went off on her. She ran to him, and he stepped up to me and said something to scold me. I cursed this man out. I had a mouth like a sailor. I called him everything except a child of God, along with every kind of racial profanity I could think to spew out of my lips. He was steaming while being in control of his temper. He picked me up and threw me over his shoulders. He carried me outside the school doors and put me on the steps. He told me not to come back that day and slammed the school door shut.

I came back the next day. The counselor was assistant to another counselor, a white man. I went into the boss's group. His boss had a professional, respectful attitude, although he was not as handsome. As separate groups, we still shared the same gym. The counselor didn't say anything else to me, nor did I speak to him or her. I forgot about it. I was in a new group and classroom. She didn't forget. I got dirty looks from her, and I ignored her. I didn't have to see the counselor and her cuddle together for the rest of the summer.

Two days before the end of summer school, we all were in the school yard playing kickball. She moved close to me and attacked me. We fought. She knocked me down and kicked me in my stomach one time. That was the most painful thing. My body crumpled over, and I could hardly get up. The two counselors were there. I looked him in his face, and he was so happy she won the fight.

She didn't beat me up. I fought back but apparently not hard enough. She caught me off guard, now that I reflect on it. She resented me because I cursed out the man she had a crush on and liked. When I verbally attacked her, she couldn't stand up for herself. She didn't care about herself, her appearance, or her hygiene; she cared only for him. I had cursed him out and created this hoopla.

His boss analyzed it and figured out why I did something like that. After that incident, the counselor broke away from her and acted more professional. He started treating all the girls equally and was not so close to her. All the time that I picked at her, she refrained from arguing with me; even when we were fighting, she remained silent. I considered her quiet, dirty, inconsiderate, and inappropriate. I admit I had a lack of sensitivity toward her because of her behavior toward him.

My yelling and screaming at him brought him back to reality. He checked his behavior and response to her affection. If they were in the South, he couldn't lose his job over this underage girl. Even if he had sex with her, he could have behaved any way he pleased and gotten away with it.

If he slapped me a couple of times for speaking to him in that manner, I'd get the blame, not him. He could do whatever he wanted with impunity. We lived in Harlem, New York, in the 1960s, and he could have lost his job for dealing with her.

They both disappeared after the summer ended. Maybe she found some other older man and had sex with him. I hope she realized that her desires were taboo and went on to live a happy life.

The next bullying incident happened when I was twelve years old I went away to summer camp. I spent a weekend in the countryside of New Jersey. At the time, my mother couldn't find a place to stay, so she resided at Miss June's. I remember packing and taking a large bottle of her Avon Cotillion perfume. She allowed me to borrow it and bring the rest back.

After I got stomped in my stomach, I should have become more docile and timid. My thoughts made me angrier and more negative than ever, especially with my mother living at Miss June's. Her energy got me all fired up, and I wanted to fight. My finances were high. Harlem had these summer-only programs for inner-city youth. I received a weekly salary to participate in activities and trips. I got paid seventy-six dollars every two weeks. That's a lot of money for a teenager.

The program started in late June and ended in August. The Vietnam War had not happened as of yet. So many black youths were coming of age in junior high and high school, about to graduate and turn eighteen. Young, healthy men crowded the Harlem streets. The government had strategically planned every move right up until the Vietnam War.

As a form of economic control, the politicians who represented our district got funding for these programs and put them in place. It wasn't a success, because there were still poor, uneducated black people. As youths, we had money, and we spent it back in the community, which then paid taxes. They even had summer programs that paid me to go to school.

I accepted all the opportunities that were offered and attended. I also had a summer job. I was getting paid to go on a four-day summer camp vacation. At 6:00 a.m. sharp, nineteen junior high and high school girls and I were at the program's headquarters. We all boarded a private bus to New Jersey. The trip was our vacation gift for working with the program. It was an experimental project that the government offered to keep the inner-city kids off the streets, and it worked. It gave us something to do during the sweltering summer days in New York.

Our job consisted of collating paperwork and taking a census to see how many people lived in Harlem. After we had finished our work in the morning, the afternoon consisted of fun, games, music, and field trips. A largely air-conditioned storefront converted into an office contained us for eight hours. Two adult female counselors accompanied us on the bus. Everyone took a seat, and the bus pulled off. Two hours later we all arrived in New Jersey at a large two-story house. The house had ten bedrooms, two bathrooms, a large kitchen, and a living room. Two girls shared each room, and five girls shared a bathroom. We all shared a huge kitchen with two long tables and benches.

A female cook prevented us from coming and going freely in the kitchen or snacking between meals. She closed the kitchen after breakfast, lunch, and dinner.

As soon as we got there, I started gossiping and stirring up trouble. I knew all the girls from working with them in the program. I had no desire to start trouble with them in the city. When we got out into the country, with its quiet and serene surroundings, I realized I was not a country girl. The city with its hustling and bustling pumped excitement into my veins. The noise didn't stimulate me in the country. All I could hear were the crickets and owls at night. Even in the city at night, there were miles of street lamps that lit up the street.

When I looked out into the pitch-black, deserted country, I became restless because I didn't see another house in sight. I couldn't stand being cooped up with all these girls; I couldn't take it. This whole communion-sharing thing wasn't me. I kept running back and forth, talking about everybody to everyone else.

Unbeknownst to me, all the girls were communicating, telling one another what I was saying about each of them. I had to get out and walk in the countryside. I couldn't stand being around them in the house, bonding. I wanted to be free in Harlem. I went home after five during the week, without making allowances for anyone. It was my first time at a camp, and it didn't dawn on me that I had a phobia of being trapped and locked in.

Once we arrived at the house, the counselors seemed to disappear. In the big kitchen, we all sat down and had breakfast, lunch, and dinner. I stirred up so much gossip. Sunday arrived, and I had to pack and get ready for Monday's early-morning drive back to the city. When I returned to my room, there were nineteen girls lined up and standing in my doorway.

I thought my roommate had died or had an accident. To my surprise, they all were waiting for me to return to my room. They all were aware that I had been talking about them. A leader of the group thought my punishment should be walking a gauntlet and getting hit by all the girls. The room wasn't big enough for me to walk a gauntlet. They decided to stand in line and one by one punch me in the arm. They also rummaged through my suitcase and threw my clothes and personal belongings all over the room, including my mother's perfume bottle, which they broke.

I stood there and took the punches. I didn't cry, back out, or run to the counselor. I took my medicine. My arm was sore for a week as if I had gotten an injection.

Now I understand the saying, "You hit like a girl." That's what their girly punches felt like, and it didn't faze me. I was thinking about how was I going to explain this to my mother when I got home—her Avon perfume bottle had broken, and the perfume had evaporated into the suitcase. I wondered if she'd go into a fit of rage and beat me over a new, lovely bottle full of fragrance.

When I arrived home, my mother didn't beat me in front of Miss June, and she did not go into any of her gorilla frenzies. I could feel her negative energy bubbling under the surface. Her negative energy affected me.

Miss June had a calming effect on her. Miss June's presence in the home seemed to ease the pressure of being a mother and being responsible for a child. I stayed on my toes and kept alert, living on edge, waiting for my mother to explode. When we got back to the city, the program ended. I told her about the perfume; I didn't say what the girls did to me. Underneath, I could see her anger, but she didn't say anything. I told her it was an accident—the bottle broke in the suitcase.

Acting became my way of dealing with my mother. I spent most of my childhood coming up with creative ways to cover my ass. I didn't have to face the girls or see any of them ever again. None of them lived in my neighborhood; they lived in Upper Harlem or the Bronx. They didn't hang out where I socialized. I did see one girl when I became a successful young adult. She remembered me from the program. I reminded her of the incident when everyone punched my arm. I felt I deserved some type of retribution. I didn't sense that I would be ganged up on in that manner. I thought that was a horrible situation for anyone to experience.

This massive opposition took me by surprise. That taught me to deal with opposition. If I didn't like a group, then I didn't join it to be popular. I stood alone; it was nineteen girls against me. I didn't like them personally. I knew they were cowards. None of them dared fight me alone. They laughed at the things I said about them, because they were funny. I fought if someone gossiped or talked shit about my mother and me. I'd experienced being the laughingstock. My fierce pride made me champion my image. Kids can be cruel.

My name was Aminata Warsuma. The kids laughed, so I changed it to Amina Warsum. After my mother left school registration, I told the teachers not to call me by that name; it made the kids laugh, and I wasn't proud of that.

I made it through elementary school with Amina Warsum. When I got in junior high school, I put the *a* back on my last name. I started taking pride in my name, Amina Warsuma. In seventh grade, nobody knew me; my personality shone in front of strangers. New people opened up the warmth and leadership qualities inside me. They hadn't met my mother, and I could make my past as big as I wanted it to be; they had no ammunition to knock me down.

Also, I didn't wish to come to terms with the reality of what had happened to me. I didn't want anyone to know that my mother neglected and abused me. I didn't deal with the reality of being treated like a stepchild, a secondhand Rose who wore secondhand clothes. I was still a teenager, and I hadn't yet made my mark in the world, so I wasn't proud of my parents or where I came from.

My mother brought shame to me; society people looked down on her. I was the one crucified for her irresponsibility as a mother. Strangers and new people allowed me to escape and act as if none of the bad things happened to me. If anyone wondered if I had a great childhood like any other kid, I assumed an attitude of don't ask, and I won't tell.

I had the respect of the other children in the class. They laughed with me and not at me. Until one day at school, when I saw a boy who lived on my block. I had grown up with him, and we used to play together. His mother gave me clothes that her kids grew out of. They were quality hand-me-downs. He knew all about me and my mom. When he entered the classroom, he had been in another school or class.

Spring had arrived. By that time, all the kids thought they knew me. I was Miss Popularity in class, and everyone was happy and getting along. The way I acted around the block was different than how I behaved in class. I liked myself when I wasn't around the block. I was extroverted, and I remained that way when he entered the class.

Around the block, the other girls who had mothers and fathers were the leaders and had the extroverted personalities. When he saw how popular I had become, he had to rain on my parade. He knew if he revealed information about my mother and past, then the kids were going to see me in a different light. He told everyone in my class that my mom was from Africa and wore African clothes, which none of my classmates knew. I had been the queen of the class until he transferred in.

I reigned as a queen until they found out about my mother. My popularity started to decline—or maybe I acted differently, withdrawn. When I lived with Miss June, all the kids saw my mother speaking on the street corner. Virginia dressed like an African militant, and they would make fun of my name. He knew all about me and my mother. He knew she left me for five years and that his mother gave me his sisters' clothes. The class started laughing at my name, making African jokes. I had a bone to pick with him.

"Meet me outside after school," I defiantly said.

"OK," he calmly replied.

I felt like I was being bullied and made fun of by someone I grew up with and played with and knew. After school, the boy from my block and a gang of males kept hitting me with their books. I had a sharp-circle making tool in my hand, but I failed in my attempt to stab them. I had to level the playing field.

Then I said I would fight him by myself. I told them to back off, and they did. We started fighting. I scratched his face up. He wrapped his arms around my legs and threw me to the ground. I grabbed the car door handle again so I wouldn't go to the ground.

He kept punching me in my temple until I almost passed out. He and the other boys ran off and left me lying in the street gutter.

You are supposed to protect your head in boxing, and I didn't do that in this fight. He lived in the next building, and his sister did my hair. I went to school the next day. I didn't ever speak to him again. He got left back, and I told everybody on the block. It spread like wildfire, and he had to go to summer school. The kids laughed at him all summer.

He kept a low profile now that he knew what shame felt like and he could empathize with me. That didn't stop me from fighting all through junior high school. I kept fighting bullies, and they were boys, not girls. There was one girl who was skinnier than I, and I picked on her. When we had our tuberculosis test, she tested positive for TB. I stopped antagonizing her. When she coughed, everyone spread out. It looked like Moses parting the Red Sea; there was a clear path between her and the class.

Another girl from another class was picking on her, and they did fight. Surprisingly, she fought back. That was the way of the ghetto jungle. Boys snatched my umbrella and tore up my rain caps. I fought bullies even if I had to chase them down to get my belongings back.

I loved to run zigzag, stop, turn around fast, and run. I'd been running all my life. The more I did it, the faster I became. I learned to duck and dodge the ironing electrical cords that my mother swung at me. It made me aware that there had been a constant danger in my life of being physically harmed. In time, I developed fast reflexes and the ability to run incredibly fast. Bullies could not catch me.

I should have avoided many of my fights. Being chased after school by a group of bully boys is nightmarish. For some kids—like me—it was a way of life, a problem I had to face head-on and change. I didn't stay home for anyone or hide. I had to get out and bravely go where others feared. The group of boys had a leader they respected. I'd quickly hit the head of the gang in the face and run.

Nobody stopped or chastised them in class when they balled their fists up at me. The boys balled up their fists, touched both eyes, and then pointed to me, implying that this assault on my eyes was going to happen to me after school.

Around two, I started gazing at the clock on the classroom wall. By the time it struck three, I had devised my escape plan. One boy in junior high was waiting for me at the bottom of the five-step entrance to the school. I leaped off the steps, flew through the air, and landed on him like a wildcat. I grabbed his face and scratched the skin off it with my long nails. I kept scratching as he fell to the ground. I kicked him in the ribs and ran home. Miss June lived seven blocks from the school.

I entered the house and didn't mention the fight. The next day I courageously came to school as if nothing had happened. I ran into the boy in the hallway. His face was a bloody, horrible sight, all scratched up and covered with welts. He never bullied me again, and neither did most of the other boys. I fought until I broke the cycle of being bullied in junior high school.

Surprisingly, after passing all my courses, I didn't graduate from junior high. The board passed me on to high school because of my reputation for being belligerent. They did not wish to leave me back and have me stay another rough year in that school.

Mr. Basch, the assistant principal, was a fearless man with a commanding baritone voice. He was in his fifties, and his hair had receded far back on his forehead, like Dagwood in the comics. He even dressed like Dagwood in suits with pleated pants.

If he said something to a student, he yelled or spoke in an embarrassing tone. He was a white man holding his own in an all-black ghetto school. The board of education in New York dumped him there. He had been there for twenty-five or thirty years and had become the ultimate bully. Mr. Basch didn't ask; he commanded in a loud, nasty way. I can hear him yelling, his voice reverberating in the school's hallway.

"Warsuma, Samuels, get out of the hallway," he would yell. Samuels and I were close in the sixth grade, and we roamed the hall together. I refused to get left back like the other kids.

Junior high school changed. Instead of starting at the seventh and going through ninth grade, it began in sixth through eighth grade. When I arrived, I attended the sixth grade, and a group of girls attacked me in the gym.

Big-busted women graced the cinema screen, and I desired a bigger bust. Implants didn't exist at the time. I used cotton to stuff my bra. The girls in the gym noticed it—particularly Theresa, a big, tall girl. Out of all the girls, she was the leader of the pack in the gym. My whole body shouted healthy bones with curves. Theresa was fifty or sixty pounds heavier than I. When we were changing into our gym uniforms, a piece of cotton fell out of my bra. Theresa spotted it as it fell onto the floor, and I quickly scrambled to pick it up. Embarrassed, I scurried out of the locker room to stuff the cotton into my bra.

A large, removable, thick blue mat lay on the floor in the corner of the gym. That cushioned the students from the hardwood floors. I liked to be the first one there so I could have the mat all to myself to do my warm-up exercises.

I started warming up with a few exercises. Theresa and six other girls, dressed in their gym uniforms, were congregating in front of the locker room door. She told the other girls that I had a fake bust. Theresa rallied the six girls on the gym floor, and they all grabbed me. Theresa, being the biggest, got me down on the big blue mat I was standing on. As they tried to open my gym uniform, I fought fiercely. The intention was to humiliate me by pulling the cotton out of my bra and throwing it all over the gym. I kept fighting, becoming as slippery as an eel.

Theresa couldn't hold my hands down so that the other girls could unbutton my gym suit. In a terrified rage, I kicked her off me, got up, and ran to the gym teacher.

I told her they were trying to take my clothes off. The gym teacher gave a speech that we were all girls in the gym. She said trying to take another girl's clothes off was not acceptable behavior. If the girls didn't stop, the punishment was suspension from school for bullying and assault.

Theresa was a big girl. She lacked my fighting experience. I'd been fighting since elementary school. I was a loner, and I carried myself with fierce pride. It occurred to me that Theresa secretly resented me. We had not had an argument or altercation. I barely knew her. Theresa's character was that of a big punk and coward who lost her power. She couldn't succeed in humiliating me or dragging me through the streets as she desired.

Theresa had to rally six girls to help overthrow me, and she still didn't succeed in her quest. After that incident, I had no problem with Theresa or any other girl in junior high school. I thought I should team up with some other girls who could fight, so I'd never be jumped by a group of girls again. Girl bullies are mean. They will drag you naked through the mud, humiliate you, and degrade you. Boys are going to push you around, then beat the hell out of you and run off with their friends.

You will have girl bullies when you blossom into a young teenager. Boys will stop bullying you and want to date you. Girls will continue to bully you into college. That first year in junior high school, sixth grade, set the tone after that gym incident. I wasn't ever going to tolerate bullies of either gender.

Then I saw that Samuels was in my class. She had a fight with another girl who wasn't in my class. The battle took place in the school yard, and Samuels beat the hell out of that girl. I wanted to be friends with Samuels, because she could fight. There was another girl named Carol who could also fight. Finally, they separated Samuels and me, and she wasn't in my classes anymore.

Carol had a quiet disposition, and she didn't have the life or adventurous streak like Samuels. On rainy days, Samuels and I cut class and ran through Central Park. All the perverts chased us with their eyes. As the dirty men in Central Park were masturbating, we could see them through the trees. Afterward, we'd go to her boyfriend's house, where they fought and wrestled with each other. I'd watch them struggle in a rough, tough, and tumble manner.

They punched each other hard with their bare knuckles like two men fighting. Samuels laughed as he hit her in the buttocks and thighs. I wasn't that tough, nor was I bold enough to be sexually active with a boyfriend. He and Samuels were so in love. I think he was sixteen years old. After they got finished boxing and wrestling, they both burst out laughing. She was a beautiful girl with a beautiful smile and a light complexion. Samuels looked like she had a mixture of Native American, black, and Latino—curly, wavy, shiny black hair. Her clean, stylish appearance made a good impression on me. She laughed and talked, and we both loved attention.

Samuels and I were courageous, daring, and adventurous together. Mr. Basch caught us walking the halls several times, and we laughed at him. He didn't hurt our feelings when he yelled. We'd skip back to class. Mr. Basch looked at us as mischief-makers and hooky players.

When Samuels left and was no longer in my classes, Carol took her place. Carol and Denise hung out together, and they sat in back of me in class. I had not noticed Carol, nor did I know anything about her or Denise. Samuels had my loyalty and undivided attention. After Samuels left, I knew bullies were attracted to boys and girls who were alone, and I didn't wish to have the image of being alone. I turned around and started talking to Carol and Denise, and they befriended me.

Carol was the opposite of Samuels; she had no boyfriend. She had five brothers, and she didn't socialize. I guess being tall, big-boned, and slender made her shy. She had light skin and sandy-colored hair. Carol was plain and clean, not fashionable or adventurous.

She dressed as if she were attending Catholic school. She wore pleated, checkered skirts, penny loafers, and knee-high socks. She didn't command attention like Samuels and I did. Denise had a darker complexion than I, and she wasn't as laid-back as Carol. Denise didn't have a unique style of dress, so she blended in. She and Carol laughed, as I was the only one talking and telling jokes. We only hung out in school and didn't cut class or walk the halls. I improved when Samuels departed. I became settled and less restless. I took a sewing and cooking class in home economics. They have abolished those classes in junior high.

When I was with Samuels, the two of us seemed like we were ubiquitous. Samuels and I weren't restricted like the other kids were. Samuels and I ventured out of the classroom. I didn't have one fight the whole time with Samuels; we were together, and no bullies bothered us. I saw Samuels a few times in the hallway going to her classes, and then she disappeared. I don't know if she dropped out or transferred to another school.

Carol, Denise, and I ate lunch together in the school cafeteria and sat together in class. A female bully from one of Carol's other classes that Denise and I did not attend started picking on her. She thought Carol was a loner, because she was quiet and not outgoing. Carol wasn't someone who reached out or made an effort to talk to people. Neither Denise nor I knew that Carol had a bully breathing down her neck.

One day we were going down the staircase on our way to lunch, and a girl confronted Carol. She had a brown complexion and a heavier body frame than Carol. I couldn't hear what the girl was saying; I paid attention to her body language as it expressed hostility. That is when Denise and I realized that Carol was a victim of a bully. A silent anger came over Carol; neither girl yelled or screamed at the other.

Carol said, "All right, let's get on with it." All of a sudden, Denise and I had a front-row seat. Carol started boxing the girl. They were in the corner of the staircase. Carol kept her head low and kept punching in an uppercut motion, and she didn't stop hitting this girl. The girl kept hitting Carol's back, head, and shoulders. They were in the corner, up close and personal.

Students crowded in the stairwell to watch the fight. Carol did not desist from punching the girl. She fought like a professional boxer, and the girl fought like a girl. Finally, a teacher entered the stairwell and broke up the fight. Carol didn't refrain from punching the girl even as the teacher pulled them apart. One of the students pulled the girl away from the fight.

She went down the stairs, leaving Carol, the teacher, Denise, and me on the staircase. After the fight, the crowd of students dispersed from the stairwell and went to lunch. Carol didn't say anything to the teacher. When he realized that she wasn't injured, he exited the stairwell.

"Carol, what is going on? What happened here? One minute we were on our way to lunch, and the next minute a fierce fight breaks out," I said.

She looked at me and didn't say anything. Carol's hair was messy from the girl pulling it. She slicked her braided hair back into place as we approached the cafeteria. I couldn't stop wondering what caused this fight. Carol declined to talk about this girl to Denise or me. The girl shocked me because she suddenly appeared.

I had no concept that Carol could fight so well. "Who taught you how to fight like that?" I said in a praising manner.

"My brothers taught me how to fight," she answered.

Denise, Carol, and I all went to lunch. Carol didn't wish to reveal the girl's name or anything about her. The girl vanished, and for the rest of the school year, nobody fought with Carol. What I learned from Samuels and Carol was that you don't have to accept being a victim of harassment, stalking, or bullying because you are a female. If you know how to fight, you don't need anyone coming to your rescue. Fight back, because you can defend yourself.

After I had gone to the eighth grade, I missed Denise, Carol, and Samuels. They were irreplaceable. I became an independent attention getter.

I had to fearlessly stand on my two feet and fight my battles against bullies. After eighth grade, I went from junior high school to high school. I had taken sewing and cooking classes in junior high, and I had it under my belt. A change came over me; I desired to express my creative freedom. I started sewing and making my clothes.

I began smoking cigarettes. My diet changed; I no longer had urges to eat junk food at lunchtime. Creativity began to consume me. *Vogue* and *Harper's Bazaar* were my fashion bibles. That summer I got a lot of inspiration from Twiggy and Naomi Sims. I also stayed home and watched TV. Channel 5 aired hours of old black-and-white movies. Edith Head was the costume designer in practically every film. All the female movie stars wore fabulous clothes. Looking at old movies, I acquired lots of inspiration.

I'd make mod fashionable outfits. I started wearing makeup—red lips and cheeks. That summer, between the end of junior high school and the start of high school, a sudden transformation occurred. I blossomed into an attractive, fashionable teenager. I made several mod outfits that were out of this world, and I couldn't wait to wear them to high school.

As soon as I walked into the school door the first week of school, a bunch of girls laughed at my wild outfits and makeup. The leader of the pack was the instigator, and the others were following her. From my experience, I knew she was a punk and a coward.

"Trick or treat, you freak!" she continued yelling as I walked into the school building and down the hallway. I didn't know her; she started picking on me because of the way I looked, which was original and funky. Also, I was alone. She had a group who attended junior high school with her. Overnight I came to terms with expressing my creativity and being the person I desired to be. I came from a place where I was left to fight my battles: that's Harlem, the ghetto. Fashion occupied my time—selecting fabrics, sewing, and acquiring my modern wardrobe. I didn't have a chance to bond with any girls. Already I was being bullied.

I held my tongue and went to my class as the girl continued to rant. Her taunting went on for the first week of high school.

Out of all the girls who were with her, I noticed she was the only one ranting and following me. I went home that Friday and said to myself that if she yelled at me when I returned on Monday, I'd unexpectedly turn around, get up in her face, and curse her ass out.

That Monday I came to school. I had on a white leather fringed skirt with a leather vest that I had made with a hole puncher. I painted my lips and cheeks red. I had my hair parted in the middle of my forehead, pulled back in a tight chignon. On my ears were feathered earrings. I looked like a Native American. That was one of the fashions in the mid sixties.

Sure enough, as I entered the school building hallway, she and the girls stalked me. "Trick or treat, you're a freak," she ranted at me.

I turned around, rushed toward her, and got up in her face. "Who you calling a freak, bitch? Your mama is a freak, with your raggedy, no-fashion ass. Yeah, you got that red shit all over your face. You look like you are going trick-or-treating. Halloween is not here yet."

She quickly retorted, "You want to get down right now, right here? I am ready to whip your ass."

"You don't know me, and you have no right calling me names. Either you are going to fight or back the fuck off and mind your business."

Shock came over her face as the other girls stood around and watched me call her bluff. I wasn't about to let her mess up my outfit that I had worked so hard to perfect. I planned to wipe the floor with her and give her some of her own medicine.

Instinctively I knew she couldn't take an ass whipping. She hesitated, and fear of an ass whipping dawned on her.

"I don't have to ask you what I should wear to school. You are not going to fight, punk, so you can kiss my ass. I wear what I want to wear to school. Nobody is going to crush my creativity and self-expression. Get the fuck out of my face and stop talking to me. Don't speak to me," I ordered.

My element of surprise threw her off-balance after a week of my silence. I lit into her with a powerful force and stood up for my rights. The girls who were with her didn't say a word. It started in the school hallway, and it was going to end right there with me. A shadow of terror came over her. She feared the unknown and new people.

She didn't know my reputation in junior high school, nor did she wish to take the risk of finding out firsthand. My problem vanished after that day; I garnered respect. I boldly sashayed through the halls of high school with my hairpieces, makeup, and false eyelashes on my eyelids.

Naomi Sims was a black model at *Harper's Bazaar*. She wore blue eye-shadow rings around her eyes. I started copying that and wearing that to school along with my original fashions. Nobody said a word. I came and went as I pleased with the freedom to express myself without being bullied. Girls like Samuels and Carol didn't exist in my high school. The girls were more into fashion, and the boys were more into the girls. There was also the drug culture that spread like wildfire in the sixties.

Forty-five percent of the high school students were using heroin. They were either sniffing it or skin-popping it. I started sniffing heroin in my nose and acquired a habit; I didn't realize I had one. I was afraid of needles, so I resisted shooting up anything. I didn't like tracks on my arms or body; I didn't like permanent scars that needle tracks left on a person's body. When I got a couple of bruises in a fight, my skin healed well.

One day at work, I got stomach cramps. The thing about heroin is you don't know you are hooked on it until you don't use it for a day. On a Friday I was at work, and I suddenly felt an intense withdrawal cramp in my stomach. I had to leave work and rush home. I knew drinking milk would induce vomiting and flush the drug out of my system. The milk also killed the painful cramps. I lay in bed, and I drank milk and vomited all that weekend until the heroin vanished from my body.

I can imagine what pain heroin causes for someone shooting in their bloodstream. After that, I used it only sparingly to prevent forming a habit. That is the only way you can beat that white horse. One day I stopped using it altogether, because it was so painful to kick the habit.

Some of the high school girls I'd sit with in the lunchroom continued to use dope. Two girls invited me down to Alphabet City; Avenues A, B, C, and D is lined with project houses. One of the girls lived in the project. We were in the project hallway, and one of them pulled out a syringe, a needle, a spoon, and some dope. She heated it up with a match, and the other girl wrapped a rubber around her arm and then injected the needle into her veins.

She looked at me standing on the steps. "You want some of this?" she asked.

"No."

She injected herself into the arm, skin-popping. I stood on the steps and watched them get high and go into a deep nod. They got promoted to stone-cold addicts. The guys in school were dating the girls, and they both were using heroin.

No one was forced to use drugs. It was an energy—an influence that surrounded the Harlem community and all over. Before the Vietnam War, drugs took the fight out of everyone in high school. It was the sixties, and drugs of all kinds flooded the cities. You had your choice of narcotics as a teen or an adult.

I was in my thirties when I got into college. The college had a mixture of Puerto Rican and African American students. There was a young African American woman in my class who gossiped all the time.

"I farted," she'd blurt out, sitting in the back of the class. She was a rude, ignorant, impossible creature. She talked during class and did not pay attention.

She talked about how I dressed. One day I confronted her. "What is it to you how I dress?"

"You look bad!" she kept yelling. "You look bad! You look bad!"

When my child attended the first grade, I started dressing down. All my money went to my kid's appearance and home. I was acquiring a late education. They didn't have a Forever 21 store at the time. I wore unfashionable cheap clothes to school. I had to sacrifice fashion to get my degree in business. I got bullied when I dressed fashionably and when I didn't dress fashionably.

After that incident, she shunned all communication with me. She realized I had a serious interest in graduating and not dressing to please her. Eventually, the loser dropped out of school, and I got my degree. What I learned from that was that no matter what you do or how you dress, people are still going to talk about you. I had to know when to be sensitive and when not to be.

I wanted the ignorant creature to stop talking about me, and she did. I knew she gossiped about me when she went home. There was nothing I could do about it, and I didn't care. Females are the most vicious bullies; men will harass you with the phone. I am so glad the iPhone is on the market, because you can block those calls. We didn't have computers then, so I didn't have to deal with Internet harassment.

I have dealt with harassing, spying sorts of phone calls from men I dated and men I didn't date. A man I was dating terrorized me with phone calls and had different people call me. A great depression came over me. I'd had the best intentions for him. I wanted to be his woman. I got so obsessed with that incident that I lost my courage for a while.

I couldn't figure out what I had done to him to be a victim of this type of behavior. All I got from him was cruelty and infringement of my rights. He got his comeuppance when he called another woman in the same manner, and she sued him. How strange karma is—the case was in my business law book when I went to college. I, of all people, had the pleasure of seeing this case in a law book. It seemed like fate was letting me know what happened to him. I had forgotten all about him, had gone on with my life. A court found him guilty, and there were other charges against him. The jury convicted him and sent him to jail for five years.

One day I saw him upon his release from prison. He was dressed in his orange jumpsuit; he lost everything, even his civilian clothes. I didn't derive any pleasure in seeing him standing there talking to two men on the street.

He glanced at me, not sure if it was me, the woman he had terrorized on the phone. He had grown a beard and mustache, but I recognized him. I glanced at him and kept walking. I held my head up high. His eyes observed me as I walked by him.

He refrained from speaking to me, and I to him. I had no fear of him and no desire to run or turn and walk the other way. I walked by him with courage and bold defiance. I dared him to speak to me and if he did speak, I had made up my mind to keep walking. He was a demon who robbed me of my virtues.

Changing my number was not an option for me. It was my phone number; I was paying the bill. Respect it. Use it, but don't abuse it. I have a right to enjoy my phone. I'd wait for the punks at the other end of the phone to come and get me. No one ever appeared. They were trying to manipulate or spook me with the phone.

Several men have called me in that manner throughout my life. I call it attracting the same man with a different face; life repeats some things until you learn the lesson. Phone abuse is how they treated someone who liked them. I can't blame myself for their behavior; they abused other people in the same manner.

I am amazed how abusers and bullies flatter themselves, and they have no control over their actions toward others. I don't like them. If I could come through the phone, I'd take their heads off.

I wasn't like the other females or kids who committed or attempted suicide because of phone bullying and cyberbullying, and I made sure that didn't happen to my child.

CHAPTER 11

What Goes Around Comes Around

I REMEMBER THE GOOD THAT my mother did for me. She bought me two microscopes, a Barbie doll, and a Barbie dollhouse. She took me to Hayden Planetarium. I remember at night in the 1950s when the sky was a clear, dark navy. We looked up as we were walking in Harlem on Seventh Avenue.

"Look at the stars," she'd say. There were too many stars for me to count. We went to the movies every night. It was twenty-five cents for adults and a dime for children under twelve. Every ten blocks in New York, there were several movie houses, and on Broadway, there were and still are theaters. They were like palaces, with red carpets, chandeliers, and gold decorations on the wall. They had huge movie screens with the film projector room on the third floor.

You could sit downstairs or in the second or third balcony. If you sat in the third balcony, you could see the light coming from the projector room and hear the film slithering around the reel. Films were bigger than life, and they devoured you. You had to be so involved with watching the movie to drown out the loud projector noise.

Most films were in Technicolor, which was breathtaking. There were black-and-white films too; not every filmmaker used Technicolor.

When the films were in Technicolor, you looked at the color and the story. Black-and-white films made you focus on the story. The films had to grab you; they were in competition with television. There was nothing like the movie experience. You forgot all your cares for two or three hours. When you left the theater, you felt refreshed and energized for your return to reality.

I also remember the lovely jade and gold jewelry my mother bought me. Virginia had my ears pierced, and I wore gold earrings in my ears. When she bought me clothes, they were expensive and fashionable, which instilled a sense of ambition in me to look and dress well. When she left me with Miss June, I wore hand-me-downs. All Miss June could afford to buy me were cheap shoes from Miles Shoes on 125th Street. Miss June was on welfare, a shut-in for the rest of her life. I acquired happiness, stability, and peace from Miss June. After my mother and I separated, Virginia made a complete turnaround.

A movement of black people not wanting to be called Negroes or colored was emerging. The Negro race desired to be black, which meant that Afros and dashikis were in demand. My mother started making them on 119th Street and Lenox Avenue. She worked for a lady who owned a clothing store that sold custom-made African clothing for men and women. With an American flair, she sat out in the retail's front courtyard and stitched the outfits on a sewing machine. My mother sketched and made patterns. Not once did I ever see my mom without funds. When she took the money from my shoe bank, she may have been adding to what she already had.

The sixties was a time of freedom and liberation in the sixties. You had the hippies, women's lib, blacks, Elvis, the Beatles, Motown, Vietnam, drugs, Twiggy, JFK, MLK, Malcolm X, the Black Panthers, the man on the moon, and the Cuban missile crisis. Everything was happening, one thing after another. A constant movement of changing events continued. Freedom shouted from all corners of America, and peace did not have time to breed. Upheaval was the underlying theme to all these developments that rapidly happened.

Women were burning their bras to be free of them. There was a freedom in fashion along with birth control. The sexual revolution and common-law marriages sprang up with sex and the single girl. During the winter months, my mother had a private, unlicensed day care in the Bronx. The neighborhood working women left their preschool-age children with her.

They didn't know about her past abuse and negligence of me. I think she was free, liberated, and wanted to repent. At age fifth-teen I decided not to see my mom ever again. I felt like I was a burden to her, holding her back from the life she wanted to live. What goes around comes around, because she began to feel like that to me. I became liberated, independent, and adventurous.

I wasn't in the Bronx, where I was born. I was living in Manhattan, the Big Apple, the center of the universe. Living five blocks from the Apollo Theater inspired me to go beyond my limitations. I also became inspired by the older girls who lived in the next building. A group of them made their clothes from Simplicity and Vogue patterns, and the clothes were beautiful.

Their hair was done up in cluster curls that matched their fashionable outfits. The clothes were expensive to buy; if you were able to sew, you could look stylish and save money.

Barbie had a strong influence on American girls, white and black. They all looked like black Barbie dolls. They went to see the Temptations at the Apollo Theater; attending a concert was like going to a fashion show.

A child group by the name of the Five Stairsteps started playing at the Apollo. I began to go to the Apollo on Saturdays, and I met the Five Stairsteps. The Five Stairsteps were the first child performers to appear at the Apollo, and they were our life. I looked forward to seeing them during school holidays, and it was something to live for during the summer.

When a group of girls and I went down to the hotel to visit the group, they came out into the hallway. We'd stand in front of their rooms and socialize with them, which was a definite boost to our happiness. Between that and hanging around them in the back of the Apollo, we received a double dose of their company. Fans couldn't get enough of seeing and being around them.

I also formed friendships, including one with Suzy. She and I became close friends. There were lots of girl fans. The Five Stairsteps sang love songs. I didn't dance to their music. I listened and sang along with the group. They did dance steps as they performed.

One time we all went to Newark, New Jersey, to see the Five Stairsteps. Most of the time, we paid to see them play and purchased their records. This time we were late, and the show had already started. The box office was closed, and we couldn't get in. A steady, light spring rain poured down on us. Five of us were standing outside with our shower caps on. We all huddled under the side door of the theater to get out of the rain. Suzy, CD, two other girls, and I were there.

Our first thought was to wait until the show was over and for the group to come out. We tried to go backstage; the door locked from the inside. Of the three theaters where we went to see the Five Stairsteps, the Apollo was the only show where we could go backstage to the dressing rooms or wait in the staircase for the group to come out of their rooms.

As we waited on the sidewalk in Newark, it became dark. There wasn't anyone on the street except us. Suzy and I came all the way from Harlem. CD lived in Jersey City, and the other two girls lived in Brooklyn. We had to find a way to see the group.

CD came up with the idea to sneak into the theater. That way we'd see the show and be out of the rain. CD weighed three hundred pounds and was tall. Her hair was coiffured and her nails manicured. She dressed neatly. CD was a teenager who wore women's clothes in size 2X or 3X (now they call them goddess sizes). She smoked cigarettes. Everyone, did including me. I started smoking at a young age in the sixties. I will explain about Suzy in the next chapter.

The other two girls were not in my life; they were fans of the Five Stairsteps and hooked up with us in Newark. CD picked the lock on the theater basement door, and it opened. As we descended the staircase into the basement under the stage, a clanking sound came from our shoes as we stepped down on the metal steps.

We entered the basement and realized we were ten feet beneath the stage. The Five Stairsteps were onstage, dancing and singing. Hearing their voices and footsteps dancing on the stage made us eager to see them. Old furniture and stage props aligned the basement walls. Several lamps lined the wall, but only one dimly lit lantern guided us through the corridor. The two girls and CD were in front of me, and Suzy was after me.

We walked through the long, dark corridor, hoping to find a door that led into the theater. I could only see what was in front of me, and that was a shadow of CD.

Out of the dark, coming from above me, a man's loud voice yelled.

"You better get out of here! I am going to let this dog loose on you!" *Woof! Woof! Woof!* It sounded like a big German shepherd. We took off running down the corridor and didn't look back. CD, with her huge legs, couldn't run, only wobbled from side to side swiftly. I could see CD's large body jump up and shake through a narrow doorway like a giant penguin. That let me know there was a step in the door. When I came to it, I jumped up on the stair and kept running.

I heard a loud noise. *Blam*! I listened to an awful cry of "Aaaah," then *Woof*! *Woof*! *Woof*! It was Suzy. She had missed the step on the doorway and fallen. She got back up and was not far away from me. There was no door leading to the theater, only a metal staircase. We ran up the stairs, and Suzy hopped up following me. At the top of the stairs, there was an exit door, and one of the girls burst the door open, and we all ran out onto the sidewalk. The door closed behind us and locked.

Then I realized I had left Suzy. I didn't stop running; none of us did. Neither one of us ever laid eyes on the security guard or the dog. After a few seconds, the door opened and out came Suzy, crying in pain and hopping on one foot. Two other girls and I rushed over to her. She had to lean on us to stand. We all were laughing hysterically. That made it funny, dangerous, desperate, and exciting. All of us were craving excitement. That was why we were there. Being free and far from home made us daring.

I'm not sure the dog was a German shepherd, but I assumed it was; most security guards or police officers have that breed of dog. I felt guilty for not going back and getting Suzy. I was terrified of the German shepherd, even though Pal had been my companion when I was a baby.

My guilt about leaving Suzy didn't last long. We were determined to see the group, and it had stopped raining outside the theater. Finally, the Five Stairsteps came out and greeted us for a moment. That made our day. We were addicted to the rush of excitement, and this was the Stairsteps' last stop; they were going home to Chicago that night. We bid them farewell, and CD got on a bus and went to Jersey City. The rest of us boarded a train to Manhattan and Brooklyn.

When I got home and went to my room, I reflected on what happened in Newark, New Jersey, and laughed myself to sleep. Every time I tell the story to friends, we all laugh. Those were the days when I truly had my taste of freedom. I learned not to ever break into other people's property.

A couple of months later, a girl named Stella lived on my block. She had short, nappy, uncombed hair and psoriasis all over her face and body. The kids and I refrained from making fun of her or laughing at her condition. She used to chase a group of us with her German shepherd. We all ran into her hallway, and I hid under the staircase.

Stella chased the other kids up the stairs. When she and her dog were out of my sight, I ran out of the hallway and sat on the stoop's concrete banister. The other kids ran into someone's apartment. Stella came back downstairs, led her dog to me, and he bit me on my thigh. I screamed. The dog's teeth left a boomerang-shaped scar on my leg.

After I had healed, I whipped Stella's ass and wiped the floor with her. The thought of Suzy passed through my mind—how we all ran from the dog in New Jersey. Suzy wasn't hurt permanently. She hit her shank on the step, and it was painful. She went home and put ice on her leg. Her legs were her most attractive asset. In the midst of all the excitement, it didn't dawn on me that shortly I would have to keep a dark secret.

This time I was the one who got bit. That was another reason I wanted to get away from my block. Everything painful happened to me, or I had to fight to keep from being victimized. Years later, I went to a friend's house. As I was leaving, her German shepherd lightly bit my heel. Luckily, I had on boots, and she didn't break the skin. I could feel her sharp teeth through my boot. I told the friend, and she scolded the dog. German shepherds are loyal dogs; if they don't know you well or their owner tells them to bite you, they will attack, especially if they are trained to be guard dogs.

CHAPTER 12

A Taste of Freedom

ALTHOUGH I LIVED WITH MISS June, I didn't hang out on the block. All the kids knew about my mother. In their eyes, I was the image of the tall, skinny orphan child who wore hand-me-downs, whose mother spoke on the street corner. They couldn't let me forget my mom or where I came from. Being teased and laughed at sort of like my mother, I longed to escape. The Apollo answered my heartfelt desires. I met a whole new set of friends. It was as refreshing as a breath of spring air that blossomed and matured me in a healthy, promising way. At the time, I didn't realize that I had stars to guide and put me on the path of success. I went where my inner promptings led me. Society looked down on drifters, and that wasn't me. I had an inkling to pursue success as a person I didn't have the ambition or goal yet.

I felt the energy of the stars and followed the direction they led me in. I didn't have the support or a stable life like the other kids who lived on my block. It wasn't Miss June's fault Virginia appeared like magic as soon as I got settled. My mother had the power, and she used it to snatch the rug of security out from under me.

No one considered me to be a strong kid or someone who had leadership qualities. Adults didn't sit me down and say, This is how life is. I am here to protect and guide you. Being a latchkey kid, I had to pretend to be mature. Freedom and adventure allowed me to search for myself. A whole new world opened up for me. When I met the Five Stairsteps in the back of the Apollo, I met a group of girls who didn't know my past and accepted me as I was. I was free to forsake the past, and the other girls and I attended all the shows at the Apollo.

After a show, we'd go backstage and hang out with the group. We even went down to the hotel to visit the Five Stairsteps. It felt exciting, like the family I desired. We tracked the group to the Brooklyn RKO and to theaters in Newark, New Jersey, to see them perform. I remember having to purchase a battery-operated mini–record player.

I broke Mamie's big record player by playing "More Love and More Joy" by Smokey Robinson over and over. On my new portable record player, I'd play the Five Stairsteps records such as "Something Is Missing." They were a fabulous family with fantastic musical talent. Mr. and Mrs. Burke were good parents, and they both escorted their kids on the road. How lucky they were; they had what everyone hoped for: success, money, travel, fans, and an entire family. That is what attracted me to the group. I yearned for a whole family.

Miss June gave me money for clothes in junior high school. I needed clothes to live my new life. Billie did not teach me to sew, although she let me use her sewing machine. You could get quality fabrics cheap under the 116th Street bridge market. I liked wearing pants and double-breasted suit jackets. I couldn't make the lapels tailored. My lapels came out rounded rather than square. Billie replaced an antique sewing machine with a new one. How you dressed played an important part in attaining success.

Miss June and Billie played Harlem numbers, and Billie managed an accessory store on 125th Street. They hit the numbers, so they had money endlessly. In the summer, I worked at Harlem Youth Opportunities Unlimited (HARYOU), a Harlem community program. Later on, I started working at a coffee shop and a record store. All the excitement was on 125th Street, the life force of Harlem.

When I was a child, 116th Street had two movie theaters, the Loews Theater on Seventh Avenue and the Morningside Theater on Eighth Avenue. RKO and the Loews and Apollo Theaters were on 125th Street.

CHAPTER 13

I've Never Told Anyone

I'VE NEVER TOLD ANYONE ABOUT Suzy, one of my best friends, a very dark-skinned African American girl. She was sexually active, adventurous, and loved to party and meet new people. We were both fourteen years old in the 1960s. Suzy had a well-built figure with a well-toned body for a young girl who didn't go to the gym; Mr. Burke, the father of the Five Stairsteps, gave Suzy the nickname Muscles, because she had muscles naturally without working out. To show off her powerful legs, she looked especially good in gladiator sandals, shorts, and miniskirts. Suzy was five two, and I was five six and still growing. And I was skinny.

At the time, the Five Stairsteps were a young family singing group of four boys and one girl. Each one was a different height, so the name Stairsteps fit them. Finally, the group had an everlasting hit single titled "O-o-h Child." They were on the scene a few years before the Jackson 5.

You forget the phone numbers in your life. I will remember Miss June's phone number for as long as I live. I was glad to be in Harlem, away from my mother, who vanished anyway.

At the Apollo Theater, many singers appeared there, such as Ike and Tina Turner, Stevie Wonder, Diana Ross and the Supremes. James Brown, Mary Wells, the Ronnettes, the Marvelettes, Otis

Redding, Marvin Gaye, the Delfonics, Little Anthony and the Imperials, Smokey Robinson and the Miracles, Etta James, Michael Jackson and the Jackson 5, and much more. In January, they would have the Jewel Box Revue, a show with drag queens who performed in great costumes. The Apollo Theater was the foundation and birth of soul, rhythm and blues, and pop music—all on one stage at one place: the Apollo Theater.

The old Apollo was decorated like an opera house in red, gold, and light beige, with red carpet. All over the lobby walls were photograph and collages of stars who had passed through the Apollo. All the fan action was in the back of the Apollo, a brick building. The theater's black back doors were locked, and a fire escape led to the dressing-room windows. Just like the back of any theater, the Apollo Theater was packed with excitement.

We mingled and socialized with the groups between shows. Although we were fans, they made us feel like friends and family. We screamed when they were onstage performing, and we were civilized fans backstage, having a block party with our favorite singing groups, their families, and friends. We also got to know the backstage concierges.

There were no security guards, bodyguards, or police. Fear and panic didn't exist; a sense of courage and happiness permeated the air. It felt right and good, and it made us come back again and again.

Across the street was Public School 126, and attached to it was a huge school yard with a gate that was open. The yard seemed like it was half a block long. We could see the view through the school yard fence of the St. Nicholas projects on 127th Street, a conglomerate of thirteen bright-red fourteen-story brick buildings surrounded by green trees. It was a beautiful contrast to the old faded-brown, back wall of the Apollo Theater.

Racism was a hot topic in the sixties. We didn't have to deal with it. Harlem had a vital creative energy; all the black dancers who were in Broadway shows lived and hung out in Harlem. Life was so much simpler and happier when we didn't have to deal with racial segregation and integration.

Can I make money and go about my business? That was a question black people asked. That became increasing impossible for black people in the sixties. The civil rights movement came to a head along with several issues that were happening all at the same time. The Apollo became a great escape, a glimmer of hope for a glamorous life. Music made you forget all your troubles or not remember that you had any. The Apollo was a social place to gather and meet new friends and acquaintances.

Being a fan is fun. We forgot about ourselves, and we poured our affection upon the singer or star. That person is the spectacle, and you are there to see him or her. It was not like a group of friends who got together to entertain one another. As fans, we were there to share the excitement of being entertained by the objects of our affection: the singers, groups, and stars.

Suzy and I became friends through the fan club, and I became friends with two other girls, Alise and Gloria. Clarence, the oldest brother of the Five Stairsteps, called Gloria "Paleface." She was brown-skinned with an hourglass figure, and she had a whitish ash color to her face without any shine.

As a Gemini, Suzy shone all over, especially with those muscular, moisturized legs of hers. Suzy was the oldest in a big family that included three sisters, one brother, a mother, and a father. Her mother was a tall, dark-skinned African American woman with short hair. She told me she was taller than her husband. Suzy's mother described her husband as a short, muscular West Indian man with hazel eyes and smooth, light-brown skin. They lived on 123rd Street and Eighth Avenue in a railroad apartment. Suzy's abode was messy, with clothes everywhere, junk, and dirt, a sign of poverty.

Black kids ran around with snotty noses and nappy hair that was uncombed and smelling of sweat. Suzy's mother worked and smoked cigarettes. She liked me and talked to me. I was tall like her, and she saw my ambition and intelligence. She loved the TV show *Mission Impossible*. She told me if I didn't watch it from the beginning, I couldn't know what the plot was.

One day, I went home with Suzy to change her clothes, because we were going to see the Five Stairsteps. Her father was at home. I didn't like him. He came off as a smart aleck and a bully, a little Napoleon with a West Indian accent. I ignored him; he was insignificant to me. He'd come into the room and try to be humorous. I refused to laugh for some reason. I was waiting for Suzy to get changed so we could go.

I saw her father a couple of times. I didn't go to her house that much, because we were on the streets all the time. A couple of months later, a magazine did a story on a poor black family, and it aired on television. It was about Suzy's family. The magazine bought Suzy's family house in Queens. It was down the street from James Brown's famous white stone house. The magazine took Suzy's family out of the ghetto. Harlem was a mixture of poor and don't-know-what-poor-is dwellers. When you have food on your table, clothes on your back, a beautiful apartment, and possessions, and you live moderately, you don't know what being poor is—depending on how clean and uncluttered you kept your apartment and appearance.

Miss June told me she could have five cents in her pocket as long as no one knew it. Some families had money, and some were struggling with low self-esteem. They didn't care how their children or apartments looked or smelled. The magazine picked Suzy's family as the downtrodden, poverty-stricken family to do a front-page magazine story on to show what poverty looked like in Harlem. The magazine moved them to Queens, into a spacious five-bedroom, two-bathroom home, a two-story white house on a block surrounded by beautiful roses and violets. The streets were lined with green trees far from Harlem. One Saturday Suzy invited me to visit her.

I took the A train from the 125th Street station on Eighth Avenue to Forty-Second Street and Eighth Avenue. I changed to the E train to Queens. I arrived in Queens, got off the train, and walked to Suzy's house. Suzy had a big kitchen, and that day she had baked a cake. It tasted delicious; it was a yellow cake with chocolate icing. Later on that day, we had a glass of milk and ate peanut butter sandwiches with syrup on them. Suzy's mother had her house decorated in beige and white. It had new furniture, and it was clean, neat, and big. Suzy and her family took pride in their good fortune. I did not spend the night there. I left before sundown to catch the E train back to Manhattan.

One day Suzy and I were hanging out on the street in the back of the Apollo waiting for the Five Stairsteps. By that time, we both were smoking cigarettes, and Suzy told me a secret.

She said her father took her virginity and had done it to each of her sisters. She worried about her ten-year-old sister—that when she turned eleven, her father would take her virginity. Suzy's sisters were thirteen, twelve, and ten, and her brother was eight years old. Her father came into their room at night and raped his daughters. He'd put his hand over their mouths to keep them from screaming.

"What does your mother say?" I asked.

"She says nothing," Suzy said.

It became apparent to me that Suzy's mother turned a blind eye to the sexual acts that her husband was perpetrating against his daughters. Suzy made me promise not to tell anyone. I never told Miss June, who never liked Suzy. Miss June loved my other friends, but she said Suzy didn't look clean.

I never told Suzy's secret to Billie or any of my other friends Miss June approved of. My other friends laughed when *The Addams Family* came on TV and said Miss June looked like Grandmama on *The Addams Family*. They laughed because Miss June's hair was gray-white and long, and she had a knife in her hand, cutting apples or peeling potatoes. I was taught not to make fun of people. Suzy never made fun of Miss June or anyone.

Suzy and I stayed out of her house and in the streets as much as we could. When Suzy lived in Harlem, she wanted me to come home with her to change her clothes. Suzy asked me to come upstairs with her, and I did. When she moved to Queens, that was too far away; I couldn't escort her home. She carried a change of clothes with her.

She brought a pair of shorts or a miniskirt in a little plastic grocery bag. Suzy did whatever she could to avoid going home. Her house was a house of horrors.

One morning in Suzy's kitchen, her mother was cooking a big pot of grits. Her father was sitting at the table, eating breakfast. Suzy's mother finally got the nerve to confront her husband about raping their daughters. They argued, and he hit her. She retaliated and threw the hot grits in his face, severely burning his whole face.

Suzy's father went to the hospital and stayed for a couple of weeks. Then her father returned home. I guess out of shame, Suzy's mother didn't report the sexual abuse. A month later there was an explosion in the house. The boiler blew up, and Suzy's father and brother died.

Suzy's mother didn't have home insurance. They had to move right back where they came from on 123rd Street, this time between Seventh and Eighth Avenues in Harlem. Suzy and I were still friends. I lent her my other friends' clothes—the fashionable ones so we could get all dressed up and go to the back of the Apollo. I'd go to Suzy's house and pick her up now that her father wasn't there. Suzy's mother had been friendly and talkative to me. I didn't dare tell her what Suzy said to me.

One night Suzy and I went to Andre's, a bar on 124th Street at Eighth Avenue, right around the corner from the Apollo Theater. We were only fifteen, going on sixteen. The doorman at that time didn't ask for ID. Wearing eye makeup and eyelashes, we both looked older than we were.

It was a beautiful bar, decorated like a grand eighteenth-century French cancan saloon. It was painted black, gold, and red, and it had dim lights. I remember the song playing on the jukebox by Diana Ross and the Supremes: "No Matter What Sign You Are."

Suzy was sitting on my right side at the black bar. I wore bell-bottom jeans and a stylish red top. She had on white shorts and a black crop top showing her perfectly formed waist. Suzy loved to show off her flat abs along with her muscular legs. As I was talking to her, I felt someone looking at me. I looked up from Suzy, and my eyes met his. He was tall, light-skinned, African-American, and gorgeous.

"Suzy, look! He's staring at me," I said.

Finally, he came over and introduced himself. The guy's name was Davy. He was a dancer in the Broadway hit show *Hello, Dolly!* He came from Chicago and was friends with Michael Peters, whom I met later on through another friend of Davy's. Who knew that twenty-five years later he'd choreograph the dance steps to Michael Jackson's "Thriller" and "Beat It" songs?

I put my age up to be with this man, who was twenty-five at the time. Two months later, Suzy got jealous and told him I was fifteen, going on sixteen, and I was still a virgin. That killed any romantic notions Davy may have had for me. Although I never told her secret, she revealed mine.

It broke my heart when Davy scolded me. He said he wanted to talk to me and took me into a building around the corner from Andre's, where we all hung out on hot summer nights after his Broadway show performance. He went off on me in an adult way and started remembering all the childish things I did. They validated what Suzy told him. I cried a river in the hallway in front of him. Everyone knew I loved him, especially Suzy. We both went to Andre's bar and hung out with him. After that, I distanced myself from Suzy. My other friends and I still spent time with Davy, excluding Suzy, who wasn't on my scene anymore.

When I was sixteen years old, Miss June got tired of me staying out late and kicked me out of her apartment. I moved in with Billie down the street. Billie gave me the freedom to run the streets at all hours of the night, as much as I wanted. The following spring I ran into Suzy. I was coming out of Billie's apartment, and there stood Suzy.

Standing outside my door in the hallway, I was drinking a half-pint carton of school milk.

"Can I have a sip?" Suzy asked desperately. I gave her the milk; she took a sip and handed it back to me.

"You can keep it."

"What happened to us?"

"We went our separate ways," I said.

Suzy seemed desperate. She didn't say another word. I rushed out of the hallway and went on with my new life and friends. Neither

Miss June nor any of my girlfriends liked Suzy. Even when we were around the fans, they only tolerated her because she was with me. Davy and the girls who hung out with us didn't ask what happened to Suzy. I befriended her in spite of them; they were kind enough to tolerate her. There was a bit of selfishness on my part.

Everyone I knew was paired off with a friend. I wanted a friend for myself. Suzy was a loner. She happened to be in the back of the Apollo, and we clicked. Miss June was the only one who expressed her dislike for Suzy, and my other friends weren't chummy with her.

Suzy had seen my other friend in a cute mini dress, and she wanted to wear it. Suzy begged me to ask my friend to lend me the dress without telling her it was for her. I lied to my friends and got the dress and promised I would get the dress back to her the next day without being damaged. Suzy wanted it to look attractive to go to the back of the Apollo with me. I made her take it off that night so that I could return it to my friend. I ignored all the signals that Miss June and my friends were giving me about Suzy, because Mr. Burke and the Five Stairsteps liked her a lot. That is why I had to escort her home to change her clothes.

That way she could look stylish for them, and I was unknowingly protecting her from her father's advances. I thought because she had a serious, reserved demeanor, she'd be loyal to me. She flirted with men, and the girls shunned her because she appeared to be more mature. Maybe she thought I should have been honest with Davy. I planned to reveal my age to him in time, thinking he'd wait until I became eighteen.

Her telling him destroyed his trust in me. I couldn't look in his eyes after. Suzy's betrayal destroyed our bond; she wasn't a friend to herself or anyone else. Some months later in the mid afternoon on

123rd Street and Seventh Avenue, I saw Suzy's mother waiting at the bus stop on her way to work.

"Hi. How are you doing?" her mother asked.

"I'm doing fine. How is Suzy doing?"

Her mother shook her head in disappointment. "Suzy went down in the gutter and died of an overdose of heroin."

"I'm sorry to hear that. Take care of yourself," I said, and I walked away. Even then I didn't tell anyone else that I knew Suzy's secret. Until this day, I have kept Suzy's secret. I've never told anyone.

My father told my mother that the women in Somalia performed female genital mutilation. This ritual was supposed to happen to her and me when she returned to Somalia with him. It was the custom of Egypt and Somalia. When I was seven months old, she left him, horrified at what awaited her. She kept it a secret and told me later on. My mother kept in touch with my father after he went back to Somalia.

His mother, father, and he were born in Egypt. When he became an adult, he moved to Somalia, and he traveled back and forth. I wrote to him when I was in Italy. A war happened in Somalia, and I didn't hear from him. I can only guess that he and his family got killed by a warlord. I am glad I wasn't born in Somalia. I never told Billie or anyone else.

I think he had plans after marrying my mother. He became an American citizen. He had a job where he made a significant amount of money as a cook. When he told her of FGM, and this was a standard procedure for women in his country. Virginia jumped ship and annulled their marriage. They moved out of the apartment and went their separate ways. After her mother kicked her out, she rented a room from Mrs. Johnson and brought me along with her.

I didn't know that Miss June lived in the apartment next door. I was two or three, and I remember Mrs. Johnson's boyfriend, Herman, molesting me. I remember having on a maroon corduroy jumper, and I had a hole in the seat where the seam was split from stretching and climbing on chairs. He was sitting in Mrs. Johnson's living room while she was in the kitchen. Herman was friendly with me when he visited Mrs. Johnson, and that day I climbed on him while he was sitting in the chair.

Herman was in his fifties. All the kids between two and four climb on adults. I was laughing, and I got my arms around his neck. He ran his hands down my small body, tickling me, and then he put his hand in my crotch. His finger found the hole in my crotch.

He moved my panties aside and dug his finger with his dirty nails into my vagina. I felt a burning sensation. The dirt from his nasty, dirty fingernails caused an instant infection. At the time, I felt what he was doing was out of ignorance, so I remained silent. Mrs. Johnson came out of the kitchen, and he snatched his hands out of my crotch and slid me down off his lap. I remember a mild burning sensation. I never told Mrs. Johnson or anyone else. I never got up on his lap again.

I don't remember him visiting Mrs. Johnson after that. Maybe they broke up; that was his last visit to her. Maybe she saw what he did to me and was too afraid to say anything. I remember being very promiscuous with the boys I played with when I was five, six, and seven. I didn't understand why I was like that.

After age seven and my birthday party, and up into my teens, I felt all this guilt. I became afraid of sex and men who were sexually attracted to me. At thirteen, I received my first French kiss. It was a guy named Ronald, and we were playing spin the bottle in the park. His kiss blew me away, and he knew it. When he saw me on the street, he called my name. I'd run like the devil was after me. He was tall, dark, and handsome, and he must have been seventeen years old. He spoke well and in a wheedling tone. He was intelligent, and the chemistry I felt from his kiss scared me to death. I was tomboyish and athletic, running and jumping—having a boyfriend was not in my plan.

All the other girls I associated with had boyfriends and were having sex. Other girls embraced it. I became terrified and didn't know why I ran away from it. At age seven, after being promiscuously curious as a child, I began to analyze my actions and saw it was wrong for a child to initiate any sexual activity. I realized why I was acting in that way: because Herman molested me. After I turned seven years old, I changed my behavior as a result of guilt and fear of sex.

I lost my virginity at age seventeen to a bisexual male model. It was the most horrible experience. I had to go to the doctor the next day. I was all cut up inside and bruised. I spurned him after that, although I did see him out, and he tried to speak to me. I never responded, and I felt ashamed that we were friends. I didn't suspect that he was a sadist. I couldn't believe it, but he told me after I gave him my virginity. He got AIDS and died I've never told anyone about him and I.

When I was sixteen years old, some of my friends were having an orgy. It included a guy I was dating. I had introduced him to my buddies, and they became his friends. They all got together and wanted me to participate in the orgy. At the time, I was a virgin and terrified of sex. They all held me down and took off my clothes. My two best female friends were in on it. At that time, I protected them, but in spite of my loyalty to them, they didn't protect me. Because the guy was impotent, the rape didn't happen. I was shocked that my two best female friends had done this to me. They both got up in my face and bragged about how those guys were my friends, and now they were their friends.

We all took an LSD trip, and one of the girls who betrayed me couldn't stop laughing. My male friends wanted to throw her out the window to prevent her from laughing. I was the voice of reason; my instinct to protect my friends was sincere. I rushed to tell her to stop laughing, or the guys were going to throw her out of the window. The apartment was on the second floor, and if she didn't die from the fall, then she could have been severely hurt. I told her to go and lock herself in the bathroom if she couldn't stop laughing.

She locked herself in the bathroom, and the guys formed a circle. They began to discuss how they were going to grab her if she came out of the bathroom laughing. They were going to drag her to the window and throw her out. She stayed locked in the bathroom until the guys came down from their LSD trip.

I saved her life from danger one other time. We had come back from a restaurant, and she had gotten a plate of takeout food. It was in the fall around eight o'clock. To enter her building, you had to unlock the downstairs door in the hallway. An African American man appeared. He had on a gray pea coat and a gray cap on his head. He had his hand in his pocket.

"I have a gun. Let's go up on the roof," the man said. She had the door halfway open, so we entered the hallway. We stood there for a moment. I felt that he didn't want me; he wanted her, and she knew it. My friend became afraid, and she started crying.

"Get on the elevator. We're going up to the roof. I have a gun," the man said again in a low tone. His hand remained in his pocket, hiding the gun.

We didn't want to call his bluff and ask to see the weapon. All three of us got on the elevator. My friend lived on the third floor. She was still crying while she pressed the elevator's third-floor button. The building had five floors and the roof.

"We are going to the top," the man said again. He tried to convince us that he had a pistol and we should do whatever he said. Unlike my friend, I didn't shed a tear. He didn't make any attempt to press the fifth-floor button. Nor did I, and I was standing close to the elevator door. He and my friend were standing in the back of the elevator. He had his hand in his pocket, pointing the gun in my friend's ribs. When the elevator stopped on the third floor, my friend was still holding the takeout plate of food in her hand. I grabbed her arm. I pulled her halfway out of the elevator door. The man grabbed her other arm and tried to pull her back into the elevator.

A tug of war began. I snatched my friend out of the elevator, and he pulled her back into the elevator. She was crying, and I pulled hard. Her arm broke free of his grasp. We both fell back and hit the hallway wall. The door to the elevator closed, and we both ran into her apartment. My friend's family kept her apartment door unlocked her family member was always there. She had a police lock, a long steel pole that bolted up against the door. I don't think they make those locks anymore.

That night her mother was asleep in the back room, and she wouldn't have heard anything if that man had taken us up on the roof. It amazed me that she still had the plate of Hoppin' John takeout food in her hand. I was her friend to the end.

She and my other female friend helped take off my clothes, and the group of guys held me down and tried to rape me. I had been dating one guy, and she wanted him for herself. My other female friend was sleeping with the previous guy who had a crush on me. We were friends; I couldn't imagine him as a romantic interest. He had a little jealousy and resentment toward me. The thought occurred to me that he was sleeping with my friend to get back at me.

Thank God, the guy I was dating was impotent. It must have been from taking all the drugs. The rape never happened, except I never forgot the terror and humiliation of the attempted rape. Some habits you learn from your teen years, you keep with you, and others you discard. It depends on your moral compass.

What you do as a teen and the relationships you have as a teen affect you throughout your life. I changed on the inside, although I refrained from confronting them about the incident. I still talked to them. I kept a happy face as I distanced myself from her and my other female friend.

Once I got my break in modeling, I left them in the dust. It was a silent wing departure. I saw the whole group out and about once in a while. That gave me the opportunity to gloat about my success. I was generous with my friend because we spent good times together before her betrayal. I gave her some old designer clothes I had. My other friend, who was a friend of hers and who was a part of our group, scolded me for giving them to her and told me she had no place to go to wear those clothes, so why would I give them to her?

I delighted in hearing that, because then I knew they had no loyalty to me or to each other. I made sure they didn't get into my new circle of wealthy, talented friends. I realized that my power prevented me from becoming bitter or discontented.

That taught me to be discreet about my associates. I learned not to share my partners, especially with people who have hurt me because they want to get to people I know. Also, I started to evaluate my friends; some people deserved to be left in the past. In my twenties, I started dating a dangerous man who took me back to his place. He had a woman there. He beat me up, pulled a gun on me, and raped me. He also inserted all kinds of sexual toys inside me. He made the woman who was there rape me also, and he tried to make me give her oral sex. I didn't, and he beat me. I was dating him and trusted him. All I can remember is seeing blood on my face from him hitting me in the nose.

I fought back, and then he pulled a gun on me. After the rape, he escorted me into the bathroom and made me take a shower. He pulled the toilet seat down and sat on it with the gun in his hands. He watched me in the shower to make sure I washed all evidence off me. He was seething with anger beneath the surface.

"Now you know not to play games with me," he said in an angry tone. "The truth hurts worse than a lie when it's told at the wrong time." That was his famous line. Then he said he had grown up with five sisters, and he hated them. "A true Scorpio," he said after the beating he gave me, meaning I could take an ass whipping. I didn't scream or holler for mercy.

"Why don't you kill me and get it over with? I give up."

I remember telling him that I was not deriving any pleasure from this. He backhanded me across my face again. Without fear, I rolled my eyes at him. There was some respect mixed up in his madness toward me. We were coked up, numb like vampires needing more. What triggered him to do it? I wonder now that I reflect back on it. I wanted to know how he felt about me out of bed, and he was casual in his answer.

"I know you feel more than that. Because when we made love the other night, I could tell you like me," I said and giggled.

He perceived himself as being less powerful, vulnerable, or weak—or seeing me with the upper hand. That wasn't the case. I wanted to know where I stood with him.

I liked him. I didn't want to continue to date him if it wasn't going anywhere. There was a logical drive in me to be number one. I didn't look closely at the guys I dated. I didn't like to be questioned, because I had secrets, so I didn't like to ask guys in the beginning. I wasn't going to give straight-up answers, and neither were they.

I got a signal from him when we were waking up, and he received a phone call. He was blowing up and cursing out the person on the other end. I was half-awake, and I could hear him yelling into the phone.

"F this person. MF that person. You calling me with this BS, F you too." He hung up the phone, and he said nothing. I took it that someone was calling him with you-say–I-say drama, in the morning, and he went off. We woke up and showered, and he took me to breakfast.

I didn't ask questions up front, and when I started asking questions down the line, it set him on a path to be out to get me.

"The only power you have is in bed." That was another famous line of his. He set the rape up to show me he had the authority. After I eschewed him again, he'd be in his car, see me, and call my name. I kept walking or ran across the street for fear he'd try to run over me with his vehicle. I think he went to jail or got killed in prison. I heard he cut some woman's face up with a broken beer bottle.

That is what happens when you take drugs. You have some good times and some bad times. You meet friendly people, and you meet dangerous people. Drugs don't discriminate, and it impaired my judgment. I have been drug- and nicotine-free for thirty-five years.

CHAPTER 14

A Path Not Taken

A MAJORITY OF YOUNG ADULTS and teens were taking drugs in the sixties and getting hooked, including me. I decided not to go down the same path as Suzy, Alisa, and Gloria, along with most of the girls from 121st Street. Girls I grew up with were overdosing and dying from shooting up heroin. That was a path I wasn't taking.

I kept going to the Apollo Theater and met a whole new group of friends when the Delfonics appeared. The Delfonics were a pioneering Philadelphia soul-singing group popular in the late 1960s and early 1970s. Their most notable hits included "La-La Means I Love You," "Didn't I (Blow Your Mind This Time)," "Break Your Promise," "I'm Sorry," and "Ready or Not, (Here I Come)."

Songwriter and producer Thom Bell and lead vocalist and founder William Hart wrote all their hit songs. When I met William Hart, he was very generous with his time. I was a teenager, and he was a man who spoke the language of love like he knew what it meant. I was in awe of this man. He dressed in the latest fashions and sang classic songs. He was a renaissance man who was very sure of his talent. He quietly observed his surroundings; nothing missed his eagle eye. I got a sense of fashion, talent, and showmanship from him. I thought about those things; that is what drew me to him, and he inspired me.

Even though I was making my clothes, I was so skinny that my fashion was limited to double-breasted pantsuits and pants. My body was functioning as a woman, because I had my period apart from not having a woman's body at all. While the other girls were full figured and had boyfriends, men didn't find me attractive. I was skin and bones. I guess if they wanted bones, they could go to a butcher and not date me. I didn't care. I had the excitement of the Delfonics and William.

One night I stuck my head into William's car to say good night. He French kissed me. He was the second man who French kissed me. I was flattered, and he made me feel attractive and shocked all at the same time.

"Oh, they don't want you," Billie said, and I believed that no man wanted me.

That didn't stop me from talking to boys in an adventurous, curious way. I felt I wasn't the girl they wanted romantically. I was their female twin who was spiritually connected to them. What I wanted for myself, I wanted for them. Whatever they were doing career-wise, I was totally for it. It means so much to a man when a woman is totally for his career and admires him. They didn't have to win me; they wanted to please me and give me happiness. I wasn't sexually active or making special demands on them like their lovers or the other girls did.

I didn't breeze off from William or respond to the kiss. I had no fear. Being around him made me courageous. At the same time, he wasn't going to wait for me to grow up and then marry me. I looked older than I was because of makeup.

I could come into the dressing room and be around him and his brother Wilbert, and I felt safe. I was inspired to have beauty and music in my life. I remember William singing "A Taste of Honey Is Sweeter than Wine." He was a classically trained singer.

Eventually, William met this lovely woman, and he introduced me to her in his dressing room. She was a schoolteacher, a full-figured, gorgeous woman. His fiancé dressed in the best mod sixties fashion. I was thirteen going on fourteen, and she was a woman. That was what William needed, a real woman, not a girl fan. At night, I didn't see him, but I frequently saw him during the day at the Apollo. William started dating her and got serious about the relationship.

All of a sudden, the Jackson 5 appeared at the Apollo on a Wednesday night, which was amateur night.

I'd go to amateur night, because it made me laugh. The acts would get booed off the stage if they were not good. I was there to see the show that night. Michael Jackson won the amateur night. Michael and his brothers came on the stage wearing blue satin shirts and white pants. Their standing ovation brought the house down. The prize was to appear professionally for ten days at the Apollo. They wore the same outfit the whole week they were at the Apollo.

I was excited to see them dance and sing, and Michael looked like a little person. He sang all these adult songs that adult artists had written and sung. I know they had a jive manager. I was not sure if he was their road manager, and Mr. Jackson was their manager. Their cousin Johnny was with the group. He dropped out when they got established.

When I saw the show, I didn't know I was a witness to music history. Many adult groups had come and gone in a flash. Or they made one hit record and went into oblivion. The Jackson Five was a kid group. The Five Stairsteps had disappeared, or maybe they were playing in other states.

Michael was the cutest little boy, and the Jackson 5 were excellent. Michael had good manners, and that is what made him stand out from the rest. He could sing and dance without the music; he had the chops. It was a young child's voice that could sing grown-up songs and be believable onstage. That taught me that you could start out with nothing and gain the world through hard work. None of us was taught to work hard; instead, we learned to take the easy way of a simple life with few or no dreams.

If it was difficult, it meant it was impossible. Only white people could do the impossible. The Apollo Theater gave black entertainers the courage to dream and inspire the black youth. Anything is possible when you work hard and dream big. Michael and his brothers got to open the show for the Delfonics, who were big-time. I was impressed with Michael Jackson, and he with William. Michael sang falsetto, and that is what William sang. We watched William, and Michael could learn from him how to dress, sing, and move onstage. How to be a man and carry himself like a star.

There was a certain way to behave with class, and you didn't respond to hostility or someone else's bad behavior, harsh words, or opposition. You ignored it and surrendered to the peace. Their influence took a lot of the fight out of me, even when I was attacked, instead of fighting back fiercely as I had once done. I became a martyr rather than a fighter for a period in time.

Also, I was encouraged to work on the inside and not try to control the outside. Later on, at times, outside events beyond my control affected me when I was immobile. William was my first inspiration—other than Superman and Wonder Woman. He was real and had a different way of living and dealing with life, fame, and talent on a large scale. Michael and I were into learning and growing, and life was the classroom.

William fell in love and married Pam, and they began a family. I didn't know they'd be married forever; they are still married. He wrote about love, and he knew how to love and how to keep love. William and the Delfonics were men, and for them to take the time to be around young girls and not get anything from us except inspiration and fandom set an example of what real people were.

Wilbert Hart was jolly and fun, with a young spirit, and a professional voice. He wrote good songs. He had several kids of his own. For whatever reason, a lot of us didn't have fathers.

Michael Jackson came to the Apollo for five years, and I never missed his visits. He would appear five times a year: Easter, Christmas, summer, and two more times between July and August. Those were the times that we were out of school. It was a wellspring of inspiration to have kids my age to show me the way to go. Michael did that for me, and I was smart enough to follow him. He was smart enough to follow William. Whatever he learned from William and anyone else, Michael took it to the next level. That experience is priceless. I can't put on a price tag on it. My idols were in my life, in the flesh and not on Twitter or Facebook.

I could feel and touch them; it was real. Looking at your favorite pop icon and not being able to spend quality time with that person as a role model—in my youth, it was unthinkable. I had DC comic book heroes to adulate. My mother said that I would yell "Superman!" in my sleep. I'd be dreaming of being in the comic books. I had three or four boxes filled with DC comic books. That is the excuse she used for throwing hundreds of my comic books into the garbage. Those DC comic books are worth a fortune today. I had to replace my DC comic book heroes with the acts at the Apollo.

Michael Jackson was an excellent role model. He was a child like me. At the time, I didn't imagine he would have his cartoon show. As a young girl, I lived in the now. I didn't look or think too much about the following years. My stars led me to Michael. I used to sit in Mr. Jackson's van and wait for Michael to get off the stage and sit with him. When the others came downstairs from the dressing room, all of us would rush into the PS 126 school yard and play tag and kickball, while the boys played basketball. How convenient the school yard was, across the street from the back of the Apollo.

Brimming with energy, we ripped and ran in that school yard. Michael didn't play, because Mr. Jackson was afraid he'd get injured in the rough-and-tumble game. Everyone looked out for Michael, including me. He was the star of the show; he couldn't get hurt or sick.

A show must go on, and being in that position made performers reliable. Mr. Jackson was a father figure to me, and he received our respect. We addressed him as Mr. Jackson. I don't know how much of the bad stuff could have happened. They were on the road, working in the public eye. Back then they did not have all the technology and the Internet. They had to work and be happy about it. They couldn't fool the public. If they didn't like that life, eventually the groups broke up, or the singers stopped singing.

At a time when black boys were being arrested or shooting up heroin, these were six energetic youths, including their cousin Johnny. Mr. Jackson was quiet and serene, and he spoke in a low tone in the midst of these active boys and ten or twenty young girls.

He sat in the van, read his newspaper, and tuned everyone out. He was the father figure, and he was the mother hen. Many times I sat in the van with Mr. Jackson and quietly waited for Michael to get off the stage. I'd go down to the hotel and spend the day with Michael, his brothers, and Mr. Jackson. We went to the arcade and played the Fascination pinball games. Michael loved those games, and afterward, we would stop and get ice cream. I didn't want any.

Michael offered me some of his ice-cream cone—he was so well mannered. I had to say no thank you. Then we'd ride the A train back up to Harlem and walk down 125th Street to the Apollo. There were eighteen of us girls who escorted them around. I lived five blocks from the Apollo, so I was there first.

Mr. Jackson made me feel welcome. Michael had the best manners; he was so loving and gracious. I felt like they were my family, even though I was a fan friend. We played tag and kickball in the school yard. I made an aggressive, sustained effort to support Michael. I've heard that some people didn't want him to sing or perform. How could they even think such a thing? When Michael Jackson opened his mouth and sang, he brought so much happiness to everybody.

Back then there was a lot of segregation in the South and with our music. The Apollo was our place where we could enjoy our music and talent. Nobody was ripping anyone's clothes off or pulling a guy's hair and going berserk. We had pure love, admiration, and respect.

When they went to other cities, they had to run and hide. Women were throwing their panties up on stage at them and the Delfonics. Those fans in other cities didn't have the pleasure of their company, and I in Harlem did. Being in their presence and spending time with them was a treasure. They were our inspiration and a picture of the good life we could only imagine. It was pure excitement and happiness, like waking up in Las Vegas every day. You forgot your troubles and cares.

When they were not in town, life was real and not exciting. Some of the girls who were fans started using heroin, got hooked on it, and fell to the wayside. Again, that was a path I was not taking. There were too many other drugs, like LSD.

Marijuana was potent in the sixties, and it made me paranoid, so I didn't smoke it, although I did smoke cigarettes and drink wine. I couldn't drink hard liquor; it was too bitter, and I had no taste for beer. LSD enticed me and drew me to it in the sixties.

I had a group of friends who liked to take LSD, and they introduced me to a man who used to make it. David was white and wealthy; he didn't sell LSD. He was a conservative and a hippie. His family was wealthy, so David had money and didn't have to work. He had a psychedelic loft with a sound system that ran through the abode. David also had a white chair shaped like an egg. It had two speakers inside on the right and left side. Music filled my life, and LSD enhanced it more.

I don't remember having a conversation with David, other than hello and thank you for the LSD. He didn't talk. He was quiet and polite. I'd sit in the egg chair and listen to all the music flow through my ears and head. David played a lot of the Beatles, Jimi Hendrix, Janis Joplin, and Led Zeppelin. He mixed music together in a continuous flow.

In the winter months, by the time our trip had worn off, the sun had risen. We left David's warm loft to greet the icy, snowy ground on the New York SoHo sidewalks. Everything looked so beautiful and bright with the fresh snow on the ground. I couldn't smell the fresh air; it smelled of a chemical candy from the LSD. A couple of times I tripped at David's house. It wasn't a habit; it was more of an exhilarating mental experience. David had a large number of albums and tapes, and he turned his loft into a successful disco club.

He was excellent at mixing music, and the position fit him. I went there once or twice, and I had to squeeze in through the door. His loft became a sardine can of jammed-in people. There were other clubs—Oh Poofs, Hippopotamus, the Electric Circle, Trudy Heller's Trick, the Dome, and the COCP in Brooklyn. The COCP was a teen club with no liquor or drugs.

The teens had to dress up to go every weekend to do the Brooklyn hustle. To do the hustle, you had to hold hands and dance together.

That brought the boys and girls together. The boys had to have a jacket on with a dressy shirt and pants. The girls were Fashion City; they looked like they stepped out of *Vogue* magazine. Even if they weren't thin, they dressed elegantly. I stopped taking LSD and got into dancing and going to the clubs.

When school started, my high school reading teacher suggested I try modeling. She was adamant about me becoming a model. She even photographed me. Mrs. Lawrence was a model herself at the Ford Modeling Agency (now Ford Models). Mrs. Lawrence took me to see Eileen Ford, who met with me and looked at me from head to toe and from side to side. Her verdict was that my look would be sellable in five years. I went back to my life.

I knew what I'd be doing for the next five years: devoting my life to being with Michael Jackson and the Jackson 5. We all hung out and played together, and I connected more with Michael. William and the Delfonics stayed in my memory. They didn't come back to the Apollo as much as Michael did.

They had done their time there and were in demand all over the world. Michael had to build up his fame and work hard for his success. The Jackson 5 were young in a grown-up world of show business. There weren't any consistent black child family groups. The Five Stairsteps disappeared, and the Osmond brothers hadn't appeared yet for the white race. The Jackson 5 were all we had that represented our age group.

Adults responded to the songs Michael was singing. He had the teens and the adults for his audience, and Michael worked for everything. No one gave Michael anything. He earned his success. Michael didn't have to do anything for himself; people waited on him hand and foot like he was a king, and the other brothers had to fend for themselves.

Jackie, his brother, had a crush on me, and I think if I had taken that path, I might have married a Jackson, before the girls started using Michael to get next to his brothers. The New York fans never used Michael for anything. I loved Jackie like a brother. I didn't get intimate in the beginning and as time went on, because if I got close with Jackie, Michael was going to say I used him to get to his brother, and he wouldn't forgive me.

Every time I saw the Jackson 5, I kept it friendly and respectful. This beautiful, talented group of boys felt like family to me, so a sexual relationship felt like incest, a path I was not taking. I did all I could; I spent five years of my life as a devoted fan. I felt I was supposed to do more with my life. Modeling was a suggestion, not a guarantee. I had my sights on it, and I wondered if it could happen.

CHAPTER 15

Breaking Ties That Bind

BINDING TIES WERE MADE THROUGHOUT the sixties. I had ties to my mother, Miss June, the Five Stairsteps, Suzy, Alisa, Gloria, my female friends, the Delfonics, Michael Jackson, Reggie, and Davy. With each tie that bound, one relationship would fade, and another one would replace it. The Five Stairsteps faded. Suzy, Alisa, and Gloria got on drugs, overdosed, and faded. The Delfonics came into view, and then they went on to greener pastures and disappeared from my sight. Michael replaced them, and when he got his Motown deal, he faded into success. I learned you could have nothing and attain success.

Five years flew by fast. Michael Jackson released a hit single, "ABC," under the management of Diana Ross. My life was like a movie—people, places, and things appeared and then faded out.

Through Davy, who was a Broadway dancer, I met Clifton Davis, who was dating Melba Moore at the time. He wrote the hit song "Never Can Say Goodbye" for Michael Jackson. Michael had hit record after hit record. Davy took me to Miles Davis's house and Dizzy Gillespie's jazz concert at the Village Gate club.

I was forced to live my life. Miss June and I were coming to an end. I relinquished the responsibility of coming home early. I was still a virgin, meeting all these creative, exciting people, and they didn't demand anything from me except admiration. The freedom felt overwhelming and compelling. I was so busy forming my public life that I didn't notice Miss June had a drinking problem. Billie knew about Miss June's drinking and kept it secret. When Billie arrived home from work every night, she'd call Miss June. She could tell from the sound of Miss June's voice whether she had been drinking. I didn't know. I hadn't called Miss June while I lived with her.

I didn't have a key, so I had to knock on the door at two am. She got up out of her bed and let me in. The door opened, and it was pitch-black in the apartment. Miss June stood behind the door with a broomstick. I ran into the apartment before she could hit me with it. I ran down the dark hall into my room and closed the door.

She did not follow me into my room. Once I slept for two days straight, and she thought I was dead. Miss June pushed my door open as she walked swiftly by in fear. When I finally woke up, she said, "I thought you were dead."

Hanging in the streets was exhausting and exhilarating all at the same time. It seemed like every time Miss June was drinking, I happened to come home late. Miss June assumed I was supposed to stay home and be a shut-in like her. When I was a small child, she could control my life. When I became a teenager, my life began to take form. She had no control over my life, and I wasn't in control of it either. I was moving forward and going with the flow. I had no direction. I was out there to see what was happening and to jump in to my opportunities.

I didn't have a watch at that time to keep track of time. One night I came home around three o'clock, and she was drunk. I started spending more time with my Broadway dancer friends. She opened the door, and it was dark. I could see a large, glistening, cooking fork reflecting the fluorescent light coming from the hallway outside the apartment. The door was hiding Miss June as usual.

I couldn't believe she had a large cooking fork, and she was going to stab me. I had nowhere to go. I had to cross the threshold and enter the apartment. I was wondering if I could run into the flat, get to my room, and close the door before she could stab me. I would be safe. I can't recall her ever following me into my room, whereas this time when I ran across the threshold, she tried to stab me with the cooking fork.

I ran to my room and turned on the light. Miss June chased me, swinging the large fork several times. I moved from side to side. I hadn't seen the film, *Psycho*. Later on, when I became friends with Anthony Perkins and his wife, I looked back on that night. Miss June to me resembled the old lady in *Psycho* who was swinging the knife at Janet Leigh in the shower.

Although I was in my room fully dressed, I managed to knock the fork out of her hand, and she gave me a head butt. I pushed her away and ran out of my room into the bathroom in the hallway and locked the door. The bathroom door had a weak latch and hooked on the door. She tried to open the bathroom door. Fearfully I grasped the doorknob and held the door shut. She couldn't rattle the lock open as long as I held the door shut tight.

I knew she had the cooking fork in her hand. Miss June cursed me and called me all kinds of whores. She accused me of sleeping with different men. Suzy was doing all those sexual acts, not me. I wasn't hanging out with Suzy anymore, nor was I a confused teenager. Her harsh words hurt me deeply, for she was accusing me of acts I wasn't doing.

I still didn't know that Miss June was drunk or drinking. I thought she was in her right mind, and that was what she thought about me. The fact that she was trying to stab me pissed me off, and I held the door shut as tightly as I could. I cursed her back. I screamed and hollered until the ties that bound us together broke. Miss June got quiet, went into her room up front, and went to sleep.

Finally, I came out of the bathroom, went into my room, and went to sleep. Later that day, I awoke and got dressed. Miss June was standing at the window in her room. A quiet, solemn atmosphere penetrated the house. Billie was there, and she told me I had to move. Billie said I could come and stay with her. At the time, I was thankful for a place to stay.

It didn't dawn on me then that I was financially profitable to Billie. She knew Miss June was drinking and deliberately kept it from me. It was like she knew Miss June and I eventually would get into a fight. I knew Miss June could curse like a sailor. I couldn't fathom that my staying out late would cause her to try to kill me or do me bodily harm. Billie knew Miss June longer than I did because Miss June was her mother.

I think there was a bit of jealousy—competition for me because I was Miss June's pet. She and I were the same skin complexion and are considered brown babies. Miss June connected with me. Billie was not a racist; she knew what being dark-skinned meant. I regretted that our relationship had descended to the point of no return. I think Billie should have given me a heads-up—even let me come and live with her before the harsh words and the attempted stabbing that forced the separation.

Billie didn't want Miss June to be angry with her. At the same time, she wanted my relationship severed with her mother. Why? Because it benefited her. At Miss June's, I didn't have to pay rent; at Billie's, I had to pay rent. Billie was a woman who looked out for herself.

Also, an inheritance from Miss June had to be of some value, and she didn't want me to have any of that either. After I unaffectionately visited her Miss June, had a prophecy, and she predicted, "When I am gone, you are going to wish for me." I only came to see her when I wanted something. I was trying to make it, and I had to go out at night to all the necessary parties. I wouldn't be viewed as a second-hand Rose and looked down on. My life was forming, and I was meeting exciting, creative people. I felt compelled to meet individuals to change my life.

It hurt me that Miss June didn't want that for me. Maybe in her mind, she thought she was going to die soon, and I should be there day in and day out until it happened. I thought she'd live to be 110 years old.

She talked about her aunt Rosa, who did live to be 110 years old. Miss June was sick. She had been sick all my life and functioned well. My promotion was now. I had to abandon my past, and Miss June wasn't my future, even though I had seen Billie every day at Miss June's.

When I visited Billie's house at Christmastime, all her friends' kids were there. She treated them better than she treated me. I remember she hit me twice, once while I was still living with Miss June. Billie approached me, saying someone had told her they heard me cursing like a sailor.

"Oh no, not me," I said.

"If you are cursing, I will catch you," Billie answered.

"Oh no, I don't curse," I convincingly swore to her face. One day I was walking with a friend, and we were hitting a ball back and forth to each other while we were walking.

I missed the ball. "Oh shit! Motherfucker!" I said.

Billie was across the street and heard me. She rushed across the street.

"Come here," Billie said in a commanding tone. I started to run, and she caught me. "Don't run from me," Billie yelled. She slapped me across the face a couple of times with her heavy hand. "I told you I was going to catch you cursing. I didn't hit you for cursing. I hit you for running."

I had picked up cursing from her mother.

I was living with her the second time I got hit. She was talking on the phone with one of her friends, and they talked for an hour. I was in a hurry to get her to answer a question. I felt she could have told the party on the other end of the phone to hold on and then ask me what I wanted.

Instead, she yelled, "Don't you see me talking on the phone?"

She took the phone receiver and hit me on my collarbone with it. I can still feel the pain. Those phones were of thick plastic. You could kill a person with a phone. Nothing was said, and I went to my room at the end of the hall. My room had a curtain for a door. It was right by the beautiful wooden door that had a large frosted glass square window in the center of the entrance door. Every time somebody came into the apartment or went out, the air from the door opening and closing blew open the curtains to my room. She never hit me again. I realized that she couldn't rent my room out. I could have lived with her earlier.

Later on, the lodger moved out of the next room, and I took that room and paid rent. She had done that with the three remaining bedrooms.

My old room at Miss June's wasn't vacant for long. Miss June had gotten two lodgers, Walter and Allen, who paid rent.

Billie had a place for everything, and if you moved something, she knew it. Billie had lodgers all her adult life. She never locked her room door, and everything was perfectly in place. She worked every day on 125th Street for Mr. Gus. He had an accessories store that sold beautiful leather handbags, gloves, and hats. She was his manager of the shop. Only she and his wife worked there. She managed the store when his wife wasn't there. Mr. Gus had a couple of stores, and after six o'clock every afternoon, he would stand outside Billie's window, which was on the second floor. She'd throw a bag with money in it out the window to him.

He trusted Billie, and he gave her a $10,000 bonus plus her commission. She hit the numbers, and lodgers' money consistently flowed to her. She had never paid rent; the lodgers were paying the rent. The slum landlords were never there to know what was going on. Downstairs the hallway smelled like piss where men went in a corner under the staircase in the back of the elevator and urinated. Billie sprinkled lye on the floor so when they went to pee, the lye ate off their shoes. The smell of piss never left the hallway; it was embedded into the marble floor. When you got up into the apartment, perfume filled the air, and it smelled good. Billie kept her bedroom, kitchen, bathroom, and living room spotless. She had to clean only four rooms; the lodgers cleaned their rooms.

When I was small and spent the night with her, she gave me a shower, washed me down, and fed me. She cooked all the time. Every Christmas I received a nightgown and robe, or one or the other. I noticed I was treated like an orphan when her friends were there. Billie would talk bad about my mother to her friends and not to me. Billie's friends from Mobile were loyal to her. They never disclosed what she said about Virginia.

One day her friend Money slipped as we talked on the phone and said, "God said honor thy mother and thy father. He didn't say what kind of mother." Billie's friends liked to talk down to me like they had a better life, and they weren't orphans nor were any of their family members.

Billie acted like a warden in that apartment. Everything had its place, with not a grain of rice or a drop of water in the sink. Billie wanted perfection. I had small weak hands, unlike Billie's big feminine hands. She kept her nails done and her hair styled. She had a large dishrag that I couldn't wring thoroughly. It dripped water. I'd twist it slightly after I washed the dishes, and then I'd go down the hall to my room. Once in my room, I'd sit down and get comfortable.

All of a sudden, I'd hear Billie yell, "Amina!"

I'd get up and go all the way back down the hall to the kitchen. "What is it?" I asked.

"Get this drop of water or grain of rice out of the sink and wring the water out of this dishrag."

"A drop of water or a grain of rice. You've got to be kidding to call me all the way back here to clean it up," I replied. OK, the dishrag was dripping water. I had to wring the dishrag three or four times before I could get all the water out so it didn't drip.

Billie was a seamstress and made her evening clothes. She had the most beautiful evening clothes, jewelry, and furs. I acquired a fashion sense from her, and while Billie worked, I looked at old movies. She never really pushed me to amount to anything, and she never encouraged me.

She kept her secrets. There was no guidance. She kept her wisdom to herself. I knew how to clean, cook, sew, and shop. My domestic knowledge came from watching her.

I started smoking and didn't tell her. One morning we finished with breakfast, and she had lit a cigarette and placed it in the ashtray in her bedroom. Billie stepped into the kitchen and left a lit cigarette in the ashtray. I went into her bedroom and took a long drag off her cigarette. She walked in on me.

"Are you smoking?" she asked.

"No," I said and looked right into her face as the smoke was coming out of my mouth.

"The smoke is coming out of your lips. Somebody told me they saw you smoking," Billie said, looking at me. She didn't get mad; she made me buy my cigarettes. It was like I couldn't sneak and do anything without this spy of hers telling or reporting on me.

I learned from her how to dress and keep myself clean; I kept my hair and nails groomed. Billie's ambition focused on packaging: how you were put together in appearance and mannerism, how your surroundings were organized, and if your kitchen was spotless. Billie's philosophy was everything had to have a place. She knew where everything was in her house, and she knew if someone moved something out of place. Billie didn't teach me how to make it in the world. There is a spiritual way you operate in the world, and I had to learn that for myself. Billie didn't share her wisdom about life in the home with me.

I went out more than I did when I lived with Miss June. I desired to get out of Billie's sight and reach. When I stayed out all night and didn't come home for days, she didn't care. I never called her or told her where I was. When I left the house, I'd tell her I was going to a party or downtown with my friends.

If I was bringing my fashion or Broadway friends by so I could change my clothes or get something, I called her and told her I was bringing some friends to the house. She was the perfect lady; my friends were somebodies. Davy introduced me to Reggie, who was friends with Michael Peters, who later became Michael Jackson's choreographer. Reggie was a model with Wilhelmina Models. He was a dancer on Broadway, and when Michael Peters was in town, we all socialized together.

Reggie's show on Broadway ended. He was out of work, living on unemployment, and we were together every day. He would take me on his go-sees for modeling jobs. The photographers were interested in me. They wanted to photograph me and do test shots. That is when I started taking modeling seriously. After a year of not finding work, Reggie booked a show in Paris for six months to a year.

His friend Melvin and a drag queen named Miss Lynne moved into his apartment. Melvin made this beautiful black wool hooded maxi cape with white fox trimming. I looked like a countess when I wore it, and I received lots of attention. New York was all about what you looked like and how you dressed.

While Reggie was away, Melvin and Miss Lynne and I became close. Miss Lynne had a box, and I didn't know what was in it. I thought it was a cat that I had never seen. One day I asked what was in the box. She told me it was her snake, Miss Hainty. Then she took her out of the box and let me see her. Miss Hainty, her snake, was part of her dance act. She had a résumé photo of herself in drag, with Miss Hainty around her neck.

I wasn't scared at the thought of sitting on the mattress, which was on the floor. All this time the box was right there beside me. Miss Lynne never told me there was a snake in the box. What if Miss Hainty had gotten out and started crawling on me? The thought of that happening scared me.

I told Billie about the snake; she was terrified of snakes. She stepped on one as she was running barefoot on the grass in Mobile, Alabama. As a child, she hated wearing shoes. But since she was horrified after that incident, she wore shoes.

Billie became petrified of a man at a carnival in Mobile. He had a fake snake that curled around a stick. They had those at Coney Island in New York all the time. He waved the fake snake at her. Billie thought it was real. She had a soda bottle in her hand. She threw it at the man as hard as she could, and it missed his head. The man realized Billie in her fearful state of mind could kill him, and he backed off with the fake snake.

I knew Miss Hainty and Miss Lynne wouldn't be stopping by Billie's to see me. After a while, Melvin, Miss Lynne, and I got busy and drifted away from one another. I became involved with photographers. Reggie came back from Paris. Melvin and Miss Lynne moved back to Chicago. Reggie started dating one of my girlfriends. By that time, I was on my way. Photographers were photographing me. I was making my clothes and doing my hair and makeup. I had a little money. I'd work part-time jobs. I couldn't keep a job, and neither I nor the universe wanted me to. I desired to be a model. Billie started pressuring me about paying rent.

I told her I was trying to make it as a model. Her friend Gwen struggled and walked in the snow all winter and never made it. Billie didn't see me as an original; again, no encouragement. I insisted that I wanted to make it as a model.

Billie said, "You better get you a job. You are not going to make it."

Because Gwen didn't become a model, she thought I would have the same fate. She didn't see me as an innovator.

I remember when I was a little girl, I danced in front of Miss June. She laughed at me and said I couldn't dance. My mother didn't approve of me being a dancer. She said too many dancers were gay, and she didn't want me around them. She never supported my hopes of becoming a ballerina. I had seen success with the Delfonics and Michael Jackson.

Two doors down from Miss June's house in building 223 lived Miss Ida Forsyne Hubbard. She was a dancer and Billie's friend, who came to holiday dinners on many occasions. In 1904, she went to Russia and danced in St. Petersburg and was the Queen of the Cakewalk. She incorporated Russian dance in her solo act for eleven years. Miss Ida spoke Russian fluently and danced all over Europe, including the Moulin Rouge in Paris. Miss Ida was a dark-skinned, petite woman.

Her show business name was Ida Forsyne, but we knew her as Ida Hubbard. She talked to me about her dancing and being in show business when I visited her on occasions. Being eight or nine years old, I didn't understand show business. I only saw the glitter and bright lights. Miss Ida always smiled when I visited her, and there was an aroma of peppermint in the air. She had so much stuff in her bedroom, I never got a chance to see the rest of the apartment, although the architectural design was identical to Miss June's apartment. I remember her having classy 1950 party dresses stuffed in boxes from the days of her wine and roses. There were photographs of her on New Year's Eve. Her birthday was January 1. She had two drag queens as lodgers.

I think they were dancers from the Jewel Box Revue's January show at the Apollo Theater. The show cast only drag queens. They had incredible costumes and did a terrific show.

"What are those two men doing together?" I asked out of curiosity.

"They are sticking each other in their butts," Miss Ida blurted out.

"What?" I said. She acted like I should have known. Miss Ida had been out in the world at an early age, and me being an orphan, she assumed I had the same experience. Therefore, she didn't feel a need to hold her tongue. Miss Ida took me to the Loews Theater on 125th Street. The film was in Technicolor, and one of the actors said, "He's using cocaine." Miss Ida, sitting next to me, burst out and laughed, and she repeated, "Cocaine." That was my first time hearing of the drug. I didn't know what it was.

When World War I started, work became scarce, so she left Europe and came back to America. Miss Ida found out quickly that she couldn't get work as a dancer because of her dark skin. Miss Ida acted in three movies and danced with a few shows—not nearly the success she had in Europe. She was forced to get a job as maid and elevator operator, which were two unknown job skills for her. She had to learn how to adjust.

Miss Ida never discussed her downfall with me. As I did the research, I discovered this information. Miss Ida had retired at sixty-five, before I was born. When I knew Miss Ida, she was in her eighties, and she always talked about show business and dancing as if she never said good-bye. Although I had never seen her dance, Miss Ida seemed happy about being a performer and the life it afforded her.

Billie had seen the downside, and she didn't want me to talk to Miss Ida. She never outright said it, because she had photographs of Miss Ida dressed up and at parties, and Miss Ida autographed the photos. In 1969, Miss Ida went into a nursing home and resided there until her death in 1983. Billie visited her and never took me to see Miss Ida. Billie would take me to the cemetery to Manuel's grave. Once or twice we visited Miss June's grave. Every time I talked about show business, she'd throw ice water on my dreams. Billie only saw the failure and assumed my fate would be the same. I didn't understand why she couldn't see me as a success, being that Miss Ida had made a success out of herself.

She kept telling me I was weak and not raised in a stable structure. Because of the way my mother dumped me on Miss June, I didn't come from anyone who thought I was important. I wasn't supposed to be nurtured to become a success. I felt like Betty Davis in *Now, Voyager*. I owed Miss June, and Billie's jealousy blocked me from mending my relationship with Miss June. Billie always reminded me of how Miss June and I got into an argument, and Miss June said awful things and I never forgave her. Billie seemed mentally relieved that the bond was broken between Miss June and me. Billie never attempted to be a mediator or to encourage Miss June or me to mend fences.

Billie made me feel I owed everything to her. I was in bondage to her. I became a deep thinker, looking for answers; Billie was reluctant to give me any answers or guidance. I kept my ambitions to myself. I didn't want others to react the way Billie did if I revealed my dreams to them—one thing she taught me other than domestication.

I couldn't lean on her; I needed to be independent. My rent was a mere hundred dollars a month, and I bought my food. If I asked her for a cigarette, she charged me ten cents. She stayed home, and she took care of her house, except for my room. Being free like my mother became my objective. I didn't have any kids. Not ever having a stable home life conditioned me against any ties that bound me mentally or physically—especially the kind that prevented me from living in a public world. There was an ongoing conflict between my home and career, which consumed my public life. At the same time, I yearned for a stable home life; I didn't know that it wasn't in my destiny to ever have one.

CHAPTER 16

Jealousy Can Kill You Physically and Emotionally

FROM THE AGE OF THIRTEEN to twenty-five I experienced life to the fullest. I was never jealous of what other people had. When I was with my mother, she bought me expensive jewelry, clothes, and toys. When I was with Miss June, individuals who lived on the block gave me clothes, and they were decent. They weren't as expensive as things my mother bought for me; they were hand-me-downs.

Every neighborhood in Harlem was different. Our block had more working people and a small mix of alcoholics and welfare people who lived across the street. In the heat of summer, adults drank and got into fights. They cut each other in the face with switchblades. The ambulance took them to the hospital emergency room. They came home to heal; still, the scars on their faces never went away.

When I lived with Billie, I walked through the long block of 121st Street all dressed up and going to see my photographers. I didn't get any jealousy from the people on the block. After all, it was the older girls who dressed and made clothes as if they had stepped out of *Vogue*. Most of the people on the block worked for rich white people or in a factory. From building 219 to 233 were the same five-story twin buildings. Apartments on the east and west side were the same as Miss June's apartment.

The rest of the block consisted of brownstones, with a mixture of working and poor welfare tenants. Billie's building, 201, had seven rooms to an apartment, and prosperous people lived in the building. Miss June's building, 219 to 233, housed affluent people, and their kids had every kind of toy and doll that was on the market. My mother bought me bicycles and ice skates.

One of the girls I used to play with had ice skates, and the blade on each ice skate was twenty-four karat gold. Her full name was engraved in script on each blade. We'd go ice-skating at the Central Park rink. She had a pogo stick I could never master.

We were poor, although nobody experienced homelessness or hunger. The other girls I played with had loads of toys. I knew another girl, Raina, whose mother bought her everything. She wore a lot of gold jewelry as a child.

Raina, being a couple of years older than I, precipitated my jealousy of her, but not because of her material possessions. She had light skin, along with a prim and proper manner, in spite of her dirty, yellow teeth. As a result, I became jealous of the way her mother groomed her. She never had a fight or had to fight for anything. A lot of kids were jealous of her and rumored that she was adopted. Her mother forbid her to ever come outside on the street to play with the other children. One day her mother let her stay at Miss June's and picked her up when she came from work.

When Raina stayed at Miss June's for a day, I picked on her and pulled on her. She'd yell at me to stop. She swung at me a couple of times in annoyance, but she never actually fought. Raina got so pissed off at me, she told her mother she didn't wish to stay at Miss June's anymore. I visited her at 229, up the street, and her mother was there. Of course, I behaved exceptionally well, and I had to leave before dinner. That was a rule: don't eat at anyone's house; come home when it's dinnertime.

A boy lived at 223, a couple of buildings down from Raina. We all lived on the odd side of the street. I had a secret crush on him and a couple of other boys on the block. They never liked me. I was too much of a tomboy. When Raina and the boy became teenagers, they started dating and then got married.

Most of the women who lived on the odd side of the street had good jobs with wealthy, white city dwellers, and they acquired money and material things. Their husbands had good jobs, and most of them fought in World War II. They were postmen, truck drivers, janitors, superintendents, or factory workers. The rich white people threw money and gifts at them, and they went happily to work.

Those who didn't care about how they looked and had low self-esteem were talked about shamefully if they didn't comb their hair or if their house was dirty or if they wore wrinkled, dirty clothes or mismatched colors. On the other hand, as black people, there was sympathy toward this unfortunate group. We all felt like we were in the same boat.

Several people who lived on the block had homes down south and visited in the summer. They knew what segregation and discrimination were.

In New York, the affluent white population treated their workers well; they didn't want for anything. They stayed on for many years as workers until they retired. Even though none of the wealth was mine, real beauty surrounded me at a young age. What other people had regarding money and material things did not make me envious.

When I started going out and away from my block, I started seeing the haves and the have-nots. Even some of the fans who were coming to the Apollo didn't have expensive taste. I never looked down on them. I knew they were never around people who had quality things. There were a couple of girls who had money and stylish clothes that their mothers bought them. I got into an argument with one of them, and we fell out; she was jealous of me.

When I got away from my block, I made my clothes, wore makeup, and looked fashionable. Nobody knew about my mother. I became a new person who departed from the past. I had a warm and cheery, outgoing, starlike attitude that attracted people to me. I felt if you acted like a star, you appeared to be classy and well groomed. I grew up admiring Jackie O and Elizabeth Taylor, not ever thinking I'd meet Elizabeth Taylor, and she'd be in Michael Jackson's life.

"Jackie O is pure class," Billie said whenever I mentioned her name.

When I started to become classy and well groomed, I attracted envy. I didn't have a lot of money. I had personality, style, and a great sense of humor. I wanted to live a peaceful life full of beauty and prosperity.

Harlem became flooded with heroin addicts who were robbing people. I purchased a .22 automatic pistol from someone in the street. All kinds of goods became available on the streets.

I loved to go to the different bars in Harlem to see the fashions that paraded into the bars. I befriended three girls in a bar, Reenie, Corine, and Fidela. Reenie had a car, and she offered to drive me around to different taverns we attended. Reenie and Corine were best friends; Fidela tagged along. Reenie asked me to come along so Fidela wouldn't feel left out. I was riding along in the car, and we were stopping at different bars, having fun. When you walked into a bar in Harlem, the Bronx, or downtown, people talked to you. They wanted to know about you, what street you came from, and who you knew.

They wanted to see if you knew the same people they knew and find out if you had something in common.

I hadn't achieved success yet. I was on my way up the scale of life, and there were obstacles to success. I never imagined that riding in Reenie's car could be one of them. All of us except Fidela had gangster boyfriends who gave us money and gifts. I never saved a dime; I spent money on clothes and fur coats. I never bought jewelry, because I was afraid someone would snatch it off me as I walked the streets. The boyfriends weren't the problem; it was Reenie's car. At the time, cars did not have seat belts. One weekend Corine didn't come out with us. I sat in the front, and Fidela sat in the back seat.

Reenie was driving and hit another car. My forehead hit the windshield. There was no blood; even so, my head hurt from the bump. That should have been a sign for me not to sit in the front seat of Reenie's car. The bump went away by the following weekend.

I saw Reenie at the bar. Corine was not there. Reenie, Fidela, and I exited the bar to go to another bar. When we came out to the car, Reenie insisted I sit in the front and Fidela in the back. We were driving around, trying to figure out what bar we were going to.

"I am Reenie's friend, and I don't appreciate you taking my friend from me," Fidela said to me.

I was shocked. I knew Corine was Reenie's best friend. She hadn't been out with us in weeks. Reenie was seeing Corine during the week at her house.

Fidela accused me of trying to steal from her friend. Reenie didn't want to set Fidela straight as to who her best friend was. She didn't want Fidela to turn on Corine. I was a better target. I don't know if Fidela looked up to Reenie or was using her as an excuse because of her jealousy toward me. Fidela kept trying to start an argument with me in the car.

I asked Reenie to drop me off at a bar, and I got out of the car. I went into the bar as Reenie drove off with Fidela. I enjoyed myself that night and met a guy with a car. I hitched a ride with him to a different bar. Then when we got to the bar, he wanted to stay with his friends. I met another guy, and he was going to another bar. I hitched a ride with him. Luckily for me, he was barhopping all night.

We picked up and dropped off people who were on their way to the same bars as we were. I had forgotten all about the drama between Reenie, Fidela, and me.

I went out to a bar the next night. As I approached the bar, Fidela approached me and verbally abused me. A guy who knew her told her to leave me alone, but she kept on cursing and threatening me. The man stopped a cab and escorted me into the cab. I went home, got a hammer, and put it in my shoulder bag.

Fidela was smoking angel dust, a drug made from embalming fluid. The drugs heightened her envy. I had no fear, and I wasn't staying home and hiding. I had to walk the streets. No one was going to stop me from doing that. I went back out to another bar. While I was sitting at the bar, Fidela came in and walked up to where I was sitting.

She started threatening me again and challenging me to a fight. I turned my back to her and faced the bar. Fidela kept ranting on; she refused to be quiet. Thank God the people in the bar liked me; she was a stranger to them.

A woman sitting next to me said don't ever turn your back on your enemy. I turned around and faced Fidela. Profanities flew out of her mouth, and she called me all kinds of names. Hurling her fist, she swung at me and hit me. I jumped from the barstool, and I hit her back. We engaged in a fight. She pushed me, and I tripped over a barstool and fell. Fidela landed on top of me and pinned me down. Then Fidela pulled out an ice pick. For the first time in my life, terror came over me, because she had a sharp weapon. I couldn't believe what was happening. I went into shock. She raised the ice pick and was about to stab me in the face with it.

My eyes closed. I didn't want to see what was going to happen. Fidela was sitting on my hands, pinning me down. I thought this was the end of my life and my dreams of becoming a model. I suddenly felt her weight lift off me, and I opened my eyes. A woman in the bar picked Fidela up and pulled her off me. Fidela was standing up, and the woman held Fidela by the back of her collar and her arm. That gave me a chance to jump up quickly from the floor. I can take an ass whipping. I can't live with being ice-picked and mauled to death.

Grabbing my bag by the barstool, I quickly pulled out my hammer. I charged at her with my hammer as she fled the bar. I swung the hammer at her. It barely scraped her back because she ran so fast.

The crowd from the bar and I chased her down the street. It was a summer night in Harlem, and everyone was out on the street. Being known has its merits in a time of need. The mob and I chased Fidela as she ran in the streets for her life. Guys stepped out into the streets and put their feet in front of her to trip her up. She fell, but a man grabbed her, and she got back up swiftly. He tried to hold her as the mob and I descended upon her. Fidela wrangled free from him and ran.

Fidela had broadcast all over Harlem at every bar that she was going to kick my ass. All the people on the block jumped on my side for this witch-hunt. The crowd was in a frenzy; they wanted her blood. My hammer was going to do their bidding.

Fidela ran away and disappeared into the night. The excitement of the chase was all the crowd needed. Everyone dispersed, and the mob and I went back to the bar. We drank the night away as if nothing had happened.

I came out the next night, thinking Fidela's silly quest of destroying me was all over. As I approached the bar, a guy ran over to me and said Fidela was looking for me. Fidela had a jar of lye acid she was going to throw in my face. I turned around, went home, and got my .22 automatic gun. I had to take care of myself; the cops were not going to do anything until after she had thrown the lye on me and scarred me for the rest of my life.

I went back out to another bar. Fidela knew all my watering holes. When I got to the bar, I didn't see her.

Before I entered the bar, a girl approached me and warned me not to go down the street. Fidela was sitting down the street with a jar of lye that she was going to throw in my face. I looked down the street and saw her sitting on top of a car with the jug of lye beside her. I was determined not to be ruined for life because someone gave me preferential treatment. That was Reenie's choice, not mine. The situation reminded me of Cain and Abel. Reenie and Corine disappeared. I did not see them during this whole ordeal.

Then it dawned on me that I was set up, and Fidela was hung out to dry. I found out that a guy who was pursuing me was Corine's boyfriend—something I didn't know about until after the hostility started. Many men wanted me, and I liked the attention after growing up as an unattractive girl.

I had blossomed into Cinderella at the ball. I loved to make my grand entrance with beautiful attire, hair, and makeup. The public looked at my outfit and scrutinized me if it wasn't right. Being style forward, I blended fashion from the past with the contemporary. Fidela had become a thorn in my side, and I had to stop the demon. I came to the conclusion that it would all end here with me.

I avoided her for the rest of the night until after the bars closed. Arriving at the after-hours spot, I saw Fidela there without the jar of lye. Everyone who was there had heard Fidela threaten to throw lye on me. Her threats spread all over Harlem, and people had seen the jar of lye. Being well liked in that after-hours spot had its benefits. I had been there many times and spent lots of money. My men friends who accompanied me there spent tons of money.

A couple of she-wolves I knew were dressed in sheep's clothing and pointed to Fidela.

"So what are you going to do?" one of them asked.

"Wait until the sun comes up," I replied. We had a couple of drinks and blows of cocaine, and in a few hours, it was six am. Fidela was still lounging on the couch against the wall. She hadn't spent a dime all night, yet she was the troublemaker.

I got up from the bar and walked over to Fidela. "This is bothering me. Can we go outside and settle this beef between us?"

"Yes," she said without hesitation.

Five other girls, Fidela, and I left the after-hours spot. Our eyes adjusted to the bright daylight glaring down upon us.

"Let's walk around the corner to talk," I suggested. Fidela willingly walked with us around the block.

I don't know if she was high on angel dust or not. My mind was made up as to what her fate was going to be. Fidela was escorted a little way into the block until we cornered her against a basement rail. Most buildings had a basement rail fence that came up to a person's waist. If someone pushed you, you would fall over into the cellar.

Once you tell everyone you are going to do something to someone, you have to do it. Everyone waits for you to do it, and your reputation is your word. That was when I realized that words carry weight. Sooner or later Fidela would have made good on her threat to throw lye on me.

With that thought, I pulled out my gun, and the five girls held her so she couldn't run.

"How dare you threaten to throw lye on me over some bullshit? About a man I was no longer seeing and a car seat I was no longer sitting in. How ironic. Neither he nor the car seat belonged to me; they both belonged to Corine. The car belonged to Reenie, and she gave Corine the honor of sitting next to her," I said calmly.

I didn't want to wake the neighborhood up with yelling or have witnesses. It was my problem, and I had to face it head-on. I put my .22 automatic gun to her head and pulled the trigger. God must have been watching over me, because I pulled the trigger several times, and the gun jammed. Fidela had a razor hidden in her hand, and she broke away from the girls. I grabbed her to keep her from running. She cut my finger and ran away. It wasn't a big cut—a nick from the razor—but some blood spilled.

I saw Fidela walk in the bar and walk back out the next weekend. She appeared to have a quietness about her; a reformed attitude emanated from her. As she walked by me, she never said another word to me or about me. I couldn't control what was out there; I could only control what was in my environment. I don't think there was anything I could have done to curtail Fidela from stalking me. Reenie and Corine focused their and Fidela's jealousy on me.

They both used Fidela as a tool. I should have never gotten into Reenie's car. I allowed myself to be an unsuspecting victim. Perhaps I became too comfortable around them and paid the price. That made

Fidela assume I was an easy opponent to destroy. Fidela came to her senses and realized that her life mattered. Her life was worth more than her jealousy toward me.

She didn't need Reenie's and Corine's approval. I vowed to be aware of signals and more prudent in selecting my inner circle of friends and associates. Black lives didn't matter; girls and guys went to jail for life for selling drugs.

For murder, you didn't do any time at all unless you killed someone white; then you did time. Girls were getting their faces cut by other girls because they were dating the same guy—or thought they were. The man told one about the other, and he got them both riled both up in a jealous rage. Both women exchanged harsh words, and then there was a confrontation, and then a fight. One of the girls pulled out a razor and cut the other one's face, scarring her for the rest of her life over a man who didn't care about either one of them.

I will never fight over a man or demand any respect for him. A real man is going to protect his woman. "I chose her over you, and I don't wish to see her get hurt. You and I are finished. It's over." That's what a real man says. A real man makes that very clear and means it; he doesn't double back.

When he and his woman or wife break up, he's not going to cheat with you. Only a punk likes to play games with a woman's emotions. That will get a woman unnecessarily and severely hurt by another woman. Why? Because one of the women he is seeing or wants to see is beautiful, and he's jealous of her beauty. He's threatened by other men wanting her, even though it was a fact that he was seeing another woman.

He knows she's beautiful and another man is going to eventually take her away because of the situation he created that is feeding his fragile ego. The other woman he's seeing is aggressive and possessive.

She's not as beautiful or attractive. He doesn't care; he wants to see both of them get hurt.

I learned there are no surprises in a fight. A couple of months later at one of the bars I attended, I started dating a guy because of his good looks. All my girlfriends were swooning over him. When I came in the bar, he sat in the back at a table with a girl. They were talking and flirting. I sat at the bar, waiting for him to acknowledge my presence; however, he ignored me. I had a couple of drinks. I couldn't stop looking at the two of them having a pleasurable time.

I got up from the bar and went to confront them.

"Excuse me, could you get up and come over to the bar and sit with me?" I defiantly demanded.

"Don't you see he's sitting here talking to me?"

I was not aware that she was the barmaid's friend, and this was a setup. I was high, and I was jealous.

"Who asked you? Shut the fuck up, bitch," I yelled in anger.

"Don't you call me a bitch," she retorted. I yelled and screamed and called her an MF, B, and a whore. She stood up, and then he got up from the table and escorted me out of the bar. I scolded him for sitting at the table with her and ignoring me. He escorted me to his car, parked across the street. We got into the car, and he sat in the driver's seat. I sat on the passenger side, and his window was down. I was fumbling in my handbag for some lipstick.

I looked up, and there was the barmaid, standing at his window. "You had no right talking to my friend like that," she said with a cigarette in her hand.

"Fuck that, bitch. Jeff is my man, and if I want to tell him to get up and leave, that is my right. Mind your motherfucking business," I said, and on that note, she flicked the cigarette into the car, and it landed on my eyelid. I screamed and brushed it off my eye.

She walked away, and he drove me home. I felt a burning sensation on my eyelid, and I kept looking in his rearview mirror. All I could see was that a small circle of top skin on my eyelid had peeled. I didn't see any pink skin. I assumed that the cigarette didn't break the skin.

When I arrived home, I showered, put some Vaseline on my eyelid, and went to sleep.

When I awoke at ten o'clock, my eye was completely closed. The eyelid had swollen to the degree that it flopped over, appearing as a protruding, hooded eye. I was stunned that she had the nerve to come over to the car after I had left the bar. She couldn't confront me in the bar because she was working. I put on a hat and a pair of John Lennon blue spec shades that covered my eyes. I called one of my she-wolves named Janell who wore sheep's clothing to meet me at a bar.

It was around noon. We were in the bar, and I was telling her what happened. I took off my glasses and showed her my eye.

"She threw a cigarette in your eye? If someone threw a cigarette in my eye, I'd be like Hercules. I'd kill that motherfucker. Come on, let's go down there and get that bitch now," she said in awe.

We exited the bar and walked down the street to the bar where the incident happened. Guess who I saw standing outside the bar—the girl who was sitting with my boyfriend. In broad daylight, she looked humongous—a tall woman with a large bust, small waist, a king-size ass, and supersize thighs. She wore tight boot-cut XXL jeans. Her short, sleeveless top displayed her large arms. I looked down at her small feet. She had on red open-toe sandals with a heel. They made her tower over me. I had on my fighting clothes; it was too late to back down. I silently approached her.

"It's going to be a fair fight; you don't have your buddy with you. We are going to come back tonight and get that bitch," the she-wolf Janell said.

I attacked and threw the first punch. I had my shades and hat on. I didn't want her to see my swollen eye. All she had to do was hit me in my eye, and the fight was hers. I made sure that didn't happen. I boxed and scratched her. I dug my nails into her scalp and tried to pull her face off. My nails bent back when I tore the skin off her face. There was my blood and her blood under my broken nails.

She threw me up on the car. I held my head down, and I kept punching her. She was on me and knocked me off the car onto the street, in front of the car's front bumper. I said to myself, this humongous bitch is not going to sit on me as Fidela did. My hat fell off; my glasses were still on. I was on the ground, and she rushed toward me and stood over me. I started kicking her hard in her vagina, thighs, and stomach. She backed away, and I got up quickly from the street.

Her face was bloody from the scratches. My footprints were all over her jeans and lower body. She backed down and didn't wish to fight anymore. A taxicab drove by, and she hailed it, jumped inside, and drove off.

With bloody broken nails, I turned to my she-wolf Janell.

"I'm going home to sleep and tend to my hands," I said.

"Meet us at the bar tonight. All the other she-wolves will be there. We're going to the bar and get that other bitch," she-wolf Janell said enthusiastically. I rushed home, showered, cut my nails, and put bandages on my fingertips. My eye was still swollen and sore, so I applied more Vaseline, lay down on the opposite side, and fell asleep.

When I awoke, that night. I got dressed and put on my sunglasses. On my waist, I placed a .38-caliber pistol inside my jeans. I didn't wish to risk taking the .22 automatic for fear it would jam on me. I threw a poncho over me to cover the pistol. I went to the bar, and all the she-wolves were there, seven of us altogether.

My she-wolf Janell started bragging about me.

"Amina beat that bitch's ass. I was there. That was a big bitch. I could have handled her," she-wolf Janell said. Then she got on the bar floor and demonstrated me kicking the girl. She chuckled.

The elder she-wolf Sadie was the judge; she was the one who pulled Fidela off me. She agreed that what happened to me wasn't right. If I was cursing, they both had mouths. They should have cursed me back, not thrown a cigarette in my eye. I could have lost my eye, and that was a serious offense.

"Let's go. I got my gun," the elder she-wolf Sadie said.

We all marched out and headed to the bar to get the barmaid. When we burst into the bar, the elder she-wolf Sadie pulled out her gun and waved it up in the air.

"All right, here comes the judge; here comes the judge. We want to get this case settled," the elder she-wolf Sadie shouted.

I walked to the back of the bar, where steps led to the stage for the bands. I ascended the steps and got on the stage. I had my hand on my gun under my poncho, so they couldn't see I had a gun. She-wolves were in the front of the bar, and I was in the back. Patrons were between us, along with the barmaid.

"What happened to me last night wasn't cool at all. You were bad last night. Come out from behind the bar," I loudly said.

She refused to step out from the bar. I felt like I was in a Clint Eastwood movie, and I was ready to pull the trigger. A lady who owned the tavern and her two adult sons were there, but no one said anything; everyone froze. I stepped down off the stage. I was going to the bar to get her. I wanted to kill or injure her beyond repair. As I walked toward the bar, her man jumped in front of me.

"Can we talk about this? Step over here, and we can talk. Please don't kill her. She is the mother of my five kids, and if you kill her, they won't have a mother," he humbly pleaded.

"You see what she did to my eye? That's a death sentence," I answered.

"Please don't hurt her. She has to take care of my kids."

"Get her over here. I want to know why she threw a cigarette in my eye," I said.

He signaled her to exit the bar, and she approached me.

"You buy drinks in here all the time, and you never tipped me. That is why I did what I did," the barmaid said.

I thought back, and there were two barmaids. The other one waited on me, and she was the one I tipped. I couldn't remember her ever waiting on me, and if she did, I didn't remember tipping her.

"If that's the case, do you want to fight me?" I asked.

She pulled out a box cutter razor.

"Baby, I don't have any weapons on me. Are you going to cut me?" I asked in a sweet tone, showing her my hands. She didn't know I had my gun hidden on my waist.

She looked at my hands. I was up close and personal, and this was her chance to swing the box cutter and cut my face. She didn't take the bait. I could have blocked her swing.

She did the right thing and did not swing. She wasn't ready to die.

"I am sorry if I didn't tip you. Honestly, I don't remember tipping you," I said.

"I'm sorry for flicking the cigarette in your eye," she replied.

We shook hands, and my she-wolves and I left the bar. The only reason I didn't shoot her full of holes was that she had five kids. Also, she didn't swing the box cutter. I gave her a second chance to vent her jealousy. She backed down, the case was closed, and I never had a problem with her again. The big girl never came back to that bar. My boyfriend and I eventually broke up. He dated another woman, and she got pregnant. My she-wolves protected me. Michael Jackson loved one of them. He even wrote a song about her.

She was a wolf in sheep's clothing. She had a shoot-out with the police in a hallway and survived without a bullet hole in her body. I never told Michael, because she and I went to see Michael a lot. We grew up playing with him, and if she and I had gone to Michael and asked for help, I am sure he'd have helped us. We had fierce pride because we all started with nothing.

Getting the chance to dance with Michael, I considered myself lucky. I never imagined I'd be in his history forever.

She did not get the opportunity to see Michael. I told him when I saw him she said hello. He asked where she was; he wanted to see her. I couldn't tell him what happened to her. That she fell in love with a man, and he broke her heart so badly. She cried in pain in a she-wolf Janell's mother's house.

She-wolves couldn't fight one another, so when she found out a she-wolf Janell was sleeping with him, she suffered in pain. We had one another's back to such an extent that we couldn't fight over a man, no matter how much we loved him. Then I had to ask myself if the man was that good to begin with, or was it all an illusion, a game that he played.

My eye healed. I still have a slight scar that you can barely see. I cover my eyes with eye shadow, and you can't see it. A woman threw a cigarette into my eye, and I could have been blinded or had my face sliced up. I could have shot and killed a mother of five kids and may or may not have gone to prison. It was all because someone was jealous of me, and I was jealous of my so-called man, who was sitting and talking to another woman. Their plot had been set, and I fell into the trap.

Luckily, the gods were with me, and I came out of it all right. I can't say the same about my next two associates. I sat in the bar with an associate named Del who wasn't one of my she-wolves. We all knew her brother. My she-wolves and I unknowingly beat up a female friend of his.

One Saturday night we all went to a Bronx after-hours spot. We had on our white minks, fox coats, fur hats that matched, and diamonds, which I didn't wear. White boots and miniskirts. There were seven of us, and we ordered champagne. The elder she-wolf Sadie drove the blue-and-white Cadillac Coupe De Ville that took us from place to place. We were in a spot crowded with patrons, and we were all standing by the bar, waiting for our champagne.

You could see we were affluent or were being kept by wealthy men. An ordinary woman walked by, bumped into the elder she-wolf Sadie, and didn't say excuse me.

"Can't you say excuse me?" the elder she-wolf Sadie asked.

"Fuck you! Who do you think you are?" the woman said.

When the elder she-wolf Sadie hit the woman in the face, they started fighting. The elder she-wolf Sadie knocked the woman down, and she began crawling on the floor to get away. She-wolf Sadie kicked the woman in the butt as she was crawling, trying to escape through the after-hours spot. A crowd of people moved back and made an aisle. They watched her crawl. Finally, the woman got up from the floor, and from somewhere, she grabbed her handbag. She ran out of the spot into the hallway, and we all followed.

A fight was exciting, no matter where it took place. The doorman was trying to figure out what was going on. The woman started going through her handbag.

"What do you have in the bag?" the elder she-wolf Sadie demanded.

When the woman didn't answer, the elder she-wolf Sadie grabbed the handbag from her and emptied it on the floor. A knife fell out onto the floor. The woman and she-wolf Sadie began to fight in the hallway. The woman got knocked down on the floor again, and we all kicked her, because she had a knife and was going in her handbag for it. Pulling out a knife wasn't considered fair. The elder she-wolf Sadie picked up the knife and opened it. She held the knife so tight, she cut her hand. The doorman broke up the fight.

Del's brother witnessed us kicking the woman. Obviously, he had feelings for her, and he wanted to protect her. He didn't dare go against us, so he never tried to break up the fight. When we returned to Harlem, he approached me. He wanted me to feel guilty for kicking the woman. Her jealousy got her ass kicked. It was a fair fight until she went in her handbag. His sister Del and I had become bar buddies. She drank ginger ale and sat at the end of the bar alone in the corner by the door. Del wasn't a she-wolf, meaning she was not one of my protectors or in our gang. Del was at the bar by herself all the time. I was curious to find out more about her.

I approached Del politely, and we took to each other, so I'd sit and keep her company. Del was pleasant and loved to communicate. She seemed intelligent. Del had a misunderstanding with one of the young she-wolves, named Vickie, although Vicky wasn't my protector.

Vicki, had a close bond with my protectors, and sometimes we all hung out together. She was extremely jealous and possessive of Johnny, her man. Unbeknownst to me, the young she-wolf Vicki had insulted Del on many occasions outside the bar. One night, the young she-wolf Vicki came in and went to the back of the bar.

"I am going to hurt her," Del said.

"Why?" I asked.

"She always has something nasty to say to me. I'm going with Johnny, and she's going with Johnny," Del said. She didn't say anything more about it, and we started talking about something else. I knew the young she-wolf Vickie was loud and not a wolf in sheep's clothing. Vicki was an attractive girl with beautiful, clear skin—a full-blown young she-wolf with no emotional intelligence, ready to start a fight. Del was plain looking, quiet, by herself, and well behaved. She didn't drink, smoke, or take drugs.

I didn't think much of Del's threat. I forgot all about it. Within the next couple of days, I came to the bar and sat with she-wolf Janell, my protector, and she began to say, "I told Vicki to wait for me and not to fight; I'd be right back."

She didn't wait. Del and her sister approached Vickie. While Vickie and Del were fighting, Del's sister held Vickie, and Del took a razor and cut Vicki's face. Blood poured everywhere in broad daylight. Vickie was screaming as Del continued to cut her face open. Her face was split in half from her forehead across her eye to her lips and chin.

By the time I got up close enough to do anything, Del and her sister had run off. I couldn't see her eyes because her face and clothes were drenched in blood. Someone called the ambulance, and they took her to the hospital," the she-wolf Janell said with a feeling of guilt because she hadn't been able to prevent the tragedy from happening.

I felt bad too. I had no vision that Del was going to do such a horrendous act. When the smoke cleared and the men got questioned, neither one of the women were dating the same man. The only thing they had in common was that both of their men were named Johnny. Del and the young she-wolf Vickie assumed they were dating the same man. All their animosity and jealousy arose from an illusion and misunderstanding. Later on, I found out Del had been in and out of mental institutions. The young she-wolf Vickie had a scar running down her face for the rest of her life. Every time she looked at Johnny, it reminded her of that day. She lost her beauty, and she and Johnny broke up.

Another incident involved Chancy, a beautiful girl I knew in passing. She started seeing a well-to-do fellow who was seeing another girl.

Being indiscreet, he parked his car with Chancy in it in front of where the woman he was dating lived. She lived on the third floor in the front of the building. She could look out of her window and see and hear them. He opened his sunroof so she could see down into the car. He kept a lot of drama going on between them. He liked to see women argue and fight over him.

Chancy was beautiful, and she had a beloved figure. She could have snared another man in a heartbeat. She had chemistry with him, and so did the other girl. The other girl he was dating wasn't as beautiful as Chancy. He and Chancy got out of the car and leaned against it to talk. He flaunted Chancy in the girl's face, and he flirted with other girls. This time the girl yelled out the window at Chancy. An argument ensued.

"I am going to whip your ass," the girl yelled.

"Come down here and do it," Chancy yelled back at her.

A few moments passed, and the guy got in his car, leaving Chancy standing in front of the girl's building. Chancy was not backing down, running, or telling him to drive her home. She had no protection. She was not a she-wolf. The girl exited her building and confronted Chancy. She hit Chancy, and they fought fiercely. The girl pulled out a razor and slashed Chancy from her forehead all the way down to her stomach.

The guy got out of his car and finally stopped the fight. Chancy was bleeding profusely; the scar would be forever on her face and chest. He rushed her to the hospital, and she bled all over his car. She had to stay in the hospital for a while until her skin meshed back together. The guy went on to date someone else, and Chancy's face was marred for the rest of her life.

The person who did the cutting or splashed the lye on you walked around freely.

I don't know if they claimed insanity, drug addiction, or whatever. The perpetrators never did any time for those mutilation crimes they committed. I became judge, jury, and executioner. Although I didn't kill, I managed to get a few dangerous enemies off my back. When you murder, everything changes. Do I have a killer instinct? Yes. Do I kill? No. Life is precious.

Knowing there are people in this world who will destroy your life in a moment of jealousy or bitterness, misunderstandings or false accusations, hurts me deeply. I've come in contact with men who provoke envy in me. They harass and make spying phone calls. They bring drama and conflict to me with other women. He would be vying for my attention, because he was jealous of my beauty and capabilities.

He may want me to get wrapped up in his game, so I can get hurt or hurt the other woman. He cares nothing about either one of us.

Because I have chemistry with a man, that doesn't mean he's right for me. A viper can magnetize me, and if I'm not careful, he'll jump up and bite me in my ass. No matter how much I desire a man, I will never put myself in a compromising position in which I get hurt by his drama and conflict with other women.

I'm never going to fight over a man; she can have him. If I am not his one and only? If he's not man enough to be loyal and stand up and protect me? I'm never going to demand respect from him or anything from another woman on his behalf. He needs to have the guts to stand up, be sincere, and make it clear to the world that I am his only woman.

I'm never going to do it for him. I know better. He's no man of mine, and I don't want anything to do with him. He's not worth my emotions.

God was telling me it was time to move on and cast aside the past. I began to focus on my career as a model. I was rising in a position. I couldn't afford to associate with everyone. A few individuals treated me snobbishly, while at the same time teaching me to be open and friendly. Be kind to everyone, because you don't know who will come to your rescue. I had to separate being courteous from being involved. I became aware of other prominent women in relationships. The boyfriends became jealous of their career and mad at the break-ups. They set out to make a scandal to destroy their image and career over nothing of importance.

Recently in Nashville, I was talking to a producer, and his young girlfriend kept circling us like a shark. She introduced herself as his assistant and told me I was beautiful. I asked her to join us.

"Do you mean that from the bottom of your heart?" she asked. Feeling the jealousy come out in the tone of her voice didn't scare me. She was a young girl in her twenties, attractive, not knowing her self-worth. I was a real woman doing business. I was trying to get money for my film. I had no interest in him whatsoever. He was twenty years younger than I and not my type.

I put my hands on my hips. I didn't feel flattered; I was offended.

"Am I misrepresenting myself? I'm trying to get twenty million dollars for my film. Please don't cheapen me. There is nothing free here, nor do I wish to have that image. I'm a professional. I'm here to sell my film," I stated.

He extended his hand, and I shook it. He never introduced the woman to me as his assistant or as his woman. He ignored her and kept talking to me about films. I kept my cool as she confronted me. I wasn't going to solve his or her problem. I didn't give a shit about either one of them. They both were rude and looked appalling; there was no need for me to offend them.

He should have been a man and introduced her, or she should have been talking and representing him about financing films. She was circling like a guard dog. She tried to discourage any attractive woman from doing business with him. What if he were secretly gay? Would she stop men from doing business with him too? If she only knew what I've been through to become the person that I am, her approach might have been kinder and gentler. She is going to get hurt by an angry woman. A woman is going to wipe the floor with her, because that man cares nothing for her safety.

If it were the old me, she would have been embarrassed with harsh words and maybe a fight. I was not lending my emotions to a situation such as that; it will never be for or over a man.

If confronted, I will defuse the situation it if it's over a man. It was up to the other woman to back off. She can have him on a silver platter. If attacked, that is self-defense. I don't desire a man I have to babysit or run after. I need my freedom for my career interests and personal space. No man who conflicts with the image I've created for myself is going to be with me. I have to live up to it.

CHAPTER 17

Focusing on Becoming a Successful Fashion Model

Turning my energy toward building up a portfolio, I had to get photographers to test me. It was unheard of for fashion photographers to charge a model for pictures. I had already tackled the challenge of getting makeup and hair products. As a woman of color, the makeup foundation had to be mixed to get the right blend. Max Factor was one of the products I couldn't live without as a model. Max Factor had an incredible powder cake that you dampened with water and used with a sea sponge to apply. It gave the most beautiful matte finish. Then I had to look around for eye shadows and lipsticks. Lancôme had the best mascara.

My other challenge was getting my hair in a style that didn't require a lot of maintenance.

Hairdressers and makeup artists in the fashion industry at that time didn't know how to work with women of color. I was left to do my hair and makeup. Manufacturers didn't create wigs for a female of color. They made a black woman look more like an entertainer than a model. Natural-looking hair maybe with a hairpiece looked the best. I had to have creative ideas and create a complementary appearance.

With no help from Billie, I kept getting on the train even if I didn't have money. I'd hop the subway. At that time they didn't fine you $250 as they do now. I went downtown and walked to as many photographers' studios as I could.

Walking kept me skinny. I walked all over and knocked on doors. Some photographers said, "No, I am not testing you," and some said, "Yes, I will take your photo." Looks were defined then: actors, actresses, entertainers, singers, Broadway dancers, and models all had their distinct look, whereas today you can't tell an actress from a model or dancer.

Davy took me to Miles Davis's brownstone downtown. Miles was sick at the time, and he had his hospital bed set up in his living room with a curtain. We entered the living room and sat down on the chairs. Miles sat on the edge of his bed. He had the aura of a king, so regal and secure. I wasn't into jazz. I knew he was a great musician and a trailblazer in the music world. I had never heard him speak, so his small, raspy voice startled me.

Words of wisdom came out of his mouth, and I had to listen to hear him. I told him I was trying to model, and he asked me to stick with it. After we left, I asked Davy what was wrong with Miles's voice. He could hardly talk. I felt bad for prompting a conversation with him. Davy assured me that Miles's raspy voice came from playing the horn. I took Miles's advice, and I kept pursuing modeling.

Davy and I drifted apart; it was a romance that was never going to happen. Things started happening fast; instead of me swimming against the current of life, I realized I needed to go with the flow and let it carry me up the stream.

One day I went to see a photographer on Fifth Avenue. He did the ads for Alexander's Department Store on East Fifty-Ninth Street in New York.

When I walked into his studio, before I could ask him to test me, he offered me a modeling job for Alexander's. I'd get paid fifty dollars, and the job was the next day. I wore beige pants and a top. Both were too big for me, and the stylist had to put clothespins all down the back of the blouse and pants. I stood there in a pose, and he took the picture. My movement was limited because I couldn't show the back or side of the outfit for fear of revealing the clothespins in the photo.

After the shoot, he wrote a check, gave it to me, and said thank you. That was my first job after all the struggling, and I still had a long way to go. I didn't have an agent at the time. In New York, you have to connect with the right people and be inspiring. I was looking for a job in modeling to prove Billie wrong.

I needed more test shots. I went to a photographer's studio, and he looked at my few pictures and decided not to test me. He knew an artist named Jack Potter who was looking for models. He gave me Jack's phone number and told me to call him. I called right away, and Jack said let's meet. Jack Potter was an innovative illustrator of the 1950s who suddenly dropped out of the field to achieve his wildest dreams.

An influential teacher of drawing and conceptual thinking at the School of Visual Arts, Jack hired me and paid me seventeen dollars for three hours' work. Jack dressed as a French artist. He wore a beret on his shaved head. As a model, I had to stand still on a platform while he lectured the class. I had to stand perfectly still as the students sketched me.

There were nude models in the day classes, and I modeled in the evening classes, which were strictly fashion. I worked for him three times a week, and he paid me with a personal check. Jack knew about my ambition to be a fashion model. I had to make it as a model to show Billie.

I was more obsessed with making it than I was with the modeling. Jack didn't suspect that Billie was my motivation. I was brimming with determination to succeed and overflowing with enthusiasm. He suggested I meet another fashion illustrator named Maning Obregon. Maning, as he was known, began his career in Paris at the age of sixteen, when he sketched hairstyles for Maurice Franck, the hairdresser. He later covered the fashion openings in Paris, Rome, Milan, and London for the *New York Times* and other publications.

Maning earned prominence for sketching clothes on the runway with lightning speed and for his descriptions of well-known fashion personalities. Maning was an illustrator for Bonwit Teller and other fashion stores. He also staged fashion shows and trained models. A guru to models, he was the person I needed; I knew how to make stylish, fashionable clothes in good taste. I didn't know all there was to know about modeling.

Jack gave me Maning's phone number. I called him, and he was enthusiastic and happy on the phone. "Sure, come on over to my place. I'd be glad to teach you about modeling." He lived on Sutton Place, one of the most prestigious addresses in New York. There was a doorman in the lobby of his building, and he greeted me. I announced that I was there to see Maning.

Arriving upstairs at his apartment, I saw that it was fabulously decorated. Menoush, his friendly Siamese cat, greeted me at the door. Maning knew fashion and how to walk the runway and pose. He dressed in fabrics and wraps with his trousers, along with Swedish red caps on his head. Maning could wrap colorful scarfs around his body that made a fashion statement. He let me stay at his apartment. I slept in the extra bedroom. We talked, and he sketched me.

He was very generous with other models and me. He introduced me to Stan Schafer, a contemporary American fashion photographer.

He shot for *Vogue, Interview,* Bloomingdales, and Victoria's Secret. Celebrity subjects included David Kennedy, Halston, Mariel Hemingway, and Andy Warhol.

In 1970, he had a big loft for a studio. It was antique wood with Tiffany lamps. It looked like a romantic version of the old West. Everything was brown wood, leather, and copper. No matter how sunny a day it was outside, when you entered the studio, an amber glow light dimly lit the loft. As you entered the shooting area, bright daylight filled the room.

Maning convinced him to do some test shots of me, but he never hired me. We all hung out at his studio; my look wasn't in, and I had to continue to build my portfolio until I found a look that clicked. Success happens fast for some models. A girl named Paula Klimak, who went by the name Pola, came to stay with Maning. Even though Maning let me stay there, I'd go home and change my clothes.

Pola arrived from Los Angeles. I visited Maning's every day, and Pola and I became friends. When she became a success, she had been photographed by the best. Beautiful Pola—even without makeup, she had the most romantic, dreamy eyes. One black-and-white eight-by-ten photo of her in the rain shows the sandy-blond, wavy, shoulder-length hair that graced her face. She was wearing a black, zipped-up motorcycle jacket. Pola sent a copy of the photo to the Wilhelmina modeling agency. Wilhelmina saw the picture and put her on a plane right away to come to New York.

Maning was training her to be a model. Pola, Maning, Stan, and I all hung out together.

Pola whined and cried about everything. She was a Capricorn, and she suffered from depression. Pola wasn't a bitch; Pola was sweet and weak. I never thought she wasn't going to make it as a model. I didn't cheer her on, saying, "Go, girl. I know you are going to make it." Wilhelmina brought her to New York, so obviously, she had it made. Pola wasn't competitive. I knew the models were going to tear her to pieces—if not verbally, emotionally. She couldn't see the bright side of anything.

We visited Stan's studio, and he took pictures of her. Right away they started dating. I remember one time she hit her foot on a rail at his studio. Pola started crying, and he hugged and comforted her. Stan was kind and supportive of Pola. She did not stop crying. She cried at the drop of a hat.

Back then we didn't know that much about depression. Pola wasn't bipolar. She didn't have high energy like me. I was jumping around, dancing and laughing. Pola was quiet and solemn. When she talked, she expressed her unhappiness about something. I never really knew the root of what was making her so unhappy. I felt protective of her, and we had dance in common. She did ballet and gymnastics, and I did modern jazz and disco.

Pola asked me to accompany her to her gymnastics class. When we got there, she worked with her instructor. Pola could do most of the positions; she was slow and methodical in her movements. She took one step at a time. I thought that was strange; most gymnasts move fast. She worried about her weight. She couldn't see how beautiful she was.

A mild, doubtful anxiety overshadowed Pola, and I didn't take it seriously. From what I could see, she had no physical problems. She wasn't using drugs. She viewed her life as serious, sad, and negative. Pola asked me to go with her on her go-sees to see photographers. I did, and they loved her. They wanted to test her. Photographers viewed my portfolio; some wanted to test me, and some didn't.

I never took any photos with Pola. Her modeling career took off. Wilhelmina kept her working. She modeled in catalog magazines and made $2,000 a day so she could afford an apartment. Pola moved out of Maning's place. She and Stan broke up. Pola was too depressed all the time. It wasn't because of him or anybody; it was a chemical imbalance in her brain.

Stan had his photography work to do, and he couldn't babysit her. She had the confidence to be a model. Modeling exposes all your insecurities. Wilhelmina pushed her career as a professional model. Pola repeatedly cried the blues, saying the other models weren't sympathetic or supportive, nor did they offer her any happiness.

Catalog modeling was OK for Pola when she got into high fashion. It became mentally and emotionally dark for her. High-fashion models are freer and more competitive. Catalog requires you to work a lot by yourself or with one other type all day, and it's restrictive. With high fashion, you have all these aggressive personalities you have to deal with that wish to be the center of attention. Emotionally, she was not fit for modeling; she wasn't babied or mothered. With all the crying and whining Pola did, I should have picked up the signals.

I thought she was in New York by herself; she needed her family. I never suspected depression or that it was so severe with Pola. As two professional models, we both became busy and went our separate ways. I'd run into her on the street, and we'd talk. I thought she was doing well.

Maning introduced me to Scott Barry so I could do runway modeling. Scott wanted me to do the show for free, because this was my first fashion show. He agreed to give me a pantsuit that I wore in the show. It was a light-wool, red, collarless jacket with red pants. I needed the money. Scott Barry was a successful African American designer. It was an important show for me, because a lot of buyers and magazine editors attended. I did the show and took tips from Maning on how to walk.

After the show, I met a very handsome man by the name of Bob. He asked if he could take me out. I said yes, and I gave him my phone number. Bob said he'd call me on Sunday. Maning introduced me to another designer from Puerto Rico named Edwin Santos. He had the same type of designs as Stephen Burrows. I hadn't met Stephen Burrows yet. Edwin liked me, and I became the perfect model for him. Edwin gave me so many clothes, and I got more test shots in his clothes.

I used to wear a lot of colors and gold on my eyes. Maning said, "Take that gold shit off your eyes. The most beautiful women in the world wear black around their eyes. If you don't want to work for *Vogue*, come after five o'clock." I kept those tidbits of advice in mind when I wore several colors of eye shadow.

I never forgot to line my eyes with black eyeliner or pencil. Now I had a designer from whom I could get clothes to do professional fashion test shots. I used to make my clothes, which got photographed. I needed new clothes, and Edwin supplied them. I started going to see Edwin frequently for fittings, and I spent time with him. Edwin and I laughed all the time; he had a sense of humor—until his investor pulled up in a black limousine and entered the showroom. Escorted by two bodyguards dressed in black, he was a Mafia boss who lived in New Jersey, according to Edwin. The investor was a tall, dark, and handsome man. He wore dark shades and tailored dark suits.

A pervasive tone of quiet intimidation dominated the atmosphere. The backer looked at me.

"Hello," he said with a smile.

I shyly smiled back. "Hello," I stated in a pleasant tone. The backer and his two bodyguards went into the back room. He picked up the money and the account books, and they all left. He should have waited downstairs and sent in an attractive woman to collect his money and books. Seventh Avenue is the garment district, and it made buyers and people uncomfortable when he and his bodyguards visited. He didn't have to say a word. His very presence shouted Mafia and gangster. Maning is the one who introduced Edwin to the investor. Edwin was the designer, and it was his business; he was only the investor and had no say or knowledge about fashion design.

During the day in the showroom, the buyers were there looking at the clothes and my modeling. The backer unexpectedly popped in whenever he wanted to. The presence of him and his bodyguards scared the buyers off. He didn't think to visit at night, and I don't know if he had a key to the showroom. He could have had Edwin meet him at night or on Sundays in the showroom. He had to let everyone see him and his henchmen.

Once the buyers and editors got spooked, Edwin couldn't compete in the fashion industry. Also, the fashion industry is very discriminating and discreet, and Edwin didn't know the business side of fashion. Before he could ever have a fashion show, he went out of business.

A small fashion paper gave him some publicity. It had a little article about him and his clothes. Edwin needed a rep to deal with the buyers, and he didn't have one. Maning went off to Europe to work as an illustrator for Valentino. When Edwin's business folded, I became discreet about my power. I never revealed my investors, and real investors don't disclose their investments. That is confidential information or trade secrets. I protect my investors; you don't know who is telling who what. It may not be the image that you wish to project.

Buyers and editors were telling people that Edwin was mixed up with the Mafia, and he wasn't. The man came in to pick up his money and books, said hello, and left. That was the only dealing Edwin had with the investor. I was sorry to see that people did judge a book by its cover.

I had met the photographer Bill King and auditioned for a test shot. He wanted a group of people half nude in a poster. I didn't do the test shot, being positive I did make a connection with Bill King.

There were many delays, and Billie wanted me to pay rent, so I had to get a job. I had given up my ambitions and put my modeling career on hold.

They say when you give up, everything starts to happen. Maybe my desperation to make it and my worries blocked the universe from rewarding me. When I gave up, I replaced despair with a calm faith. An assured confidence emanated from within me. The camera picks up what's on the outside and what's on the inside of a person.

CHAPTER 18

Beautiful Clothes and Beautiful People

LOWERING MY PRIDE, I GOT a job at the upscale department store, Henri Bendel. Billie kept hounding me to get a job and forget about modeling. The name Stephen Burrows, an African American fashion designer, was familiar to me. What a coincidence that he had a showroom on an upper floor and a boutique section on the ground floor of Henri Bendel. I had been working there for a month before I met Stephen Burrows.

Henri Bendel employed me to work in a new self-service department. They gave me one brown work dress that I had to wear every day. I'd leave the dress in the locker and put it on when I arrived at work. On the top floor of Henri Bendel was a cafeteria. I ate lunch there every day. Stephen Burrows and his assistants ate there also, along with Henri Bendel employees.

Stephen looked around the cafeteria and had made eye contact with me a couple of times. Hector Torres, his assistant, came over and introduced himself to me. Then he presented me to Stephen.

"Why don't you come down and try on some of my clothes? I am tired of seeing you in that brown dress," he blatantly said.

"OK. I'm trying to be a model. I need a designer," I replied and laughed. I went and tried on his clothes. He hired me and put me in his fashion show at Henri Bendel. I looked fabulous, and all the cameras were flashing as I walked the runway.

My photograph landed in the *Daily News* and the fashion section of other newspapers. It was fashion week in New York, and I was the new kid on the block. Things started to move fast for me. I was getting swift, positive responses and messages of love—after four years of walking the pavement and struggling, waiting for my time to come. Of course, I never told Stephen or anybody how I struggled. I acted casual, maybe a little arrogant. Being a diva, I complained about everything I didn't like.

Bobby Breslau made leather bags for Stephen and lived with him. He'd run and tell Stephen everything that I said.

"Oh, fuck her. Oh, fuck her," I'd hear Stephen say. I felt I deserved to have an attitude. That said, this is who I am—Amina Warsuma. I spoke a little about my Somali father and Egypt.

Maning called me the uptown Egyptian diva. I didn't want them to know too much about me. I didn't want anyone to challenge my position, and models will do that; they are so competitive. Models were like Billie. They didn't care how gorgeous or beautiful you were. Billie used to say, "No man is cuter than me. I'm the cutest, sweetest, and the best. They don't get any cuter than me." The models had that attitude about other women and models.

Billie didn't want anyone to be smarter than she was. Billie had to use her brains and whatever she had to survive. Before the sixties, women were in competition for money, a husband, and a house. Billie always challenged my efforts, telling me I was not going to make it as a model. Pola wasn't too far ahead of me in our quest for success.

When I got the job at Henri Bendel, what seemed like a setback or delay was a blessing in disguise. I didn't think I would meet Stephen. I knew his clothes were sold there, but unbeknown to me, he had a showroom at the store. Stephen's clothes were on the floor below where I worked. It's unusual for a designer to work in a store where their clothes are sold unless the designer owns the store.

A lot of creative people worked around Stephen Burrows. Joel Schumacher and Daniel Paredes did fabulous window designs for Henri Bendel. Bobby Breslau did leather handbags, Hector Torres was Stephen's assistant, and Charles Tracy was the amazing photographer in the group. I lost the job at Henri Bendel and gained a new job as a professional model.

After the show, I entered a whole new world. There were seven other black models I worked with all the time. The designers booked us all for their shows: Giorgio di Sant' Angelo, Fernando Sanchez, Halston, Calvin Klein, Ralph Lauren, Betsy Gonzales, Diane von Furstenberg, Anne Klein, and the fashion illustrator Antonio Lopez. Although Stephen was our hangout designer, the rest of the industry emulated him.

Stephen got invitations to all the important parties, and he asked a few other girls and me to come along. We came to his house and got dressed. Stephen had a sewing table in his apartment, and he put us in his clothes. Bobby supplied the leather handbags. Goody Tu-Shoes provided the shoes. Joel Schumacher and Daniel Paredes were a part of our group.

We all hung out and went to the parties. Everything was inspirational and creative; ideas and atmosphere were a big part of our lifestyle. There was a thirst to drink the best, dress the best, eat the best, and associate with some of the finest people in the world. Even on New York's icy sidewalks, I was at a party, in a flowered bikini with a white fox maxi-coat to keep me warm. Nothing—rain, shine, ice, or sleet—could stop us from partying. The beautiful clothes and people were our worlds.

Times were tough in New York; for partygoers, it meant ice and not money. I wore a bikini by Diane von Furstenberg in the cold winter storm. All photos of me are on my website, www.ablackmodelinparis.com.

A few models were backbiting, one another and fighting. It wasn't a big deal, and the designers found it amusing. Black models weren't getting the same pay as the white models. I got everything carte blanche—designer clothes, gourmet food, champagne, and all expenses paid. I attended the most fabulous parties with the elite crowd of the world. Every designer I worked for in New York treated me like a queen, first class all the way. I was from the ghetto, and the other models were from well-to-do middle-class families. I can't speak for them; I can only speak for me. I carried myself with dignity when I wasn't drinking, although I got drunk and sick at parties.

There was a certain energy about me that demanded the best, and that is what I received. Everything was fine. I didn't care about the white models getting paid more. I got accustomed to being treated like a queen. I was given money and clothes on the side as gifts. I wasn't there to babysit. I was there to take care of my clients and me. The rest of the models had more parental guidance than me.

It hurt me to hear the lies that designers didn't use enough black models. They hired eight black models all the time I was working. What happened was a militant model came along and got into everybody's business and started accusing the designers of not using enough black models. She was creating a problem where there was none, and it wasn't her legal right or position to speak on behalf of other models, whether they were black or white.

After that, designers started making black models indispensable. Now, you either have it, or you don't; you can't make someone hire you. Fashion is not a communist-run industry. It was an inspirational industry. It was time for me to exit stage left. I wasn't going to picket Calvin Klein—who rolled the red carpet out for me, treating me with dignity and respect—or any other designer who was good to me.

It wasn't my problem that she couldn't get work. The militant model blamed the designers and the industry. She didn't have any class about herself; that's why she couldn't get work. Nor did she have the right attitude. That is the real reason why she only could work for one designer. Rejection besieged her. That is the truth. The industry didn't accept her as a top professional model.

My mistake was listening to disappointed people in my field and getting angered by their actions and words, because they don't count in my world. What they were fighting for didn't affect me, and it was none of my business. Their power was an illusion. They had no real authority in any industry.

Being young and in conflict with myself, I didn't realize the blessings I had. It was like a dream I was living, and I didn't want to deal with someone else's reality or struggle. I was grateful for my new life, and I had great associates. I was being taken care of, and eventually, I'd get a raise. Why upset the status quo? She had no right to bother and backbite me to the designer Issey Miyake and model agent Ellen Harth. She was trying to take away my success. Although the doors opened once I stepped through them, I had to work hard. Issey Miyake hired me anyway. I felt I didn't owe the militant model anything. Why was she backbiting me when I never gave her a second thought?

I wasn't going to get wrapped up in her drama, because it wasn't true or any of my business. It wasn't my fault that she didn't get work and that I didn't agree with her accusations or cause. It didn't affect me. I was working all the time and treated like a queen. I learned you have to be careful of whom you associate with and whom you allow to hold court with you. Sometimes you think people mean well, and you get drawn into their problem and plot—only to find out that they intended to hurt you, because you made a success out of your life in an industry they can't break into and become a success. Some people create a problem where there is none, like spreading propaganda.

It was a play to acquire power or the assumption of authority that they don't have and will never keep. The false prophets come in and act like knights in shining armor, saving the people from a problem they created. If it's not broke, don't fix it. Some things you can't fix. If you don't have a good feeling about someone or what he or she is saying or represents, get in the wind. Leave that demon in the dust.

Trust your feelings! These are warnings to protect you and your livelihood. Never second-guess your feelings. Be the captain of your ship, and you shouldn't let them on it. If I had known then what I know now, I'd probably have been in the fashion business for thirty years instead of fifteen years. Being with the beautiful people was the best thing for me.

Stephen had recommended me to Wilhelmina Modeling Agency. I had fashion shows lined up, and I didn't have an agent. I also had a portfolio of test shots I had taken with different photographers. Stephen took me to Halston's party. I loved to entertain and make everyone laugh, and that is what I did. The designers who were there booked me for their show. China Machado was there. She was the editor of *Harper's Bazaar*, and Carrie Donovan was the editor of *Vogue*. Berry Berenson was a photographer for *Vogue*.

No one was using Halston; all the creative, together people were at his parties. Halston got inspiration and a kick out of those individuals who attended his parties and me. Halston was very good to me, and he was fabulous. He'd let me borrow his expensive clothes to take test shots.

I met Elsa Peretti and Andy Warhol through Halston. I wasn't one of his regular models. Halston had me model his clothes at Palace Versailles and Sly Stone of the Family Stone's wedding as one of his bridesmaids at Madison Square Garden. Halston invited me to several lunches and dinners. I felt honored to be asked, to be liked, and to bring happiness wherever I went. I was more of a comedian to him than a model, and who doesn't love comics? I told him my stories and jokes, and Halston laughed so hard, he bent over, holding his stomach. If I drank, he laughed at my comedic timing, and my improvisational skills were off the charts.

He also confided in and expressed his feelings to me. One thing I loved about him was that he didn't take shit from anybody. He taught me what professionalism meant.

He paid the cost to be the boss. With style, he worked hard to build his business and to keep it running. That was his identity. He couldn't separate the two; everything was all together. Halston aka H spent money on his parties, and he had the best of everything. Who's coming? What are they wearing? What is the latest funny story? It was fun. Everyone made an entrance dressed in the latest fashion.

At one party, I sat at a table with Valentino and Francesco Scavullo, who photographed me, and we laughed all night. I escorted him to several other parties and went to his house every New Year's Eve. I never saw Pola at Halston's, and she worked for him. Her energy was down. We were all happy, and we inspired one another. We were original, and there would never be another group like us.

I was Amina in wonderland, surrounded by all the beautiful, creative people, associating with and liking one another. If you came into the room and weren't wearing a together outfit, the fashion police were everywhere, and they talked about you. I never wore Halston to Halston's party. I unceasingly wore Stephen Burrows's clothes to Halston's parties and every other party. Halston loved it; he wanted to see what new creations Stephen had.

Joe Eula was Halston's illustrator, and he gave fabulous dinners. Halston called me and invited me to dinners. He gave a dinner for Lauren Bacall, and he invited me. Of course, I was entertaining. One should be when one attends a dinner party or a party. If you went to a black entertainer's party, people got up and sang, danced, and told jokes.

In the black ghetto households, that is what I saw when I was growing up in Harlem. Mamie had parties, and Billie had dinner parties, and there was laughter, dancing, and fun. I felt right at home telling my stories and making everyone laugh. Once I wore a Halston white gown to a disco. The gown had a layered tulip bottom. Even though I had on heels, it dragged the ground.

When I returned the dress to him the next day, it was dirty on the bottom, and he complained about it. I was afraid to put it in the cleaner's, worried they would ruin the color and the dress would come back dingy white. He never again let me wear a dress to a party, only for test shots. I have all the photos and test shots on my website photo gallery.

To prove that I worked and deserved to be a model, I did my makeup, hair, and styling. I had on jewelry by Elsa Peretti and clothes by Halston, Stephen Burrows, Calvin Klein, Issey Miyake, Charles James, and Betsy Gonzales. One photographer took beautiful head-shots of me, and in each shot, I looked like someone else.

The TV show *Charlie's Angels* was casting for a new angel. I had this strong feeling that if I sent one of the other pictures he took of me, they'd call me in for an audition.

Was I excited—a black angel? It was a new take on the show that the producers might have considered. My mind was on the multimillion-dollar press I'd be getting. The show attracted publicity; I couldn't think about anything else. For me, it meant a major issue in TV history—the first black Charlie's Angel.

In my zeal, I told the photographer about it. I asked him for more pictures so that I could send them to the casting director. The only reason he said no to me is that I told him somebody asked me for something, and I told them no. In the fashion industry, whatever you put out, you get back. If you say yes to everyone, everyone will say yes to you. Don't ever let anyone know that you told someone no, in the fashion business because when you asked them for something they will say no to you. Even in the movie industry people don't say no they say I'm not available or they don't say anything or respond if they are not interested.

An audition for a More cigarette ad came along, and I used that middle head shot he took of me. I showed it to the casting agent and got the job. At the time, not having the pictures to send to the producers of *Charlie's Angels* hurt me. Looking back, I realized it happened for the best. It also taught me not to reveal classified projects. Not everyone thinks big or sees the big picture like I do, and I learned to be careful about who I associate with and not to reveal secret projects.

Not everyone should be in my inner circle. I was young. I got comfortable. I said the wrong things to the wrong people. I made mistakes, and I have learned from my mistakes. I was not a civilian. I can't say or do anything I want. I have to say and do what is right for me, because I am a mirror, a born leader. People follow me, and whatever I say, people spread it. My words carry weight, and that is a big responsibility. I can't wear my mind on my sleeve and let everyone know what I am thinking.

An Asian girl came up to me in a public bathroom and told me, "Your thoughts are your actions, your actions are your character, and your character is your destiny." She said I had to learn to control my mind.

There's a question of whether I deserved to be a model. My skill, intelligence, and courage propelled me forward. Below are some of the fabulous people who contributed beauty and art to the world. I had the pleasure of being in their company, and I had the honor of working with them.

Designers: Halston, Elsa Peretti, Ralph Lauren, Fernando Sanchez, Giorgio di Sant' Angelo, Calvin Klein, Anne Klein, Diane von Furstenberg, Donna Karan, Oscar de la Renta, Betsy Gonzales, Rudi Gernreich, Issey Miyake, Charles James, Karl Lagerfeld, Scott Barry, and Edwin Santos.

Photographers: Berry Berenson, Chris von Wangenheim, Francesco Scavullo, Charles Tracy, Bill Cunningham, Anthony Barboza, Helmut Newton, Bill King, Stan Schafer, and Albert Watson.

Fashion editors: China Machado, Grace Mirabella, Diana Vreeland, Carrie Donovan, Polly Mellon, Audrey Smaltz, Eleanor Lambert, and Tina Chris Von Wangenheim's assistant.

Fashion illustrators: Antonio Lopez, Juan Ramos, Joe Eula, Maning Obregon, and Jack Potter.

Artists and authors: Andy Warhol, Truman Capote, Robin Givhan, and Paul Caranicas.

Film directors: Ivan Nagy, Joel Schumacher, Sidney Lumet, and Francis Ford Coppola.

CHAPTER 19

The Journey to Success versus Freedom

KARL LAGERFELD SAID I WAS the woman of the future. He must have meant my name. There was a lack of black models being hired who had American-sounding names. They had exotic names like Amina Warsuma. The Mafia owned half of Seventh Avenue at one point to keep any illegal unions from setting the rules. The Mafia owned the worker's unions so employers couldn't fire someone without cause.

Designers hired black girls with foreign names from other countries who were not with a group, who minded their business, and who were professional. One person can make a difference, and one stupid person can mess it up for everyone. It only takes one person to set things right. I never pleaded with any designer or client to hire me.

The other Black American models had to work hard and plead with designers to hire them. No one twisted the black model's arms to work as a model; they all went to the audition, and they got hired. If they didn't like their salary, they could have gotten a job doing something else.

The black models were educated and could have done well in other fields. The modeling agencies negotiated Their pay rate for individual models. If the black models didn't like it, they needed to have their legal representatives speak for them to the clients. If the agents didn't wish to speak on their behalf, then they should have hired a lawyer and talked to the designers in private. It's not what you do or say; it's how you say it and do it. That's the way to get respect. No one who owns a business wants someone else to have the decision-making power. The point of owning your own business is to have the power of a CEO. If anyone tries to take that power away, you resent that person. I never let any illegal, stupid person go in and speak to any boss of mine on my behalf.

I can hold my own when it comes to speaking to my boss and clients. I have power, dignity, and respect. I could go anywhere in the world, and the red carpet was rolled out for me. If a designer offered me a price that was too low, I asked politely for more money. If they didn't pay, I didn't work for them and moved on.

Getting back to the models before foreign-name black models came along, I felt like Pola came from a different place than the other models. I was from Harlem—that was another world—without the support of my family. I met Elsa Peretti through Halston and Stephen. She was from Italy without her family, like Pola. The models were very competitive with her, as they were with Pola. Only Elsa was strong and could fight back.

There's a question as to whether you can make it as a model, or if it's a key to other things. Some of the models were sweet, and some weren't. Treacherous models approached me and asked me questions. I'd say nasty things so they could run and tell everyone what I said. They asked me what kind of man I wanted. I said I wanted a rich man. Now run and tell that. They ran and told everyone I wanted to marry a man with money. They were too stupid to understand what I meant by a wealthy man.

I desired a man who was rich spiritually, in beauty, health, manners, energy, ambition intelligence, respect, good character, kindness, loyalty, and honor—not the gay gigolos they were marrying, who were discreetly sleeping with men.

They were with these types of men because they couldn't deal with a man cheating on them with another woman. Cheating is cheating. What's the difference? There are models married to the right husbands and others trying to steal someone else's man. Like they did to Pola—a model took her man. Some of the rich men they were dating did not spend a dime on them. They were cruel and slept with other models. Some of the models had good luck with wealthy men.

I had bad luck with any man I brought into the fashion industry. I learned to keep my guys out of the fashion industry. Bad behavior is encouraged when you're young and provoked, and sometimes I took the bait out of anger. At the end of the day, it was survival and growth that counted, and when it was all said and done, it was not worth it.

Elsa was older than I and like a mother to me. She took to me right away. We had a bond that filled us with happiness. All I knew was that she was a model in America by herself. I could not tell if a person was wealthy based on behavior. I knew individuals who were refined, classy, spoke well, and didn't have any money. All you have to do is read a lot of books, and you can talk well. I never had the pleasure of taking a year off to read every book past or present.

Despite Elsa's competition and her struggle, she was happy to see me. We laughed all the time. Elsa was beautiful, considerate, happy, and fun. There is no space or freedom in becoming a successful model. The pressure of modeling was an emotional torture for Elsa, Pola, and me. Even if we were quiet, there was someone saying something antagonistic.

My personal life is forever in conflict with modeling. Elsa, Pola, and I began to use modeling as a key. Not collectively, instinctively. What we had in common was that we all needed space, and we were emotional. We came from unfamiliar places. They didn't know about Italy, California, or Harlem. For Elsa, it was a key to becoming a jewelry designer. For me, it was a key to becoming a part of fashion history, and for Pola, it was a key to death. There had to be a second career, the next step, or family. The pressure was on to look good, to be on the scene.

Some designers you had to go to dinner with every night, and you couldn't have friends, because they didn't like the friends, and the business demanded that you be ready twenty-four/seven.

There was no room for a personal life outside of the prying eyes of the fashion industry. I never knew when my next job or an unexpected trip to anywhere in the world could pop up. The schedule was not my own; my modeling employment and social functions dictated my schedule. No one could do anything alone; the dependability led to whether you were a successful model.

I was very grateful that a lack of space and freedom breeds contempt. I needed space to live my personal life, to grow and be truly happy. I was independent and courageous. I'd disappear and then pop back up, and it worked for a while. Pola was one of Halston's models. I never saw Pola at one of his parties—or at all. Halston liked entertaining creative, upbeat people. All I heard about Pola was that she was working and successful.

Elsa and I became close. She was staying at Halston's old apartment on Sixteenth Street, across the street from Washington Irving High School, an all-girl school. Those girls picked at her if they saw her walking the street when they got out of school. I went down to her apartment for lunch while we were doing the shows. Elsa and I got booked on every show. Halston was her biggest client with whom I was also associated. A lady with style, she slept on black silk sheets. Furs, diamonds, silver, and pure gold dust were scattered around her small apartment, and there was the tantalizing aroma of sandalwood that Fernando Sanchez brought from Morocco. It gave a hint of fragrance that wafted throughout the atmosphere.

This woman has such exquisite taste. Elsa was happy to have her place; before that, she lived with two models. They competed with her and each other, and they continued to fight and argue, so she had no peace. Here Elsa could think about her work and put her creative visions in order.

After Halston had seen her designs, he took her up to Tiffany and made the introduction. Her vase and Roman cuffs were instant hits all over New York, and orders were pouring in from all over the world. Elsa's great horseshoe belt was another big hit that sold all over the world. Elsa and Joe Eula enhanced Halston's style. Elsa became the talk of the town with her hit jewelry, and Halston gave her his penthouse apartment on Upper East Side.

Elsa modeled her jewelry in Halston's show. She was a do-it-yourself person. The citizens of New York don't wish to do anything by themselves. It's a social town, and you need emotional intelligence to survive. Elsa and Halston could do things independently and with other people. In the fashion industry, everyone needs you; it was a very codependent business. There is no freedom, and that is when I realized I needed space.

Elsa Peretti designed a perfume bottle for Halston that became successful. Elsa worked for twelve years with Halston twenty-four/seven. She worked so hard that she sacrificed her personal life to be with Halston and the fashion industry, which is demanding. The more hits she made with her jewelry, the more she was in demand. No time for personal space. Elsa bought some land in Spain for $2,000, and she started building a village.

She had gone to school for architecture before the jewelry success. She traveled all over the world for the jewelry products and to get inspired. Halston was calling her. He needed this; he needed that. When she returned to New York, he didn't let her out of his sight. He had a houseboat, and he demanded that she and Joe Eula stay on the boat with him. When he gave parties, Elsa and Joe Eula had to sit with him. Halston's business was his life. He felt because he introduced Elsa to Tiffany that he owned her, and her personal life belonged to him. He expressed that to me. I thought he was wrong to feel that way. Then he'd show me magazine covers of Christie Brinkley and Cheryl Tiegs.

"See these girls? They are professional. *Vogue* has over ten million readers," he said.

When I started investigating these models, they were making over a million dollars a year or more and had a great personal life. He was a possessive man. Halston spent the money; he told me he bought twelve of Elsa's silver ashtrays, and he purchased a couple of her candlestick holders. Halston was a customer, client, and friend. On top of that, he was good-looking. There was something irresistible about him. I can see where the lines could get blurred without space.

I loved Halston, and I think he liked me a lot. I made him laugh until his stomach hurt with my stories. I never took anyone for granted. I was determined to live my life and not babysit. You can't put a price on personal freedom. Once those years of personal liberty were lost, you can't recoup them.

I loved Liza Minnelli. I even wanted to be her at one point. I adored her when she came on the scene with Halston. He spent his time with Liza, and she wore a great deal of Elsa's jewelry and gave it a lot of exposure. I loved Elizabeth Taylor. I grew up watching Elizabeth, and I admired her for her courage in living her full life and not apologizing for being a star. I wished I had a mother like hers, a mother who supported, protected, and molded her into the courageous individual that Elizabeth was. Elizabeth was in control. When she came into Halston's life, she took control. Halston told me that Elizabeth needed this or that. It was no more what he needed; it was what Elizabeth needed.

A couple of years ago, I was talking to one of the managers at the Banana Republic. Elizabeth Taylor wanted the Banana Republic to close the store so she could shop for a couple of hours. The Banana Republic declined to do so. I reflected back to Halston. He bent over backward for Elizabeth Taylor. She had his undivided attention.

Liza was more of a party girl. After I had learned what kind of life she had with her mother, Judy Garland, and what she did to help and support her mother, I developed great respect for Liza. I admired Elizabeth for having a high power over men. She knocked all other females out of the way. When she entered a man's life, he only had eyes for her. Halston was no different. When Elizabeth called or came by, he dropped everything for her.

Halston invited me to Elizabeth's birthday party that he gave her at Studio 54. She was married to John Warner, and he was at the party. Most of the time, he was in Washington, DC, and Halston kept Elizabeth company. When Halston introduced Elizabeth Taylor to me, she was polite. She flopped her big diamond ring in my face.

"How do you do?" she said. Halston didn't leave her side for one minute, even though John Warner was sitting with them.

Elsa's jewelry and career skyrocketed, and she had to travel a great deal. Most of her inspiration came from Spain. Elsa began a relationship with a handsome man. She moved to Spain and lived her personal life. She continued to work for Tiffany. Elsa found a balance between personal life and career in Spain. She couldn't find that in New York or being in the fashion business.

In New York, there is no personal space for life; that is your life nonstop. Elizabeth Taylor and Liza Minnelli started being with Michael Jackson. Michael built a shrine to honor Elizabeth in his house. Liza and I danced with Michael at Studio 54. As time went on, Michael and Elizabeth were seen in public. He saw Liza in private.

When Halston got sick, Elsa was there for him. Elsa and Liza were at a tribute for Halston after his death. Elsa was the best friend anyone can have, especially when they were down; she was there. I learned from Elsa that if you have education, skill, courage, intuition, and a willingness to work, then you can make it. Elsa came to America with no money or support from her family. All she needed was to meet the right people, and she did. I learned that sometimes the right people for your business might not be the right people for you. Compromises are hard to accept; respect has to be given and received. Once you make a commitment, the universe brings you in contact with the people you need. I also learned from her that no matter what, you should take care of your business.

CHAPTER 20

I'm in the Big Time

ELSA AND POLA HAD ATTAINED their success; it was my turn.

"Amina, you made yourself," Halston said. I had a lot of work lined up. Elsa, Pola and I were with Wilhelmina, and we all were around Halston. It seemed as though being a professional model was my destiny. Diana Vreeland, Carrie Donovan, and Antonio Lopez hired me to do the *Vogue* illustration fashion show. They hired Berry Berenson to photograph me for *Vogue*. When Diana Vreeland stepped down from being the editor of *Vogue*, Grace Mirabella became an editor. She hired Audrey Smaltz and Anthony Barboza to photograph me for *Vogue Beauty*. Chris von Wangenheim shot me for the Italian edition of *Vogue*.

Francesco Scavullo shot me for *Esquire* magazine. He also did a *Cosmopolitan* magazine campaign with Burt Reynolds and Jim Brown. He hired me to work as one of the girl fans for Jim Brown. Bill Cunningham took press shots of me as I walked the streets of Manhattan. Helmut Newton photographed me for *Lui* magazine. China Machado, the editor of *Harper's Bazaar*, hired Bill King to shoot me.

Realistically, I was not going to get the Christie Brinkley or Cheryl Tiegs contracts. It didn't exist for black women at that time. Because there was a lack of black cosmetic products on the market, designers didn't do clothes exclusively for black women. The designs were for all women except 1X, 2X, and above sizes.

What a wonderful feeling to be in demand, working in print and doing runway. As fast as I acquired the money, I spent it. I never had a financial plan. Money burned a hole in my pocket. I didn't tell Billie about my success. I didn't wish to hear anything negative. Somebody told her I had a picture in *Vogue*. She was hurt because I didn't tell her.

"One lousy picture in *Vogue*, and you couldn't tell me," Billie said. Billie was so sure I wasn't going to make it. When I did make it as a model, I didn't want to celebrate with her. Billie's spy told her. I couldn't do anything without her spies seeing it and running back to tell her.

When my checks came in the mail, she collected the mail and held the envelope up to the light to see the amount of the check.

"How much is your check?" she asked.

"It was for twenty dollars," I answered.

"No, it isn't. It was for a hundred dollars. I can see through the envelope," Billie retorted.

Not being comfortable about my new wealth or having money is what made me spend it so fast. I paid my rent and bought my food, and I'd give Billie money for herself. Billie liked to go on boat cruises and short trips with her friends, and I'd give her extra money to contribute to her journey. She was in the house, answering the phone. Billie was so sweet to my fashion associates when they called. When Antonio Lopez and Juan Ramos came by my house, Billie welcomed them with open arms.

She loved my fashion and Broadway friends; they were somebodies. Billie had a pleasant speaking voice and sounded like a white woman over the phone. When I went away on trips for modeling jobs, I didn't have to worry about my apartment or possessions. Billie was there with two other lodgers who had lived with her for over ten years.

Miss June became severely ill. Billie went to see her as she had done every day of her life. During my lifetime with Miss June, Billie visited her every day. Billie stayed only thirty minutes to an hour with Miss June and telephoned her every night. There had been someone there to take care of Miss June when she couldn't take care of herself. On holidays, Billie brought Miss June a plate of food after her friends left.

I had a new life, and Miss June was losing her life. Billie wanted to do everything for Miss June, and she didn't desire me to help. Her attitude was that this was her mother, and Billie wanted to do everything for her. I went to see Miss June when she was sick. I didn't think Miss June was going to die. She had been sick for thirty-two years with ten operations, recurring cancer, gallstones, and kidney and liver problems. I figured she'd come out of it and be able to function as she had done so many times before. As I became busy with my work, her illness became severe. Miss June told Billie I didn't come back to see her.

"You better go see Miss June. If she dies, you will never forgive yourself," Billie said.

I went to visit Miss June, and she was dying right before my eyes. I started crying, and I couldn't stop. I felt the energy slowly leaving her body.

I kissed her and told her I loved her. I thought for sure that at eighty-five years old, she was going to live until ninety-five. She bragged about her aunt Rosa living to 110. Billie didn't shed a tear in front of me. When I left, Miss June was alive. I had a fitting for Stephen Burrows. When I came home that night, Billie told me Miss

June was dead. Billie made all the arrangements, and Miss June had an insurance policy and a will. Billie kept all the money; that's why she didn't want me around. Billie didn't want Miss June to leave me anything.

Miss June was laid out in her coffin at the church on 122nd Street and Lenox Avenue, not far from her abode. Another model and I went to see her. Miss June looked beautiful. A few days later, Miss June's funeral was held in the evening, and I attended.

I became so distraught after her funeral that for many years, I couldn't attend other people's funerals. Maybe Billie cried when I wasn't around. I'd never seen her cry, not even at the funeral. It was spring when Miss June died, and it was fashion week on Seventh Avenue. The abundance of work took my mind off my grief.

Afterward, I wanted to go to Paris; I had to get out of the United States. I didn't know anyone in Europe. I was working and spending money, and some of my money was held up or delayed. Some clients didn't pay fast, or they paid half and promised the other half of the money when they received it. A lot of designers struggled in the fashion business. I worked for Antonio Lopez and Carrie Donovan for *Vogue*. I made about $3,000. I sent Billie on a trip and spent the rest.

Antonio told me about Karl Lagerfeld. He'd pay for my ticket to come to Paris to do his show in 1972. I didn't wish to wait for my checks to come. I'd collect them when I came back from Europe. I was off to Paris with seventeen dollars in my pocket. Credit cards and ATMs didn't exist.

CHAPTER 21

First Paris, Then Europe

COURAGE AND DESIRE DROVE ME to leave New York. I had nothing to lose, so what the hell. I was off to Paris. When I arrived at the airport, Karl Lagerfeld was there to meet me. Antonio was staying at one of Karl's apartments, the Odeon Studio on Boulevard Saint-Germain. Karl looked like a body builder; he was all muscled up and built correctly. He commanded authority; it was never an assumption.

At that time, black girls who didn't have light skin did not walk the runway; they only did print work. Paris desired something new, so Karl took a chance and put me on the catwalk. He told me he would support me for two weeks. After that, if I didn't make it, I could go back home. I stayed in a cheap hotel around the corner from Antonio.

When I walked the runway in Karl's show, I became an instant hit in Paris. Instead of going home in two weeks, I stayed six months. I worked so much that I obtained representation at Christa, the modeling agency. Christa worked me like a dog and didn't want to pay me. I had to beg, cry, and plead with her to get my money. When it comes to my hard-earned money, I have no pride. I was seventeen and in a foreign country. The French people were very good to me.

Karl took me to dinner at the best restaurants. I had a cavity in my tooth, and there was no floss on the market then. I kept picking the food out of it after dinner. That was bad manners; I admit to it now. I should have gotten up and gone to the bathroom. Other than that, I had excellent manners.

I wore Stephen Burrows's clothes, and Karl made fun of me. All the French designers did. All eyes were on me when I walked into a room, especially if I wore his colorful dresses.

"My dear, you looked like a carnival," Karl said. Karl was a funny man; he had me laughing so much. He wasn't a phony; he either hated you or loved you. There was no in-between. He treated me very well and taught me a lot about wealth and beauty. At that time, people in France pretended to be something that they weren't, like aristocrats or wealthy or successful people.

Like the Hollywood con men we have today, you don't know who they are until you are ripped off. In France, Karl was aware of who they were and who they were not. He worked hard around the clock, and he loved it. Karl had several chateaus scattered around France. He was a German baron who spoke French, German, and English fluently. Karl knew history so I could ask him about English, German, and French history. He talked about it in the funniest way. He had a strong, honest sense of who he was and who others weren't.

I never carried a handbag. I put my money, cigarettes, and lipstick into a scarf and tied it up in a ball. Karl carried a beautiful clutch leather bag and wore velvet fitted blazers, elegant pants, shirts, and shoes. He started the style of men carrying bags. We all escorted Karl out for drinks or dinner after we went to the Club Set, which later became the Palace. The man who owned it gave me free meals. I ate pasta.

Then I went to the back of the restaurant, where there was a disco. Everyone was dancing. The Club Set had a black DJ with blond hair. He played James Brown for me, and I danced the night away. It kept me thin. All the elite of Paris and from around the world visited the Club Set.

Antonio, Juan, two other models, and I went to Karl's house during the day. Karl lived with his mother, and he introduced me to her.

He was respectful to his mother. I had to use the bathroom, and Karl told me to go ahead but don't tell the others, because he didn't let anyone use his bathroom. I was thinking of back in the South when they didn't let a black person use their bathroom. A German baron was letting me use his bathroom. I said to myself, "Girl, you have arrived."

I'd seen wealth in New York through Halston, who was self-made. Karl was born into European wealth. He was confident about spending money, and he worked all the time. I was in his world; Karl was the center of attention.

Below is a photo of Juan Ramos and me. I'm wearing Stephen Burrows's fringed red dress, and you see Karl's shoulder. The picture was taken over Karl's shoulder at a dinner table in a Vietnamese restaurant in Paris.

It was sweet of him to take everyone to dinner every night. He loved his Coca-Cola. I don't think they had Diet Coke at that time.

"Coca-Cola will rot your teeth," Antonio said.

"My dear, I am not going to take my teeth out and soak them in Coca-Cola," Karl replied. "I am going to drink my Coca-Cola."

I learned I had to know who I was to start something and stick to it to prepare for the future. Karl did videotaping and photography, and he practiced video filming and test shots on me and the other girls. He was very good at it, in addition to his designs. What I loved about doing his show was that every dress fit me, and if I didn't like a dress, Karl let me wear what I felt looked good on me. When a model feels good in an outfit, he or she wears the clothes better.

I never had a fitting for him. All the clothes fit automatically. You walked into a store, you tried on a dress, it fit, you bought it, and you walked out. Karl was a genius. Ordinarily, a model had to go to many fittings. With other designers, I tried on many clothes to get hired. Sometimes you had to go back for a second fitting.

With Karl, the clothes were there; pick what you like. Karl was hot and fruitful. He was in the property class he owned several properties all over Europe that he didn't occupy. I don't think with his intelligence and hard work, he ever knew failure. In Europe, there are so many reasons to fail. I don't think any of them found Karl. He was the one calling the shots. There was a constant flow of models coming to Paris from all over the world. Karl became tired of some models and replaced them with new models.

On the go, burning the candle at both ends, I worked in the day and escorted Karl out at night. Also, I modeled for Antonio. When I gained weight from all the delicious French food, he told me I was too fat, and he wasn't going to draw me. I'd sing and dance for

Antonio and the other guys in the apartment in my bra and underwear to show off my body and let him call me fat.

Karl hated suntanned and skinny people. I didn't feel rejected or take offense; some models starve themselves to death. If Antonio or a designer said a model was fat, then the model's feelings were hurt. They wanted to model no matter what, even if they starved themselves. It didn't matter as long as they could be models.

I remember when I took Antonio to the Apollo. He was from Puerto Rico, and his face was white like a vampire. Sitting on the balcony as the spotlight shone on us, I'd say, "Antonio, your face is so white among all these black people." We'd burst out laughing. I called him Tony the Tiger and said, "Great!"

In New York, Antonio, Juan, and I, along with several others, went to dinner at the Asian Pearl restaurant. The menu consisted of Cuban, Puerto Rican, and Asian food mixed. I love food, and I love to eat. If I was around food, I was hungry; if not, I didn't eat. In Paris, we all went out to dinner with Karl. In fashion terms, I was fat, and Karl drew sketches of me on the table napkin.

"My dear, if you keep gaining weight, this is what you are going to look like," Karl said. The sketch had toothpick-skinny legs and a big stomach. We all laughed, but beneath my laughter, I became scared I was beginning to look like that.

My laughter hid my fear. By Antonio's standards, I was considered too fat for high fashion. Losing weight fast is hard. I started doing voluptuous photo shoots in lingerie that complemented my curves. Stephen Burrows gave me a lot of clothes samples to wear, and I stayed loyal to Stephen. Even as the French laughed at me, I didn't abandon him.

The other reason I stayed loyal to Stephen is because when I got drunk and sick at all those parties and passed out, Stephen escorted me back to his apartment, carried me upstairs, and dumped me on the bed in Bobby Breslau's room. I'd sleep it off. I wasn't an alcoholic—two drinks, and I was drunk. The other reason his clothes were new and made a statement was that they draped around my body like a second skin.

When I came into a room, everyone noticed. Stephen's clothes had no buttons or zippers and were not tailored. The French were used to tailored garments, and every stitch had to be the right stitch and in the right place. Stephen's clothes were in zigzag stitches. The fabric that Stephen used was matte jersey. I couldn't afford Karl's clothes. A crepe de chine scarf he gave me was $500.

One thing about Karl was that he didn't give his clothes away. He sold them to those who could afford them. Karl could pay for what he wanted, and he didn't need to give his clothes away. In Europe, there is a separation in classes, and the rich are going to buy couture clothes. In America, the rich don't always show their affluence.

I had to do shows to acquire clothes the designers gave me for publicity. It was cheaper than paying a million dollars for advertisement. Not from Karl—if you couldn't afford it, you didn't wear it. That kind of confidence was only in Europe. Good, because you didn't go into debt buying things you couldn't afford. Also, they could tell how wealthy you were by the clothes you wore. Along with the fabulous apartment, you had to have real money to live there or great beauty, skill, talent, or creativity.

I learned that to become successful and maintain success, one must have one or all these elements: money, beauty, skill, talent, or creativity, with courage, good health, energy, and ambition to fall back on. Karl's apartment on Boulevard Saint-Germain was huge.

Antonio and Juan had enough room to make a studio. It had two enormous wooden doors downstairs. In the courtyard was a garden you had to stroll through to get to the apartment building. Karl's building was right on the Boulevard Saint-Germain, where people were well dressed as they walked the boulevard. It was like a fashion show in everyday life. I'd see black-ashy African men with white blondes. I asked Gilles Dufour, Karl's assistant designer, why their skin looked so dry and ashy.

It was the French water from the faucet, and they didn't put lotion or oil on their skin after a bath, Gilles told me. As we walked down the boulevard, all the men looked at me.

"Look at those people, how they look at you as if they wanted to eat you," Gilles said. I liked my weight; the fashion industry was way too cruel to any fat. You can stay thin; it was who kept it up the longest.

Gilles was friendly. He took me to the flea market and bought me a blue silk cap for my head. I was allowed to call his home, where he lived with his mother. That was a big thing in America. Guys didn't give their home phone numbers when they lived with their mom until they were ready to introduce you to her. I felt like I had the utmost admiration and respect when I was in Paris.

Everything was fine until Juan's friend came on the scene. I loved Antonio, Juan, and Karl. Juan's friend was like a fifth wheel. When we all went out, we talked and laughed all night. Juan's friend clicked with Juan, and the rest of us tolerated him. Nobody was jealous. He was a significant person in Juan's life.

We didn't have anything in common with him. In fashion, opposites don't attract; it was all about clicking with one another or a group. Karl didn't like Juan's friend; he was unsophisticated, and his jokes were sometimes annoying. He wrestled with me and grabbed on to me, and I'd yell at him to leave me alone. Juan's friend had an evil laugh and acted like a schoolboy brat who picks at the girls and puts their pigtails in ink. At other times, he was bearable and behaved OK. Although we all couldn't see it, he loved Juan.

Juan had the most beautifully formed head; it looked like a perfect sculpture. He was a real person with common sense, and we laughed all the time. Juan knew fashion, and he dressed extremely well.

Karl didn't want Juan's friend around. It was a choice Juan had to make. The conflict continued, and Antonio had to choose between two affections, Karl and Juan. They all were staying at the Odeon Studio, one of Karl's apartments, rent-free. Karl was Antonio's and Juan's biggest client, and he was paying for everything. Karl was what Halston was to Elsa Peretti and Joe Eula. The only difference was that Antonio and Juan never had their place in Paris. Karl owned the property in Paris.

Lack of space breeds contempt. It all came to a head one night at the Club Set. That evening the tension was brewing between Antonio and Juan. They were sitting in the back of the club. Antonio needed Juan and Karl; he didn't need Juan's friend. While I was on the dance floor, dancing to James Brown, Antonio and Juan got into a fistfight.

Juan was stubborn, and he was not about to give up his friend in favor of Antonio or Karl. Antonio quickly picked up a wine glass and hit Juan in the middle of his forehead, cutting him. I jumped in the midst of the fight to break it up. The people had seen the blood as it trickled down Juan's forehead and got scared. Antonio was tall like me, and Juan was around five foot five. Antonio towered over him.

I scolded Antonio. "He's a little boy next to you. How could you cut and fight him?" I said.

Antonio didn't say a word back to me. He was steaming in anger. I could see all the tension in his face that had been building up between the two of them. Antonio exploded. If I hadn't been there, he'd have wiped the floor with Juan or cut him again.

There were no security guards, and the club was in the back of the restaurant. Antonio, Juan, and I were in the back of the club. The DJ was up in his stage box a couple of steps off the floor. After that night, Antonio and Juan decided to keep Juan's friend. Karl was not happy about that and asked them to leave his apartment. Karl was right. Juan should have kept his friend away from him and all of us. Karl demanded that Juan be with him twenty-four/seven. Juan felt that this was his life, and he wanted his friend to be there with all of us. Antonio and Juan and his friend moved back to New York.

When I arrived back in New York, I didn't want to see anyone. I needed a temporary break. I didn't have an escape plan or place. I wanted my personal space, and I didn't want to impose my boyfriend on them. Everyone was calling. They wanted to see me, but I didn't have the energy. I needed to recharge my batteries. The fashion industry doesn't understand that, especially if you have been there for a while, and you decide to become elusive all of a sudden.

When I saw Juan and Antonio, they were not working for Karl, and that was a big setback for them. They worked hard for their money. Without Karl's money, life wasn't easy, even though they still worked. New York had a clique, and Antonio and Juan weren't a part of that circle. I tried to recommend Antonio to prestigious clients I knew.

They wanted Joe Eula. Even though he worked for Halston, he lent his talent out for a high wage. I told Antonio and Juan that all those people were working together in the clique, and Halston was the leader of it. Antonio and Juan laughed. Halston was a shadow. He knew about every big deal that was going on in the fashion industry.

Antonio had shown me an illustration he did of Diana Ross for her album cover. Antonio drew her well with hard features, which were too contoured for Diana Ross's taste. The drawing had a lot of stage makeup on her face. He told me Joe Eula got the job; he drew a softer, more feminine illustration, and she wanted femininity and beauty. Juan scolded me, saying I didn't write Karl, and he'd been so kind to me. I did write Karl and sent him a postcard, although he never responded.

Then a model told him I was skinny, and I wanted to be on his show. I knew Karl hated skinny people. Karl told her I was too skinny to be on his show. I took it at face value, and whether it was true or not, I wasn't there. I moved on.

I loved Karl. He was a fabulous man. He adhered to his contract with me, as I did mine and made it in Paris. We had a lot of fun and laughed together. I loved that he showed me what real wealth and luxury is. He also taught me not to mix your personal friends with your business associates. If you stick to something long enough, you will have success with it. You can't control everyone in your dominion. Everyone is not going to be available twenty-four/seven. Some people have lives, and some people don't want lives.

Those who don't want their life may be willing to be absorbed into your life and dominion. Every industry has a clique, and if you're not a part of that group, it's a waste of time to wait around to be accepted. Have the courage to strike out on your own. Fashion was Karl's, Antonio's, and Juan's lives, and that made me realize that fashion only paid the bills. It gave me a wild public life, but fortunately for me, it wasn't my life twenty-four/seven. I needed space to live my personal life, and you can't have that in the fashion business; that is for catalog models.

The battle between space and style continued. I traveled all over Europe and lived out of a suitcase for quite some time. On my website, you can see photographs that I did for the Italian edition of *Vogue, Bazaar, Elle, Lui,* and *Linea Italiana* magazines.

I did print photos in London, Germany, Spain, and Japan. When I was in London, another model and I stayed at Mr. Allan Riser's place. He was a gun merchant who sold guns to Africa. He left the apartment to us and went to the Bahamas with his secretary to make gun deals. Before he left, he told me Elizabeth Taylor was his friend. I said great; I didn't believe it. He also said the ape gorillas raped women in the African jungle. While he was away, the phone rang. I answered it and was surprised by who I heard on the line.

"Is Mr. Riser there?" Elizabeth Taylor said in her English accent.

"No," I said.

"Tell him Liz and Richard are in town," Elizabeth said, and she hung up the phone. That taught me never to doubt someone's word until you have proof that person is lying.

In London, I had the milkman, butcher, grocer, and cleaners deliver everything. I didn't have to go out for anything except clothes. At the time, there were only three TV channels and no commercials. London's color TV was ahead of America in the quality and the way the picture looked. It was as if you were sitting in a movie theater. Also, BBC in London didn't filter the American news as it was in America. BBC did not hide anything or sugarcoat any news about what was going on in the US government.

While in London I watched a great deal of *Star Trek*, and the cinematography was beautiful. I could see it. In London, you can learn about any culture in the world. I went to Tramps nightclub and danced the night away. It was cold and damp outside, despite the warmth of the pubs and nightlife. Londoners are communicative and interested in talking to you. Years later I met George Takei, who played Mr. Sulu. I told him I had seen *Star Trek* the first night it came on, and then I had watched it in London. He was surprised; he didn't know it had played in London at that time. He had to check it out to make sure he wasn't losing any residuals.

You never know who will see your work or how wide it extends in the world. Fans were telling me they had seen pictures of me in Japan, Spain, and Germany that I didn't see. I remember the jobs, none the less I never got the pictures. I did lots of runway and fashion and hair show conventions in all the countries.

There is a whole world of non-high-fashion manufacturers and designers. That is what makes fashion a multi-billion-dollar industry all over the world. I learned I had the energy for the chapters in my life. I was willing to travel as a black model to sell my look and make money. It takes a lot of energy to live out of a suitcase.

I shopped until I dropped in every country. I didn't have an apartment of my own; I used to live with Billie. Whatever money I had when I came back to the States, I'd give to Billie. She cooked the food and took care of all the domestic responsibilities. Billie loved to travel to the Bahamas, Nassau, Bermuda, Acapulco, Quebec, and Chicago. When I was in Barcelona, there were candles everywhere before the United States used candles as a decorative statement in the home.

During the Baroque period, candlelight was the only way of lighting a house. Spain had the most beautiful candles. Barcelona was a romantic city with its monastic medieval backdrop. As I walked the streets, I ran across three African American sailors.

"Hi," I said to them so I didn't appear snobbish.

"Do you know any prostitutes?" one of the sailors asked.

"I don't know any prostitutes. I am a top model," I replied and kept walking. That was a shock. In America, men don't ask you if you know any prostitutes.

What I liked about Barcelona was that whole city closed down for siesta around noon to four. Everyone returned to work and got off at eight o'clock and went to dinner. The restaurants packed with people eating paella and fried squid, which looked like fried onion rings.

On the weekends, there were parties filled with dancing and laughter. On Sunday, the Catholic church gave a block party with huge banners, stuffed puppets, and flags. A small parade marched through the narrow streets. The only drawback was that I didn't have a man with me.

Barcelona had the best leather boots. I purchased a pair of thigh-high boots for $200. In America, they'd have cost $5,000. I still have the boots to this day, and the leather is as good as it was forty years ago.

In Japan, I was familiar with the Japanese because of my judo. In Tokyo, there was not a soul on the streets. I got sick and needed a shot of penicillin, so I went to the hospital and found the entrance lined with brown paper slippers of all different sizes. I removed my shoes before I entered the hospital.

A girl named Sukie, a white American woman, was married to a Japanese man and working in Japan as a makeup artist. She spoke English and Japanese, and Wilhelmina knew her and had sent models over to Japan to work with her in the past. That was a relief. One Japanese agent there was so annoying; she didn't leave me alone. She was trying to steal me from Wilhelmina. Sukie was so fed up with her, she wrote a long letter of discontent to Wilhelmina.

When I got back to the States, I delivered it to Wilhelmina. Wilhelmina gave me the job because one of the other models left her to go to another agency. She was mad, so she gave me the model's job.

"Tell the model when you see her that I gave you her job," Wilhelmina said.

"Yes, I will tell her," I replied. When I saw the model at parties, I never did mention it. I was very much about me in a quiet way in front of superiors. If you are arrogant about who you are, other people won't confide in you; they will keep information from you. Not being chosen first—I never liked that. Willy and the model were on cooperative terms. That meant she didn't wish to hire me for the job in the first place.

Willy didn't like being anyone's second choice either. She had to be number one. Willy was in competition with Eileen Ford. Willy confided in me about what she spent on this model and what she did for that model. An endless clique of black models were crossing her and leaving her and going to some other agent. I learned that she had the power to put whomever she wanted in whatever position she wanted them to be in as a model.

Willy made it seemed as if she was blocking their careers. Black models were leaving her left and right. Once you bring clients to an agent, the agent expects you to continue to bring in your customers and does not work to get you clients. If they were my clients, she couldn't take them away from me. If they were her clients, she had the power to give and take them away whenever she pleased.

Willy told me about the other models because I was responsible. I made myself. I organized my clients and brought them to her, whereas Willy claimed she'd made the other black girls, and they crossed her. Willy made me aware from her conversations that she wasn't going to do anything for me unless she was mad at one of them. But when she died, we all went to her funeral.

One thing about Willy, she had a backup for the client to hire—whatever model she suggested.

"The model you want is not available. May I suggest this model who is available? Send half of the money now, and the model gets the other half when she finishes the job. Send the plane ticket and hotel reservation," Willy would calmly demand. She had everything at her fingertips. She never left her desk; the clients hopped, skipped, and jumped at her request, suggestions, and demands.

She smoked three packs of cigarettes a day—a chain smoker. Willy was at her desk early in the morning, and till late at night, Willy was on that phone. She had clients calling from all over the world and from different time zones. Cancer set in her lungs, and three weeks after her doctor diagnosed her, Willy died.

She was a beautiful, tough businesswoman who was highly sensitive. She felt like the models slighted her, and she didn't take it kindly. Willy wanted revenge. "The Lord said vengeance is mine," the Bible says, but Willy seemed to forget that verse. Black women were slaves in America for three hundred years; they weren't going to bend over backward for her, a foreigner. With the help of black soldiers, the United States defeated Germany in World War II. I think deep down inside, she wanted the black models to beg her as I pleaded with Christa for my money in Paris.

Wilhelmina paid right away. She couldn't pull the crap Christa did. She was in the United States. She was a Dutch-born German-raised businesswoman with citizenship by marriage.

Reputation is everything in America. I gave her respect, and she gave me the same. I wasn't going to get wrapped up in her enmity toward other models. She never wore makeup in the office, and she was beautiful. I loved going to the office to meet with her, look, and listen to this gorgeous creature speak. Her husband, Bruce, was intimidating, bitter, and habitually drunk.

"Who recommended you to this agency?" he yelled at me, and I'd say some model's name off the top of my head. "That model hasn't been with this agency in years," he replied. I guess he thought he was getting a wife and got a businesswoman he couldn't handle. Willy was a workaholic, on top of her business day and night.

She had kids. Who was going to pay the bills if she didn't continue to make money? In Europe, I escaped the politics, color codes, and all the bullshit I had to deal with in America. Being black was never my problem; I couldn't help hearing about the plight of other black people suffering because of the color of their skin.

When I was in Germany, I did a hair and makeup show. I was glad to be in Europe so I could work with all the benefits and no hassle. I'd say yes to every job offered to me. I still missed the United States. There is no place like home, and I wasn't willing to give up my American citizenship. The thought crossed my mind to stay in Europe and never come back to America. I returned to the States because there was something I needed to do. I didn't know what.

In Germany at the hair and makeup show, I learned that if you as a makeup artist have created a look in makeup in spring, fall, winter, summer, make sure you fit it to the client's face. The same makeup on everyone doesn't look good. You can use the same colors on a different-shaped face, but you have to add colors that complement the woman's face. This makeup artist wanted me to look like Mona Lisa, and my face doesn't look like Mona Lisa. For the life of me, he wouldn't change the makeup.

First of all, I looked like I was laid out in a coffin with all purple on my face. I had to have pink or lilac to bring me to life. He refused to make changes, because it wasn't his look. I don't know what happened to him. In spite of it all, I am still here. I learned you have to accommodate the client.

In Germany, the people were warm and friendly. Germany was all gray; it didn't have the color of Paris or the white snow of Switzerland. I enjoyed being abroad. Italy has the best food. I rode the train from Italy to Switzerland, traveling through the mountains by train, snowy mountains that looked like the Christmas cards I read. I thought those cards came from the North Pole. They were an exact duplicate of the Swiss Alps. I identified with the scenery.

The train was a bumpy ride, and the waiter served sandwiches on white bread with no condiments. Once I settled in and looked out the window, the scenery on the way to Switzerland comforted me. The fresh snow and air felt like a healing blanket. No wonder the people there live longer.

Every view was beautiful, and everything felt alive. No stress. Everyone was calm as the Swiss people walked the streets. The snow started to fall from the sky slowly. Citizens in Switzerland are secure, unlike American individuals who are fighting for security that some never get. Capitalism is a challenge for some who are struggling to be accepted, to be individuals, to be creative and competitive. What they are missing is someone to bring them joy.

Switzerland had the best steak for ten dollars. I had never seen a Swiss cow until I came to Beverly Hills. They are like elephants. No wonder Swiss chocolate is the best besides Godiva chocolates. What I learned from the Swiss is that life doesn't have to be a constant political challenge, a struggle. In Europe, they gave $100,000–$200,000 parties, and I went to a few. That was their way of stating their politics. Only the affluent and prestigious attended. I was a top model—beauty is perpetually in demand. Beauty trends are repeated throughout history and updated; it is something that appeals to 99 percent of the human eye. Beauty opens doors. People like being surrounded by beauty.

CHAPTER 22

Battle of Versailles

I CAME BACK TO AMERICA for a short while and dated a basketball player. Billie was happy; she was still traveling whenever she wanted. My mother visited her while I was gone, and she told Billie she didn't like me modeling, because I'd be doing nude photos, which I did for *Lui* magazine. Billie told her she didn't care what kind of modeling I was doing as long as I was modeling.

The person who criticized me the most was my mother, who was never there anyway. Why did she think I wanted to see her or hear her opinion about my new exciting life? Do as I say, not as I do; that was my mother's motto. She could be free, live her life as she pleased, and dare anyone to criticize her. She didn't want that freedom for me, and I was happy I wasn't there to see her.

In Europe, I didn't have to deal with the drama, race, governmental requests, or haters. I went to a couple of Halston and Joe Eula's parties, and I brought along my basketball-playing boyfriend. He laughed at the scenery. Even though he was dating several other girls while he was dating me, I didn't mind bringing him. Eleanor Lambert was putting a show together in Paris to refurbish the Palace Versailles, which sounded unusual to me. Why would Americans care about the Palace Versailles? We had enough buildings in America that needed remodeling.

When the designers selected me to go to Paris, I was so elated that I didn't care about the pay. Eleanor Lambert's assistant said Eleanor knew she could get us girls at the drop of a dime. Though I had been to Paris a year before and knew the French, I felt comfortable, whereas a majority of the other models and designers had never been to Paris. I was eager to go back with all expenses paid—why not? Three designers had to vouch for me. I had Anne Klein, Halston, and Stephen Burrows.

The militant model who stirred up trouble because no one else wanted to hire her had only Stephen Burrows; no other designer wanted her. Stephen had to beg Halston and some other artist to take her. Now she acted like she was the queen of the runway and the leader of the pack. In fact, the militant model was a follower.

"I was there to take the French down," she said.

How are you going to take the French down? I thought. You have only one designer who likes you. I can't believe the arrogance of some models!

She had the nerve to tell Diane Sawyer that. She should speak for herself. I was there to do my job and be at the top of my game; that's professional. It was a show to entertain, and that is what I did. It was nothing more to me. The French elite had never seen a show like that, with a group of black models on the stage. Well, there is the first time for everything. It wasn't a matter of what was better; it was what was original and what would sell. The French designers were designing clothes and making millions of dollars before the militant model got into the fashion business begging for jobs. Not only was she begging and hustling for jobs, but she also had Stephen Burrows asking for her because nobody wanted her.

Wilhelmina booked the job for me. I had Anne Klein, Halston, Oscar de la Renta, Stephen Burrows, and Eleanor Lambert, for whom

I worked in the Coty Fashion Awards. I didn't know that the intent was to take the French down and compete with the French.

My boyfriend dropped me off at JFK airport. I was in my red fox maxi coat with my fox hat. Halston, Elsa Peretti, Joe Eula, Liza Minnelli, and Kay Thompson rode in first class. When we arrived in Paris, it was November, and snowflakes were falling. The snow didn't stick to the ground, and the weather was a crispy cold, unlike New York. I was happy to be in Paris again. We checked into the hotel, and I don't remember who shared my room with me. We went to rehearsal. Liza and Kay Thompson were doing the choreography.

Kay Thompson quit the job, leaving Liza to choreograph the show. I was taking a dance class with Phil Black in New York, and everyone was copying Bob Fosse. Liza was fresh off *Cabaret* and her Academy Award. That was a big thing for me. I wanted to do a Broadway-type show. All my friends were on Broadway. Liza did a fantastic job; she's a quintessential professional.

I was in the Halston sequence with Elsa Peretti's silver bone in my hair. Elsa Peretti was the only model who was also a jewelry designer to be on the stage in the Halston sequence with her large compact mirror. China Machado was a fashion editor of *Harper's Bazaar* and a model in the Halston sequence. She was wearing Elsa Peretti's feathered fan with a silver handle. I modeled in the Anne Klein series; I dressed in a cape and hat.

Oscar de la Renta draped me in white for his sequence. I wore blue—beauty in motion—for the Stephen Burrows series. Andy Warhol flew in from New York and was watching the show from the balcony, sitting with all the elite of Europe. Yves Saint Laurent sat in back of him. The crème de la crème attended this event.

Before the show started, it was pure chaos for the designers. The American designers got into a fight with the French artists. With all that creative energy, the competition was fierce between them. I heard people cursing in French and English and yelling. Anne Klein and Donna Karan were working together. Someone cursed Anne out, and she cried. I don't know if it was American or the French designers or who. There was fighting among the American artists, because everything went wrong for them.

For the first time in their careers, the American artists had to fend for themselves in a strange country. Also, the American designers could not speak the language. Aggravation, competition, and enmity are a universal language. While everyone was fighting, most of the models were professional and focused on their dance steps. There was a lot of waiting around. I didn't care. I wanted to see Josephine Baker. I approached her during rehearsal, admiring her body and bodysuit. I wanted one for myself. I adored her, and she liked me. Josephine Baker was dancing for the French. I was the only model that day who had lunch with her. She kept referring to me at the table.

I knew what racism was because she and I were of the same complexion. She kept saying to all the white people at the table that I knew what she was talking about regarding racism. Josephine was sadly disappointed and bitter that America discriminated against her. With all her success, she never forgot. All her dreams came true in France. There were six French police officers at the entrance of the restaurant where we were having lunch. They greeted her with "Mademoiselle Josephine Baker" and bowed their heads. The French police threw their coats on the ground so she could walk on them.

Josephine Baker had the utmost respect and protection in France. She didn't have to pay for bodyguards; they were glad to lay their lives down for her if trouble arose.

They should have anti-discrimination laws all over the world. A person can't help what nationality or color he or she is. Nor did anyone ask to be born into this world, so why should anyone be persecuted for being black, white, or whatever color? Love has no color. As a model, I did not know that the elite of Europe was attending this event. I thought regular fashion buyers and store owners or the French public would buy the tickets. Because all the elite people were flying into Paris for this show, the competition became stronger and hostile between the artists. The French were pleasant to me, because I had been in France with Karl Lagerfeld for a whole six months a year before.

I didn't detect any rudeness from the French designers. I stayed in my place as a model, and the French did the right thing, because they didn't know any other way to make their presentation. It was a preservation of their couture and the way they presented it. The wealthy social elites of Europe attended, and they expected entertainment and something new, exciting, and respectable. They didn't wish to see a show that displayed their culture they saw that every day. They were yearning for the new and original to dissipate their boredom.

Most of the black models were dancers, or they danced at night at the disco, and we knew how to move to the music. We made a story out of the dance along with what we were wearing. I went to Club Set every night dressed in Stephen Burrows and danced to James Brown, Barry White, and Al Green. As I danced and moved in the clothes, I watched myself in the Club Set mirrors.

When I was in New York, I'd go to Halston's parties and dance in front of Martha Graham. She'd watch me and tell me I was a good dancer. That validated me as a dancer. I had to be able to dance in whatever outfit I wore. Versailles was a cakewalk for me.

Going to all the parties the year before with all the elite people in Paris didn't make me nervous. At Versailles, I loved to perform, entertain, and be the life of the party. Baroness Rothschild greeted everyone who entered; she was a sponsor of the event at Palace Versailles. Princess Grace, Onassis, and other dignitaries arrived at the Palace Versailles. All the counts, countesses, barons, and baronesses of Europe showed up in their diamonds and furs.

The Palace Versailles's theater packed with all the wealth of Europe's barons and baronesses, counts and countesses from wall to wall attending the show. I felt that whatever the competition and disagreements were among the designers, it was not my business. As a model, it wasn't my place to speak in detail about the havoc and chaos among the designers. I was there to put on an excellent show, and that is what I did. All the models did their best; it was a collaborative effort. Because the black models were used to dancing, it was easy to keep up with Liza. Every one of the models, black and white, looked good. No one was out of step. We brought the house down and made the French acceptably see American fashion.

In every show, you have the stars, the supporting cast, and the chorus. We, the black models, were hired to do the chorus of the show; we stole the show—not because that was the intention, at least not for me.

As a background performer, we did something new, simple, and original. We supported Liza and the designers to such an extent, the black models appeared to be overwhelming and fantastic from the French audience's point of view. As if the god Zeus threw a lightning bolt upon the stage, the other black models and I were electrifying. No one rained on our parade that night. It was the old traditional versus the new. That night at the Versailles, the new and original won the show.

The American designers didn't have a lot to work with. They were forced to be creative with what they had. Less is more, and the artists accomplished more than they expected. The models came through for them when they most needed it. Because all the black models did an outstanding job, we were all invited to the queen's dining room for dinner. It was supposed to be only the elite. When we arrived there, they gave us another standing ovation.

I learned that entertainment breaks all color and social barriers. When you bring happiness and joy to people, it opens all doors. Throw in beauty and class, and you've got it made. All those wealthy, elite citizens of Europe were at the Palace Versailles for one thing. They wanted to be entertained and see a new, original show, and they got what they wanted.

Because the show had been so entertaining, it opened the door for American designers to sell their clothes in Europe—now the powers that be could see how alive the American apparel looked in the flesh. It validated the American fashion designers in the European fashion market. I don't think for one minute that all those elite people cared about anyone's politics or interests. Politics didn't open any doors; entertainment did. I am happy to have been one of the eleven black models who made that transition happen.

For the American designers and the whole show, I think everyone put in 100 percent, including the French artists. Their presentation was two hours long. The Americans' performance was thirty-five minutes. Less is more. I was happy that the French played first. The Americans performed last, the audience gave us a standing ovation, and they left the theater upbeat and happy, with history in the making. I am in the archives of the Palace Versailles forever as one of the black models who changed the face of fashion.

I've done big fashion shows. None has topped the Battle of Versailles. I did so not realizing that thirty-four years in the future, I'd be honored for my contribution. Audrey Smaltz found me on Facebook and told me there was a luncheon planned in my honor:

the Models of Versailles 1973 Tribute Luncheon at the Metropolitan Museum of Art, in the museum's Temple of Dendur in the Sackler Wing. The Multicultural Audience Development Initiative and the Costume Institute honored eleven models of color who walked the Versailles runway and changed the face of fashion.

The event attracted more than two hundred guests and included these remarks: "The Models of Versailles 1973 Tribute Luncheon took place on Monday, January 24, 2011. The chairs and tables were around the temple, and going inside was awesome. All the New York press was there. The room was encased with a glass ceiling and walls with a view outside of the snow and ice on the ground. Inside looked like Egypt in the North Pole."

My deepest sympathy goes out to Bill Dugan and his family. He was Halston's assistant designer and died before the event. All the models were going to a party to celebrate his death. I got invited, and I declined. I thought it was unsympathetic.

CHAPTER 23

Returning to the USA

IN 1974, I WAS HAPPY and enjoying the winter holidays. Elsa was doing well at Tiffany's. Pola was about to receive her biggest exposure yet, gracing the covers of *Cosmopolitan* and *Vogue* magazines. However, before the magazines went to print, nineteen-year-old Pola committed suicide. Both publications agreed to follow through and published the covers posthumously.

When I heard this news of Pola's death, I became saddened. Stan Schafer and I were at Elsa Peretti's house one night, talking about Pola. I took a different route than Pola and ended up working. I didn't become as rich as she; I continued to attain employment. Pola had been working for *Vogue, Harper's Bazaar*, Halston, and other clients all the time. She consistently worked, and this was going to be her big break.

The *Vogue* cover was going to put her at the top of the heap in the fashion world. She could get pampered, along with millions of dollars in cosmetic contracts for the rest of her modeling career. I was sorry that wasn't the case; she interrupted her destiny. Some said she jumped off her roof, and others told me she took an overdose. Some said a model stole her boyfriend, and she was grieving about it. She grieved about everything; experiencing success and keeping busy didn't help her. She had time to think, and that was dangerous for her. Pola gave off signals that nobody picked up on and everyone ignored.

I said if I ever saw signals like that again, I'd know the person needed to be under a doctor's care or in a hospital to save the person's life. I didn't realize that later on, I'd suffer from depression and be in a state of dejection. Pola's death was in vain. Fashion went on, and nobody cared in the fashion world.

In New York, Calvin Klein was taking the fashion world by storm. Ellen Harth introduced me to Calvin, and he hired me to do his fashion show. Also, Eleanor Lambert, who was in charge of the ABC Coty Fashion Awards, was putting on a show in primetime for TV channel 7. Calvin and I were both born in the Bronx; we connected right away. He flew me to Hollywood to do his show on ABC, and he sat with me on the plane. He was very kind to me.

Calvin told me that at my age, I could start over one hundred times. He also said that he started his business with $10,000, making me realize that if I worked hard, then I could be successful. A repeated message was telling me to perfect my job, do things on my own, and not be afraid to be at the top and alone. There's an illusion that when you get to the top, you will be alone. There will be people around. Wherever you go, the red carpet will be rolled out for you. There has to be somebody at the top who is alone like you. The saying that it's lonely at the top is what scared me from going full speed ahead.

I think that myth scared a lot of women into marrying. I'm alone with all my success. They marry a weaker man or give up their success to marry a strong man, so they're not alone. There is a trade-off, and I'm courageous. I'm not trading off. I learned from Calvin that even if nobody else thinks it's important, I need to think it's important. Calvin played the game any way he could. It was about his clothes and what was important to the growth of his business. He went through the fashion world straight to the mass public.

Calvin took care of his business. He was on the phone, making deals during the day. I also went to his home, where we viewed the TV show, and it was great. He booked me into the best hotel, the Beverly Hills Hotel, probably never thinking that I would one day move to Los Angeles.

Calvin promoted his clothes on TV. He was the first designer to do commercials—other than perfume—for jeans. Calvin and I stood on his terrace at his apartment, celebrating his success.

"How far do you want to go?" I asked.

"I am not there yet, and there is no limit," Calvin answered.

I could see he was on a mission, driven, with a goal and a purpose, and it paid off. If you have a product you believe in, perfect it and promote it. Don't limit yourself. Diversify. Don't be afraid to fail. Get back up, brush yourself off, and get back in the race. The fashion ad business itself is a race. Also, know your market, and don't be afraid of the giants in your chosen profession. Calvin dived in and claimed his spot in the fashion industry. He wasn't part of the clique. Calvin paved his way through hard work and responsibility.

Andy Warhol and I met through Halston. Before I met him, I used to see him walking the streets in New York. I used to laugh at the way he looked, not imagining that shortly we'd be close friends. When Halston introduced us, I laughed. I know it was rude. I couldn't contain myself. I think my laughter is what attracted him.

"You and I are alike, and you are so interesting, Amina," Andy said. I had the ability to empathize with whomever I happened to be around. I made people feel so comfortable with me that they felt like they were around themselves and not another person. That is a significant part of my talent as an actress: I can become other people.

Halston was pleased with me. "Amina, all the together crowd likes you," he said. "I love together people."

That's why I regularly brought together people I thought should be together. All my life has been spent getting myself together. Life is in transition and never settled. I like being inspirational to others and making people laugh with my stories. I love to observe people and translate what I see into a story. Andy suggested ideas to the people around him. They acted out those ideas without thinking it through and then blamed Andy for their bad choices.

"Amina, you don't sleep around enough," Andy suggested.

"So-and-so slept with everyone in Hollywood, and nothing happened to her. She never became successful in film or received any extra kudos," I answered.

Andy said the same thing to somebody else who slept with everyone he or she came across. Andy had the power to influence others who didn't think for themselves. I had a mind of my own, and he respected that.

He invited me to lunch at the factory and introduced me to everyone. He was very good to me. I did two interviews for *Interview* magazine, one of me and one with Geoffrey Holder, whom I'd met through Helmut Newton on a job I booked in Haiti for *Lui* magazine. An editor named Tina was a former assistant to Chris von Wangenheim. He photographed me for the Italian edition of *Vogue* at Andy's factory. On my website, there is a photo of Geoffrey Holder and a dress by Betsy Gonzalez for *Interview* magazine, photographed by Albert Watson.

There is a Helmut Newton photo of me pulling off my wig in the pool and sitting on Geoffrey's shoulders. Helmut Newton was a great photographer. He was attentive, and he kept photographing me all during the trip to Haiti, even on the plane as I slept.

Helmut had friends, and we went to dinner up in the hills. He told us stories about a woman named the Bengal Tiger—how she danced in the clubs in Berlin, Germany. That was his inspiration because he never forgot her. The trip was good, except that the makeup artist and I didn't agree on the makeup. Helmut had to step in, and I gave in. I am glad I did. The makeup looked gray on camera; it was perfect. I wanted everything to be perfect, because I knew I was making history. These photos could come back to haunt me at a later date if they were not perfect. I didn't mean to be unprofessional. I wanted perfection.

I learned not everyone else sees what you view in the mirror. Photographer Albert Watson was excellent. He made me look good. He focused most of his attention on Geoffrey, a Broadway star director. Helmut focused his attention on me. It was Geoffrey's turn now to get all the attention. Andy was responsible for my meeting Albert Watson. I met Regine Zylberberg through Andy, who had a legendary club on Park Avenue. All the jet set from around the world came to her club. I loved Regine. She was a down-to-earth lady. I did go to New Jimmy's in Paris, and there was magic in the air. Andy invited me to dinner with KISS, the rock group, at Regine's.

Andy had a grueling social schedule, and he asked me to attend as many functions as I could. I became exhausted. I don't know how he did it; he had the energy to burn. He promoted himself and his paintings. If there were an opening of a toilet seat, then he'd attend with his camera and tape recorder to catch what people did or said. I don't think people liked the tape recorder. The camera was OK. He was good to me because I was independent in thought. If I didn't like something, I'd tell him. Other people did whatever he said to do, whether it was right or wrong for them.

Andy would ask me why I didn't tell everything about myself, and I would say that if I did that, then it would prevent me from making it. Those girls and guys who were too open with themselves didn't survive. Some people, after they made it, let it all hang out and were out of the traditional group.

If you did something wrong, they'd tell it; if you did something good, they'd tell it. There was no Twitter, Facebook, or Myspace for posting it. Word of mouth was faster than the Pony Express. Those who knew you knew about what you did, and those who didn't know you knew about it. Your reputation gets there before you do.

I had met Steve Rubell before anyone was aware of him in New York. I went to a party on Long Island through Carmen, Steve's publicity manager. I rode in her limo with her and her husband to the party. We came to a big red house in the middle of nowhere. Steve Rubell held a party there, and he greeted us when we arrived. He was a good man without any pride; I had no idea he was going to open Studio 54 the next month.

He was the perfect host. My personality got me with the jet set. I loved to go to parties. Studio 54 opened, and Steve Rubell became friends with Halston and Andy. Steve Rubell was jealous of anyone Halston liked. In the beginning, some nights I couldn't get into 54, so I'd wait until Halston arrived, and he'd take me inside the club. After a while, they let me in the club. Halston and his guest sat at a booth close to the stage. One night Halston, Liza, and Elizabeth Taylor were there. I went over and kissed Halston and greeted him. There was a bottle of champagne in an ice bucket.

"Have a glass of champagne," Halston said.

I grabbed the bottle and was holding it as I looked for an empty glass on the table. All of a sudden, the bottle got snatched out of my hand.

I turned around, and it was Steve Rubell. I didn't say anything to him. He looked at me with such jealousy in his eyes. I didn't ask for the champagne back or fight with him. I ignored him. I wasn't going to lower myself for him. When I came to the club the next week, Steve was drunk.

"Oh, I love you, Amina," he said in his drunken stupor. He couldn't even stand up. The guys who worked for him had to carry him into the back office. Steve was wearing a big dark ski coat with deep pockets filled with money that he had taken from the customers at the door. He stood at the door drunk, collecting the money from the people as they entered the club. When he couldn't stand up any longer, the guys came and dragged him into the club's back room.

I suspect they robbed some of the money overflowing from his pockets. He didn't know; he was so drunk. The only receipts were from the liquor sales. He became a slave to that club. He was miserable there twenty-four/seven and not taking care of himself. He was there watching his business, and when he got drunk, they'd steal from him. Whether he was there or wasn't there, they were going to steal, so what was the point of being there twenty-four/seven? Patrons paid cash to get into the club, and I never saw a receipt.

I never paid to get in. I was invited to many fabulous parties there with catering, champagne, and caviar. Steve Rubell must have charged $100,000 for those parties. Maybe those receipts were the ones the IRS was looking for. Andy introduced me to Truman Capote after I wrote a script about models. I didn't know Andy let Truman read it. Andy told me he thought he was reading a different person's writing. He said it sounded like me, writing from the 1930s.

"Keep writing, Amina," Truman said. We started hanging out at Studio 54, Elaine's, and El Morocco. Truman and I hit it off right away. He and I danced at El Morocco. He was on the dance floor at Studio 54.

Truman loved to dance. I didn't dance with him there so much, because we loved to stand at the bar drinking and talking. Despite what some people say, Elaine was helpful to me, especially if I came to the restaurant alone. She would introduce me to a guy, then she would send over a plate filled with appetizers for the gentleman and me to eat at the bar, and of course, he would pay the bill. Truman and I arrived at Studio 54, and we stood at the bar facing the entrance. Several men entered the club and came up to him. Their demeanors looked somewhat antagonistic.

Everyone had read *In Cold Blood* and had seen *Breakfast at Tiffany's* except me. Years later I watched *Breakfast at Tiffany's* on TV. I felt like I was Holly Golightly! I was a jet-setting professional model with no money. I'd spend my money in a flash. I knew about his exile from the elite of New York. Now he was down at Studio 54, available to the commoners. One guy got up in Truman's face.

"America has a top writer, and it's not you," the man said.

"And it is certainly not you. I am a top writer. I have earned that right, and who are you?" Truman said. It was cruel and disrespectful. Truman and the guy started bantering; he was trying to be a better linguist than Truman. Several patrons of the club challenged Truman, and he spoke in an eloquent, articulate way. Truman made a fool out of them as he did his TV interviewers.

Truman knew vocabulary, grammar, and English diction extremely well. Few knew how to command the English language as efficiently as Truman. A TV interviewer spoke to Truman as if there was some doubt: how could someone who looks and sounds like you write *In Cold Blood*? Where do you get your creativity from, as if it didn't come from him. Why is it I don't have it? That is what the interviewers meant when they were questioning Truman on national TV.

Was he wrong for writing about all the secrets of his high-society friends? Yes, they told him things in confidence, and much of it was bad for their reputations and images. They told their secrets to Truman in an amusing way. He thought it was the stuff best sellers should be made of and told them he was writing a book about them.

They never said anything to stop him. Either they didn't think he had the courage to publish it, or they didn't take him seriously. After all, he was their laughter boy as well as a successful writer to his right. They didn't see him like that. He was there for their amusement. He thought it would be amusing to the public to expose them; they had money and were untouchable. Truman didn't mean them harm. He thought the public would get a kick out of all the gossip, as they had gotten a kick out of telling him.

What is high society? Image, that's all it is. Without the illusion, there is no high society. That's what they were protecting. I think he should have changed the names, country, and time zone. Truman should have added a great deal of his imagination and made it into a novel, like *Doctor Zhivago* or *War and Peace*. He was well equipped to write such a book.

Capote was genuinely witty, incisive, and intelligent. He was full of laughter and dance, and his conversations were a lesson if you listened. Most people were too busy competing or trying to upstage him. Truman should have learned that members of high society watch their backs and will throw the selfless to the wolves. Image to them is more important than money and fame. If someone came into Studio 54 he didn't like, he'd yell out, "I hate that woman, and I am not going to put her in my book."

As a model, there was a question with me too. Why should I be modeling? Truman dealt with the same issue: why was he writing?

Modeling wasn't my life; it paid the bills. Writing wasn't Truman's life; being a socialite was.

When going to all the parties and meeting fabulous people was taken from him, Studio 54 became his life. That is when he started not caring about himself. I learned that sometimes we don't know what we need until it is gone. Truman realized he had bitten the hand that fed his life force. He needed high society; he didn't need Studio 54. High society was his destiny. Studio 54 was his fate. All the high-society people were at Studio 54, and they avoided him. He felt like partying and dancing. He was courageous about his life. I loved that about Truman. He kept up a brave face. Eventually, the pain he felt from the loss of the life that he cherished engulfed him.

He encouraged me to keep writing, even though he said it would take him another ten years to write his book. He never told me what book he was writing, only that he was writing a sentence or a chapter every day. He wanted to live his high-society life, which he could no longer do. That is what ate away at him, the fact that high society took his exposure of them so seriously. I don't think he was prepared for the opposition or becoming an outcast.

He didn't have a backup plan, and Andy tried to help him. Andy had him write stories for *Interview* magazine. He wrote the most tear-jerking stories. Even then, his writing at Studio 54 was fabulous. He made you feel something. He tapped into your emotions. Truman started hanging out in the basement of Studio 54. He was lounging on the colorful red pillows on the floor. He was too relaxed in the environment, as if he belonged there. Truman shouldn't have been there. Something compelled him to be there.

That was Steve Rubell's underground VIP hangout. I didn't stay down there to watch what was going on. I liked upstairs, the main dance floor and bar, where all the elite people and movie stars were.

Then there was the third-floor balcony, where Rudolf Nureyev and other fashion people could look down onto the dance floor.

I went upstairs a couple of times, talking to Elsa Peretti and other fashion people. Upstairs you could hold a conversation without the music blasting in your ears. The main dance floor was where the show and amusement were. Truman became obsessed with the Studio 54 basement as it devoured him. He lost hope and started abusing himself. I could tell from the decline of his appearance. Truman could hold his liquor better than Steve Rubell. Truman was witty, even when he slurred his speech. I never saw him trip over people or fall on the floor.

Unlike me, he held his liquor; two drinks, and I was drunk. Designer Giorgio di Sant' Angelo and I talked on the phone about what consumed these fabulous, promising people. It was disco. They got hooked on disco, and they didn't want to take care of their businesses. Disco ate them up.

"What happened to so-and-so?" I asked.

"Well, he got hooked on disco and drugs. I've never seen him again," Giorgio said. Ads were running in the paper of people seen every night at Studio 54. Now I don't know if it was two or three pictures. The press kept the photos running—with different parts of the person's body—to make it look like that person was there every night, and sometimes that person was there every night. After a while, it didn't look good for a professional person's image to be at a disco every night.

If you were a socialite, OK. Most of them were independently wealthy. They were not selling their services or lending their talent out to hire. They could be everywhere every night; they were socialites. Truman loved that freedom of a socialite's life. As a writer, you're expected to be at home, writing. A novelist needs to live life somewhat to have something to write about to make a living. That's if they don't have a vivid creative imagination.

Andy painted during the day and went out at night, selling his paintings and making connections. He wasn't misdirecting his energy; there was a purpose to his efforts—a method to his madness. The people who were around him were living through him and his art. They did anything Andy suggested.

They didn't have the courage to say no to him. When I went to the factory, I went to see Andy, not for whom he was with or whom he knew. Nor did I care about whom he knew. I wanted to be with him, and he brought these other people into the mix. He called the William Morris Agency for me. I had a meeting with them, and it came to nothing. My writing wasn't that good at the time; I had potential. As Truman said, I had to keep writing.

Andy invited me to so many dinners that I didn't have a chance to write. I love people. I'm more of a socialite than a writer. I didn't have the discipline of a writer. I entertained the people, and Andy swooped in and sealed the deal with them on purchasing his art. I never called the factory to ask him what he was doing that night.

I never used him to social climb. I'd call to let him know I was coming to the factory and that I wanted to be with him. Then I'd stop by to see Antonio, and Andy didn't like that. Later on, he had Antonio do an Illustration for an *Interview* magazine cover. I told Andy they couldn't do anything to him; all they could do was not buy his paintings. Antonio didn't have the connections Andy had to the people who bought art. They never paid Antonio a million dollars for his illustrations. I didn't know how to negotiate an art deal, nor did I wish to know. There was nothing for Andy to fear.

Antonio had Karl hire me for Paris. I felt that was a beautiful thing he did for me. Then he had me recruited to do *Vogue*. We were professional colleagues and friends. You couldn't ask Andy for his connections. If he wanted you to have something, then he would give it.

You couldn't act poorly in front of Andy; he gossiped like a man. There is a particular manner in the way I talk to people, and there's girl talk I wouldn't even dare talk to a person about unless that person was a girl. Andy told everyone if you behaved or said derogatory things. I respected him. You had to behave like you were on a job interview in front of Andy.

I never behaved in a derogatory way so as to turn my power over to a man. All a woman has is her pride. Once she loses her pride, it's over. A man is going to talk about her like a filthy dog. They will give a dog more respect than they give her, no matter how much money she has. The Bible says a beautiful woman has to be discreet. A man can do what he wants—get back up, put on a suit and tie, and he's still a man.

He can even become the president of the United States, and all is forgotten. A woman can't do that; it's not fair. Regrettably, that's the way it is. They will drag her through the mud and ruin her name—provided she is not married to someone in power. Even then they will ruin her name. That's why Truman got banned from high society; all those high-society women married powerful men. It's about image; those people didn't want their wives exposed because it reflected on them.

Truman never viewed it that way. His perception was that they betrayed him by ostracizing him. He took it hard mentally and emotionally. That is how I know he never meant to hurt them. I learned to block gossip out of my life and to mind my own business. I wouldn't accept defeat. I had choices.

I'm broad-minded. I look at all sides and think before I take action. Andy told me to go with a rock star. I didn't like the way rock stars I knew treated models. Not all rock stars I met were wrong. Patti Hanson married Keith Richards, and he treated her very well. There were probably others I didn't know who treated their women well.

I didn't do a lot of things Andy suggested, like other people did. When things went wrong, they blamed Andy for their errors in judgment. There was once a film on the market, and Andy asked, "Amina, why weren't you in that movie?"

"I'm glad I wasn't in it, because it was a flop," I answered arrogantly. Andy wasn't going to make me feel like a failure. I answered his question because, with Andy, you had to know the answer.

When I did his reality TV show, he described me as a model who was influential who probably wouldn't make it. Andy meant I couldn't get the big makeup contract. I had to diversify, work my buns off, travel the seven seas, and still not get that million-dollar contract. The industry was never going to pamper me as it did my white coworkers. I had to do my makeup and hair for every shoot. I had to shop all over town for makeup and hair products that complemented my skin tone and hair. He knew that eventually I'd get tired and give up.

Andy also invited me to do a Channel 5 segment commercial: "It's ten p.m. Do you know where your children are?" It was a public service reminder to keep kids off the street in New York after ten o'clock.

Nipsey Russell was there. I had no idea that later on, I'd be working with him on the film *The Wiz.* Nipsey was inquisitive and wanted to know what everyone did for a living. Andy had not yet arrived at the TV station.

"What do you do?" Nipsey asked one of the guys.

"I write Christmas songs," he answered.

"Oh, that only happens once a year," Nipsey replied. "What do you do?"

"I'm a screenwriter," I answered. I didn't say model.

"You have an agent?" Nipsey asked.

"Andy introduced me to William Morris," I replied.

"They package deals," Nipsey answered.

He kept staring at me as if I didn't belong at William Morris, because they had more power in the industry than him. I expected him to say good, if you have a part in your script, put me in it. I didn't know at the time that William Morris packages their films, and he wouldn't be employed. William Morris put their actors, directors, and producers in their movies.

When Andy waltzed into the room, he had the energy of a star. He came in and kissed me on the mouth. Andy had the confidence of a smart man; there was no air of insecurity. Andy promoted himself well. Nipsey couldn't take his eyes off Andy and me, and when I got in front of the camera, he kept looking. It made me nervous. Compared to Nipsey Russell, I was an amateur. Andy and I were poles apart in appearance. I guess he was wondering what Andy and I had in common. We both liked to be out in the public meeting people. I loved people. As I did the commercial, I thought, I better be good. This man is looking at me.

With Nipsey Russell measuring me up, I felt intimidated. I didn't show it. Later on, Halston was talking about Elizabeth and Liza, and he said stars felt insecure in New York and very secure in Hollywood. He thought that was strange. Then I thought back to why Nipsey was asking questions—to see who had longevity and who didn't. In the seventies, a lot of people did that. They looked at you, and right away they could predict if you were going to be a success or failure. I wasn't a fortune-teller. I couldn't predict who was going to make it or not. I knew who I liked and who I didn't like. They'd say so-and-so isn't going to make it, and he or she made it. Then they'd say that they never thought that one could make it.

"Get the money. Get the money," I said as my favorite line. Everyone was getting the money except me. I was the only one worried about it. Based on the position I was in, I could have never made a million dollars in one lump sum. If I were a white model, for sure, I could have earned millions. Andy was making a million a month selling his paintings.

Everyone in my circle made massive amounts of money in firms. I wasn't jealous or resentful. I didn't want for anything, and they all were very generous with me. I was the kind of friend who could encourage them and push them. I couldn't do it, and they could; I was intelligent enough to recognize that. There are jealous, malicious people, and now they are haters online. I wished for all my friends everything I wanted for myself, which was money, happiness, and success.

It cost lots of money to be in business. Now you have the Internet to get the word out on social media about you or your product. You don't even have to have a product or do anything creative to be famous now. Andy said everyone has fifteen minutes of fame. The trick was to make it last. Back then it was done the old-fashioned way: hard work and lots of money to make money.

Francesco Scavullo took nude photos of Burt Reynolds and Jim Brown for *Cosmopolitan*. They were the hunks of that time. He asked me to be one of the girls surrounding Jim Brown. They were doing publicity for the spread. When I arrived at the studio, I was the only black girl in the crowd. Jim was on a platform stage, and all the white girls were screaming and all over him. They knocked me out of the way to get to him as I stood on the side.

I stood back. "Amina, get closer," Scavullo kept saying to me.

I pushed my way through the crowd of girls. Scavullo snapped away with his camera. When it was over, the girls were still surrounding him. I waited until there was an opening.

"I was scared, and I didn't know what to say to you," I said.

"I was scared too. I didn't know what to say to you either," Jim said.

Successful, good-looking black men had so many women of all colors who wanted them. Successful white males had one woman or wife; when they broke up, it was over. Successful black men never seemed to forget the women from the past; they were all mixed with ladies from the present and future. Maybe it was an African or Arabic thing to have three hundred wives and concubines. Every black man I ever dated had several women.

What I learned was not to be afraid to step out in front of the camera, regardless of how many competitors were around. I learned to be able to answer questions and not worry about why the person was asking them, and I learned not to be intimidated when people stared at me. Although it's rude to stare, it took a long time to realize I wasn't a civilian. When you are in the fashion circle, you are not in touch with reality. It was an insulated world. I guess they say the same thing about Hollywood. Other people are dictating the rules, and the game changes. Even if you have your own business, you have to keep coming up with ideas that sell. I began to feel like modeling wasn't important. I was the key to whatever I wanted to do with my future.

Designers were becoming intimidated by the black militant model. She was pressuring them to pay black models more. They only had enough to pay one black model. Halston still used the same models. Fashion was always changing, and so was the industry.

If I can't influence others to do well, I don't want to change them at all. I was about inspiration. That is how I made my living and got my investors. Fashion, beauty, creativity—it's all inspiration, and if you don't know how to inspire, then you, as a client, have to pay an ad agency to do a campaign to encourage the public to pay attention to what you are selling. The question is money. How much or how little can I spend for my dreams to come true? What is it going to cost me in time and money?

CHAPTER 24

Dark Clouds

ALL OF A SUDDEN, A dark cloud seemed to follow me. I wasn't working as much, and I had a boyfriend supporting me. He came to Billie's house sometimes and spent the night with me. Billie got mad because he was giving me money. He bought me fur coats and expensive items. Even though I was giving her money, she got mad because she was secretly dating a married man, and he had nothing to give her.

When my other boyfriends spent the night, she didn't say anything, because they had nothing to give me. She told me no man was going to screw her for nothing. Billie wanted me to feel guilty for being with a guy who had nothing to give me.

That gave her a reason to put me down. When I found a man who could shower me with gifts, Billie said I was disrespecting her house, and I had to move. My boyfriend got killed in a shootout in a bar, so I didn't move. I started dating another guy, and he never came to Billie's house. He would call me, and I would come downstairs and get in his car for late-night booty calls. I got tired of doing that and wanted more. He started making harassing phone calls to me. He had different people call me regularly. I didn't have an answering machine then. My phone rang forty to fifty times—like I know you are there, why the hell don't you answer?

I couldn't believe it was him. In my dreams at night, I could see him at a phone booth calling me.

"How do you know it's him? It's not him; he's not thinking about you," Billie said.

Calls kept coming in from hundreds of different people. Or the same ones calling around the clock as if someone was watching me. I became sensitive, depressed, and paranoid. I didn't wish to change my number. I didn't want to seem afraid. I was terrified, and that had never happened out in public. No one intimidated me or had a confrontation with me. He did this was done in the dark to get me out of the house by making my home life unbearable. I was stubborn, and the more the calls came, the more I froze and didn't budge. I wanted the callers to come and move me.

I waited and waited, and they never came to move me. I didn't think to cut the ringer off, and at one point, I didn't wish to answer the phone. Charlie, the lodger, was living with Billie.

"Answer your phone. Don't let that bastard bug you and make you stop answering the phone," Charlie suggested. That was the wrong advice. The more I responded to the phone, the deeper into depression I fell. It drained all my energy as I dealt with it.

Then I saw a TV movie with Lauren Hutton, with whom I had worked as a model. In the film, a man calls her and stalks her by phone, and her character gets depressed. The incident was happening to me, and Billie didn't believe me. Only I didn't kill my caller like in the film. He came to her house, and there was a confrontation. I never had that opportunity to confront my caller or get him to admit that he made the calls. I appeared to be losing my mind.

Billie kept it a secret that she was blind in her left eye and had been since 1953, the year I was born. The doctor told her she had a tumor on her brain, and it was pressing against a nerve in her eye.

That is what caused her to be blind in that eye. My mother had gotten terminally ill and went into Goldwater Hospital for the terminally ill. Billie was urging me to go and see Virginia. I didn't wish to go.

I was depressed, and I went to see my mother. She had lupus in the worst form. The nurse turned her over, and she had a hole in her lower back that was as big as my head. That revealed layers of pink flesh bedsore, and there weren't any bandages on it. The bedsore was open and vast. My mother kept saying that she could see my bones on the walls. I began to scream and cry.

My mother confessed, "I know I did you wrong. It was hard being a single woman with a child. I could never keep a place to stay."

I felt she should have visited me and not disappeared. When she did see me, she beat me. She blamed me for her having to be a parent. The nurse told me that my mother was a loner, and people from the Muslim community came to see her. When she was in her forties, she became obsessed with Allah to the point of being a religious fanatic. There she was, lying in the hospital, terminally ill. Her sister and her nieces came to see her. We were estranged, and I never knew them. My mother never forgave her mother for putting her out of the house with me. Her mother knew this, so she didn't come and visit Virginia. I went a couple of times to see my mom.

I was trying to get answers as to what she had been running from all her life. "Nine little brown men from outer space have been chasing me all my life. That is what I was running from, and I always stayed one step ahead of them. Sometimes I see them at the foot of my bed. That is why I didn't come home at night," Virginia said. When Virginia became angry, she'd twist her mouth to one side and ball up her fist tight. Her face contorted into an evil frown when she scolded me.

I called the hospital one day to see if her health had improved. The nurse told me that my mother had died. I wasn't the next of kin on her emergency contact. The Muslims at the mosque where she worshiped were her family, and they came and buried her. I was too depressed to investigate any claims or insurance policies.

Virginia had several opportunities to tell me where her insurance coverage was and how she wanted her burial. The Muslims received whatever wealth or belongings or insurance she had. I went back to Billie's, and the phone continued to ring. When I answered it, different people were calling, and a guy called and asked for different women. I fell deeper into depression and suffering. I felt severe emotional pain and fear. Now I thought someone was after me. I knew someone was watching me or tracing my conduct. I couldn't sleep. I went into the hospital for a weekend for exhaustion. I had anxiety and panic attacks, which I had never had before. I started seeing another guy while my ex was calling, and Billie asked me to move.

Billie had changed her will and insurance over to her friend Anne. Because Anne was wealthy, in Billie's eyes, she was in the property class. I told Billie I didn't like the fact that she was giving everything to Anne. Billie said she could get $10,000 from Anne or any amount of money if she wanted it. Billie went to church every Sunday. Her faith wasn't in God; it was for the money. That was Billie's god. Maybe that is why I worried about money now and then, and it was on my mind. I'd tell everyone to get the money, and that is what Billie was thinking and saying. She said she didn't care what people thought as long as she got the money. That kind of freedom I didn't have. My business and career image is about what other people thought.

Billie had insurance on me since I was a child, and she cashed that it in and collected the money. I was not moving. I paid rent, and I was on the lease. Walter, who knew Billie in the 1930s, was one of the lodgers. Billie had an alarm on her door. When you locked the door, the alarm automatically went on.

When Walter drank, he'd lose his keys. He had lost his keys twice. Billie had to change the locks for $300 because of the alarm. Walter did everything for Billie—shop, cook, and help around the house. In the thirties, during the Depression, he had lived with Billie and Manuel. Walter was a party kind of guy. At thirty-two, Walter got into an argument with a man and killed him. He went to prison for ten years and got out of jail at forty-two. Walter acquired a steady job, worked, and retired at sixty-five. He was sixty-eight, living with Billie, and they had gotten into an argument.

Both of them pulled knives on each other in a Mexican standoff.

"You guys have to stop; this it was going too far," I said.

"Stay out of it, or I'll cut you too," Walter retorted. Nothing happened. They weren't going to back down from each other until I intervened. If I wasn't in a fight, the sight of blood made me sick. Walter went back to his room and closed the door. He was a binge drinker, six months sober and the other half drunk. In the summer and spring months, he stayed dry. When fall and winter arrived, he got drunk. He loved the cooler weather. Walter gave Billie his keys when he started to drink. Billie didn't want Walter staying in the house when he started drinking, because he got angry and turned on her and wanted to argue. Billie's attitude was like a prison warden. Walter went down to the Bowery and drank in September. He didn't return until February.

In New York, we had Indian summer the first two weeks in September. The last two weeks of September are cold fall weather. The end of February, Walter returned. March is windy in New York. He was sober, and Billie gave him back his keys. This time he didn't come back. He got drunk and froze to death down on the Bowery.

Behind my back, Billie told the landlord she wanted to move downstairs to a two-bedroom instead of a four-bedroom apartment and to let her know when one became available.

Charlie was her other lodger. He had tuberculosis. Nobody let him move in, not even his family. Billie let him stay with her. He had one lung removed. Neighborhoods and communities were afraid of catching TB. I knew nothing about TB as a little girl. I was going to drink out of Charlie's cup.

"Don't drink out of that cup. That is Charlie's," Billie said.

I put that cup down and got another cup. Charlie had lived with her for twenty years. He liked to pop aspirins all day and look at soap operas. Charlie drank a lot too, and I guess the aspirins thinned his blood and prevented him from having a stroke. He didn't get angry when he got drunk. Billie never asked him to leave or put him out. One drinking person she could handle and two she couldn't. I think Billie was relieved when Walter died. She had Walter's body sent to his family down south.

Meanwhile, I kept getting harassing phone calls. I registered for an adult education class. I had to get my mind out of the depression. I met a girl in school, and I told her about the phone calls. I couldn't believe it was him doing that, and she said change your number and give him the new number. Then if he calls, you will know it's him doing it. I lost my appetite along with my weight. I was skinny. I did as she said. I changed my number and gave him the new number, and the calls continued. I didn't answer my phone. Everyone in the modeling industry had Billie's phone number.

Strangers asked me for my phone number. I didn't wish to give it to them because of the calls. I continued to have panic attacks. I was afraid of the unseen. I didn't know any of those people calling. I knew him. He would grin in my face when I saw him. My emotions became uncontrollable. I was crying all the time, and I had to drop out of the adult education program. I acquired a modeling job, and when I went the next morning, I started crying and couldn't stop. I had to leave the job, and some other model took my place. I decided to stay with Bobby Breslau. Stephen moved out of the apartment. Bobby needed food, and I had money for food. I went to visit with him. I bought the food and cooked it for him.

At the time, I only cooked dense food like stews and comfort food that would fill you up. I was an inconvenience for Bobby, because he didn't feel right bringing his men into his house when I was there. I went to stay with Elsa. She had two akita dogs I loved. I felt rich walking down the avenue with those dogs. Also, she had two little dogs, and they were so spoiled—not like the akitas, who were big and didn't bark constantly. Small dogs get all the attention, including hugs and kisses, and go everywhere with their owner.

Elsa was going through a crisis. Her father died, and she was depressed. I was there to console her. She loved her father, and she cried a lot over his death. We weren't as bad as Pola; we didn't want to kill ourselves. Elsa wanted to get out of New York, and she did.

It seemed like a dark cloud of energy hovered over New York. That dark cloud swept through New York, touching a lot of people. The people who were intuitive and emotionally sensitive felt it the most. I went to Studio 54. Steve Rubell had taken Halston and Truman down in the basement. I wasn't a VIP friend of Steve Rubell. I'd stop by the basement to say hello to Halston and leave.

Steve Rubell was jealous of anyone who took up Halston's time. He called Halston every night to come to the basement in Studio 54. I wasn't there every night. I went a lot of nights, dancing. I was glad I wasn't a VIP. That basement at Studio 54 destroyed a lot of people. It was like a crack house. You went in, and you didn't come out.

I can't say what went on down there. I never stayed down there long enough to see. Whatever went on was not good. Stephen Burrows was hanging out with some militant models who were running things and blocking his big breaks. Nobody liked the bossy models he was hanging out with at Studio 54, dancing a lot. He wasn't invited down into the basement; he wasn't a part of Steve Rubell's VIP group. Steve Rubell knew wealthy investors who could have helped Stephen Burrows.

As for me, no one was giving black models a million-dollar contract. I felt blocked. There was a social barrier. I was the product. I had to work, socialize, and burn both ends of the candle. It stopped being fun for me when I had to deal with the bullshit politics.

I did everything for myself. Some models had backers. Lucky for me, I didn't. I made myself, and Halston testified to that. I met Stephen's mother and told her that if Stephen could drop those militant models, he could attract investors with real wealth.

"Stephen will never give up his friends to be wealthy," his mother said. It was a crisis for me too, because I didn't like those honcho models who were all in my space, trying to boss me around. After all, I was there in fashion before they were, and who were they to tell me what to do? I didn't want to be bothered with Stephen because of militant models. He still gave me clothes, but I dreaded going to see him. I couldn't stand the models. Everywhere he went, they'd go, hanging on to his arm. He couldn't fart without them there smelling it.

Even Steve Rubell was not there with Halston in the daytime. He was in his nightlife. I learned whenever there is a conflict between your day and nightlife, the nightlife wins if you don't make a choice. Halston worked so hard to get his wealth, and he bought orchids every day to put in his office. Truman Capote worked hard. Their careers were their identity. Steve Rubell's basement allowed them to be free and relaxed, and it destroyed both men, along with Rudolf Nureyev. A dark cloud came onto the scene and wiped that whole Studio 54 crowd away.

People don't remember what you say; they only remember how you made them feel. The dark cloud touched everyone, forcing everyone to change. The change wasn't harmonious; it was like a crisis.

Every emotion in my body was screaming to get out. Abel Rapp, an assistant of Ellen Harth, called me and asked me to be an extra in a film titled *Deadly Hero*. He could only pay me ten dollars. My salary was $100 an hour. I did it to plant a seed to get out of the fashion industry that Studio 54 controlled.

Ivan Nagy was the director, and I walked up to him. "How do I get a part in this movie?" I demanded.

"Can you act?" he asked, chuckling.

"Yes, definitely," I said. I started improvising for the director.

"You got the job," he said, laughing his head off. Ivan was an excellent director. Who knew that later he'd get wrapped up with Heidi Fleiss? Sex brought about his downfall in Hollywood. The good thing was that I met James Earl Jones and talked with him about acting.

I told him he should have gotten the Academy Award for *The Great White Hope*. He was a great actor, and everyone could see his talent. *The Cotton Club* film location was in New York, and I got that job for three weeks. I got a chance to work for Francis Ford Coppola, not knowing that one day I'd be a director. I worked from five in the morning until two the next morning. I realized this was what lay ahead; this was my future.

Richard Gere and I had eaten lunch at Andy Warhol's before. He was polite and a good listener, hearing what someone is saying. He didn't have a star air about him like, Oh, I don't want to listen this shit. I think hearing made him a better actor. I had to muster up the superhuman energy to work on *The Cotton Club.*

I was one of the dancers in the background. Before *Deadly Hero* with James Earl Jones and *The Cotton Club* with Richard Gere, I had to pass through the dark cloud. I took antidepressants, and they made me not feel anything. I stopped taking them, and I got a call on Billie's phone.

"Hello, may I speak to Amina?" a voice requested.

"This is she," I answered.

"This is Universal Studios calling to tell you that you have been hired to do *The Wiz*, a film with Diana Ross, written by Joel Schumacher and directed by Sidney Lumet. Are you available?" I was silent in shock. "Well, aren't you excited?" the woman on the phone asked.

"I can't believe it. Yes, I am available."

"We will call you for a fitting and rehearsal," she replied.

"Fine."

She hung up the phone, leaving the dial tone ringing in my ear. I couldn't shake my depression. Darkness flooded my mind. I was drowning in a sea of despair, and out of the clear blue sky appeared a lifesaving phone call. I had heard nothing of the producing or the film in preproduction. After I got the call, I danced around the house and told Billie I was in *The Wiz*, and Diana Ross was in it.

"Good," Billie said, and she was genuinely happy for me.

I remembered Joel at a party one night saying he wanted to do a fantastic scene with Diana Ross surrounded by candles. He was dreaming; at the time, he was dressing windows at Henri Bendel. We all dreamed and came up with ideas. I didn't think much of it. Then he started doing the wardrobe for movies. I even met James Coburn and Raquel Welch through him.

I was on the film set of *The Last of Sheila* in the South of France. James Coburn was my favorite star. He knew martial arts, and I loved martial arts and spy films. He had a class about himself, with dignity and manners. Joel's dreams came true. *The Wiz* happened.

A tenant moved out downstairs on short notice. The landlord called Billie and told her she and Charlie could move downstairs. I was shocked that I had nowhere to stay. A friend let me stay downtown with her until I got my place. I was off to see the wonderful *Wizard of Oz*. While I was working on *The Wiz*, Billie's doctor told her she should get an operation and remove the tumor on her brain. If she removed it, she could see out of her blind eye.

She knew she was going to accept the operation, and if anything happened to her, Anne would be her beneficiary. She didn't want me in the house to oppose Anne's inheritance. Anne never washed a dish or even came to holiday dinners. Anne came to Billie's house twice.

"I was jealous of you and Billie's friendship, and that is why I was so rude to you," I said to Anne.

"You need to accept Christ, and all is forgiven," Anne answered. Those were the only two times I had seen Anne with Billie. Their friendship was more by phone. Billie had her church, holiday, and travel friends. She'd talk about Anne all the time and be on the phone with Anne. The shadow of Anne loomed in Billie's apartment without her ever being on the scene.

Anne had a couple of brownstone houses, and Billie would visit Anne. All I knew about Anne was that she was a Capricorn. Billie wanted me out of the house. I did call Billie, and she said come and see her sometime. I said OK and didn't think anything about it. I was going to go see her. She sounded fine on the phone to me. I didn't resent her. I felt I was being forced to change. Charlie said to me you don't know what is going to happen around the corner. You are compelled to go around the corner and see. I had been with Miss June and Billie all my life.

After I left, Billie underwent the operation. The tumor was malignant. The cancerous tumor had spread through Billie's whole body. Her wicked next-door neighbor named Bee had an unsympathetic type of humor. When someone who is supposed to be your friend makes fun of you when you get sick, that's wicked.

Bee was half white like Billie; they both looked like white women. She came to Billie's house every morning for coffee and grinned in Billie's face. I wondered where Anne was; she wasn't around.

"Billie's head is shaved clean like an onion. The big titties that Billie used to have, they look like two left arms hanging on her chest. If I had titties that big, I'd cut them damn things off a long time ago," Bee said.

"Bee, you talk about Billie like she was your enemy. You had coffee with her every morning," I replied.

"Billie was lonely and called me to come over every morning. Billie thought she was so high class and better than everyone else. One thing I can say, Billie was a smart woman. Billie fell fast after the operation, and in three weeks, she died. She should never have had the tumor operated on," Bee went on to say.

That is the truth. Billie was bright. I learned from her to be clever. Billie had ambition, and she wanted to elevate herself. Bee was smiling, friendly, with class in public, a retired nurse and into politics. She had the most beautiful white legs. Bee bragged about her legs. She wore stockings, and her legs never aged. Behind closed doors, Bee was a dominating, competitive, cursing, cigarette-smoking woman who only cared about her children and grandchildren.

"If a man ever hit my kids, I'd kill him," Bee said.

I was surprised Bee never had a fight in her life. She had courage and confidence, and she stood up straight. Bee didn't drink nor
inhaled her cigarettes. Bee dominated her husband and every man
she ever dated.

He worked and brought his whole paycheck home to Bee. When
he died, he left her with three kids, and she got a boyfriend.

"I was cooking and fucking you, and you're going to help me, or
you got to go. I don't need you," Bee told her boyfriend. He bought
her groceries for thirty years and gave her money to help her raise her
kids. Even though she worked as a nurse, she never slept with him in
front of her children or lived with him. She wasn't married to him
even though he and his wife were separated. He was Catholic and
couldn't get a divorce.

"I hate a crying, whining man. I don't feel sorry for them. You
and Diana Ross look like you're crazy about a man. The only thing,
you're more controlled with it. I used to babysit for Lena Horne, and
she never paid me," Bee rambled on.

She knew I worked with Lena Horne on *The Wiz*. Because Bee
was mean and dominating, Lena Horne walked out on her.

Bee's granddaughter was living with a guy, and he didn't wish to
get married. Bee went to their house and confronted him. She gave
him an ultimatum: if he didn't marry her granddaughter by the end
of the week, she was moving, and he wasn't allowed to see her again.
By the end of the week, the guy married her granddaughter.

When Bee told me that Billie called her every morning, I knew
how aggressive and overbearing Bee was. If Billie didn't call her, Bee
came over anyway. Anne came in and took everything, including all
my school pictures. I did have Anne's phone number and called her.

From the tone of her voice, she didn't want to give me anything.
She told me Billie's funeral was on the day of my birthday.

"Everyone is talking about Billie," I said.

"Billie is dead. It's over. No need for them to gossip about her," Anne replied, and she hung up the phone. I never spoke to her again. I learned if I had a tumor and lived with it for twenty-five years, don't operate on it. Just because someone visits you often, that doesn't mean that person is your friend. Closeness breeds contempt.

Companions and would-be friends resent you when you demand their time every day, and they give it.

CHAPTER 25

Michael Jackson, Light of My Life

My DEPRESSION BEGAN TO FADE when I went to rehearse for *The Wiz*. Depression slowed down my whole body. I tried to jump up on a table and hit the shank of my leg. Thank God it didn't break my leg. When the choreographer had me do the steps, it seemed like I was moving in slow motion. I could see it on her face. She was wondering how she was going to get me into shape.

After two weeks of rehearsal, I got into top shape physically. I felt like my old energetic self again. The sun shone so brightly on the first day of filming. I was standing on the Emerald City stage prop. I looked down, and Michael was staring at me. I looked at him, and we smiled at each other. When I had a break, I came down from the stage. It was like we'd never parted.

I greeted Michael. "You are thin like me," he said, and a good feeling overwhelmed me. Everyone had been saying how skinny I had become. Michael validated my weight loss; he was pleased with it. From that day on, Michael and I were together for the next six months. He was called on to do the role of the Scarecrow at the last minute. We talked about the Apollo days, and I told him that Little Bit, a girl who was one of the fans in our group, asked about him.

"Where is Little Bit? I love her," Michael happily said. He never forgot his first fans. I was amazed that he remembered me. Later on, he made a song titled "Just a Little Bit."

I came out of my depression. Michael did have healing powers; everything in my life seemed to lighten up. I could finally see the light at the end of the dark tunnel. We were together all the time, and I protected him. It seemed like a suitable position I found myself in. He felt safe with me and the fans from the Apollo. Now it was only me, the last of the original fans.

One day on the set, a gay dancer came up while Michael and I were talking.

"Are you gay?" he blurted.

"No," I said sharply.

Michael shook his head no. "Are you sure you are not gay?" he defiantly asked.

Joel was standing there. "No, he is not gay," Joel said as if he were tired of hearing that question. The dancer took off and went back to his place on the set. The nerve of him to ask Michael that in front of me and Joel, who wrote the screenplay for *The Wiz*.

After I finished filming the movie, Michael and I met at Studio 54. He met Halston, Andy, Steve Rubell, and Liza. He and Liza became friends, and all the people in my circle became friends and social companions with Michael. Steve Rubell didn't take Michael to the basement. Michael wasn't gay, and he didn't drink, smoke, or take drugs. He didn't indulge in decadence or lasciviousness. Michael stayed on the dance floor, exactly where I wanted him. Studio 54 played the best music with an elaborate sound system. As the music moved through our bodies, Michael and I danced the night away.

Sometimes he danced with Liza. She liked to sit with Halston and watch the dance floor. Liza was married to Jack Haley, who didn't dance. Liza got out on the dance floor, and we all danced together.

Michael and I were together a lot, and Liza tried to set him up on dates. When I entered the club, he'd get up and come over. He would hug me and greet me, as if to say, "Save me from this date." His dates were so angry with me; if looks could kill, I'd be dead. Oh my God, the way they looked at me as if they hated me. Jealousy consumed them; on the first date, they went wild for him. No wonder they terrified him. He liked being around nineteen other girls and me all the time. We were fans, and we were never jealous of one another or desperate to be with him or wanting to sleep with him.

We were like family—relaxed. Michael and I were together so much that people in the fashion business thought we were sleeping together—especially the militant models hanging around Stephen Burrows.

Activist types seemed to speak for Stephen when I visited him. They antagonized me and mingled in my business. The activist model undermined me with Ellen Harth, my agent. She tried to get Issey Miyake not to hire me for his show at Studio 54. She failed in the attempt. The universe was with me, even though I didn't have faith in it. She continued to complain that there weren't any black models getting work. The militant model was the only one who wasn't getting work. No one wanted to hire her, and only Stephen supported her career.

Because Stephen was a creative force in the fashion industry, people tolerated her. I had earned my position in the fashion industry, through my efforts.

Three years before the militant model came along, she had the nerve to try to lean on me. I was supposed to bow down to her like she was high power. I beat the pavement and knocked on doors for three years before I met Stephen, which is something she never did. She was too busy with Stephen and in everybody else's business. All your insecurities come out as a model, and I didn't, like my beliefs questioned.

People were always trying to find out what I believed in; I must believe in a secret this is why I'm successful. Because I didn't have the answers to my actions, I was following my stars and inner promptings. I was getting my hair done for Stephen's show, and I didn't like the way the hairdresser did my marcel hair. I kept telling him I didn't feel comfortable with the part in my hair on the right side, and he refused to listen. I snatched the setting off my head to fix my hair. The militant model jumped in.

"You should be professional and let him do your hair the way he wants it."

She had no respect for me and talked to me like I was working for her. I lost respect for her then and never reclaimed it. That was my right. I was modeling the clothes. I desired perfection. If something didn't look its best on me, I would speak up. I blame myself for being emotionally involved and listening to and responding to her unprofitable bullshit. Out of my loyalty, I had to see Stephen to pick up some clothes, and I got the third-degree questioning about Michael. They asked how big his penis was. Stephen was in on the questioning.

"I don't know. I was not sleeping with Michael. He's my friend. And he's too young," I added.

A militant Asian woman was there. We weren't friends, and it was none of her business. "You're so full of shit. You're sleeping with a big, fat, rich man," she said in a nasty militant tone. She didn't believe I wasn't sleeping with Michael.

First of all, my men were hunks, and they were in their twenties or older than me. Michael was nineteen. It was more love and a fun bond between us. A fun buddy. I guess if we were together without our careers between us, maybe a romantic relationship could have happened. I can't say. I felt like Michael was my destiny, and it didn't matter where my career or life took me in the world. A bond between us existed, and I didn't want anything to destroy our connection. That was the first time I knew what it was like to be Michael's girlfriend. From the public's perspective, this was what was going to happen to me: my life with Michael as a victim of interrogation and third-degree questioning.

Even if I dated him, my lips were sealed. I never expected Michael to deliver in an intimate, romantic way. He was with me every night, and that was enough for me. His energy embraced me and everyone around him. I was inspiring and encouraging to him. Michael sang Stevie Wonder songs to me and songs he had written. Stevie Wonder had been teaching him how to write songs. When a singer can write his songs, he can make his hits, and he doesn't have to pay a songwriter royalties. Other musicians will pay him or her to record the songs.

Being able to write songs gave Michael control over his career and made him independent. I loved to hear his voice without any music. Here was the biggest entertainer in the world singing to me in private.

I never thought for one minute to say shut up and kiss me, like the other girls wanted him to do. They wanted him to focus on them. They wanted to get pregnant by him to get a multimillion-dollar check. They were following him all over the world, trying to sleep with him when they were in their fertile cycle. Nor did the girls want him out dancing all night. They wanted him in their bed.

I loved the fact that we were out all the time. The men wanted from me what the girls wanted from him. They expressed their desire with harassing phone calls and manipulation. The girls had no shame or pride about the fact that they were sexually after him. Being with Michael was like being in Las Vegas every night. His energy was exciting, exhilarating, and electrifying up close and personal.

When I went home, sleep eluded me. I woke up energetic and ready to go and meet Michael. I got dressed in Stephen Burrows clothes and wore a different wig every night. Michael gave me a transfusion of energy that I needed to survive at that moment in time. My depression had zapped my energy.

No doctor could have written a better prescription than Michael. Michael complimented me on how beautiful I looked. He loved my hairstyles and clothes. I became a muse to him. Michael celebrated my birthday and New Year's Eve with me. Of course, I felt flattered that I was getting attention and love from this fabulous young person.

"I love you, Michael," I said to him and kissed him on the cheek. Michael put his arms around me and hugged me, and I hugged him back.

I loved holding him in my arms. It feels good to hold a baby, and that is how I felt holding him. I'd supported Michael's career ever since I saw him perform at amateur night at the Apollo Theater. I spent five years of my life being his fan and supporting him. Thanks to Michael and James Brown, I became inspired to dance. I never thought of him giving it up and putting a woman first. Marriage was second; the career and his duty came first. The women he attracted couldn't understand his fame. I could deal with the fame; I needed to have downtime. With Michael, it was nonstop action. Michael needed constant mental stimulation. I was accustomed to being in the public eye with Michael with the rest of his fans.

His women wanted him home, keeping the home fires burning, whereas I wasn't used to a man sitting around me. All my guys had somewhere to go or something to do. I like being alone at home and recharging my energy, and I had things to do around the house.

Usually, I'm preparing to go to an event or travel. I like watching TV and films, being creative, and having time to think of what to do next. I loved that there was constant action of something happening with Michael.

At an early age, dealing with Michael set the tone for my life, and I didn't grow out of it. Even in my down times, I'd get restless and yearn with pangs of desire for fame. My career formed excitement, and my public life continued, although I needed to bail out at times due to my home life.

In my uncertainty, I thought this was the end. I realized it was never ending, and I had to live my life on the edge of readiness. Be ready. Someone will call with an invitation to participate, work, or fly somewhere at the spur of the moment. My career or work continued to pull me back into the spotlight.

Michael never bailed out; he stayed on the scene. Like James Brown said, "Stay on the scene like a sex machine." That didn't bother me as long as the public didn't see us in private—although we were never alone. Fame is not a deal breaker for me. Being out in the public eye was a deal breaker for him and his women. I was thinking from a fan's point of view, not from the perspective of a traditional wife who wants to have a normal married life with her husband.

That could never be Michael; the world is a stage, and that was his life. Going out and being mobbed was OK as long as they didn't tear his clothes off and grab him, like they were the walking dead on speed. Michael was a big kid who never wanted to grow up or deal with adult matters. If you had a little child inside you, Michael made you feel and act like a child again. He had that effect on most people, except his women. His women were mature, fully grown women;

they did not wish to go back and be a child again. They wanted an adult man who put them first.

Michael's career had to take a back seat; the women wanted him to deal with adult intimacy. It became a tug-of-war: the women demanded, and Michael couldn't give or be what they desired.

He was terrified of adult intimacy. Michael was the type of person who can write love songs and sing about it as if he experienced the romantic union. He received insight by watching other men becoming emotionally involved with women. Michael was singing and writing as an empathetic sponge; few musicians can absorb feelings, emotions, and words of other people so deeply.

Environment and change became important elements in Michael's life. He needed to be around happy people, not people with deep psychological problems. Kids play by themselves; adults are in the company of other adults. If you have children, you put them to bed, and then you and your mate have some alone time. You want adult mental stimulation and intimacy, which can cause heartbreak and is why the wrong relationships test our maturity. It depends on how emotionally mature we are about the breakup.

If we have emotional immaturity, we are going to take the estrangement painfully. It seems like the pain lingers on forever, and you will never get over your ex. And then some people break up and remain friends. Michael didn't wish to go through that; he had seen his brothers get their hearts broken several times. That affected his perception of love affairs; he didn't want to be hurt.

If you are a kid and separate from your best friend or your dog dies, you get over it. Children cry one moment, and they are happy the next. They don't mope over things or hold on to things like baggage—pain, heartache, and bitterness—like adults do. They don't have to deal with old age, wrinkles, inflexibility, or great responsibility. Sometimes they even laugh at such things.

As an adult, you have to tell them it was not funny and it was not nice to laugh at such things. Most of all, with a child, there is learning, along with ice-cream cake, candy, toys, recess, and playtime. Hopefully, there's an adult taking care of all the necessary details and worries.

When some kids grow up and become adults, they start regressing back to the traumas that happened to them in their childhoods. Some can get over it, and some of them can't. Adults were around Michael most of his childhood, and good manners rubbed off on him. He played with Diana Ross's kids and other kids—mostly girls who came to see him, like me. He had his brothers and cousins to play with during rainy days. When he wasn't working, or in between shows, he was never alone. Even though there were people around, that doesn't mean he didn't feel lonely.

All the other groups on the shows with him were adults. He had a front-row seat to see what it was like to be an adult. Michael wanted no part of it; he had a phobia of getting old and wrinkled, of not being able to play and have a carefree life. He was terrified of getting his heart broken; intimacy meant taking that risk. I was around adults or people who were older than me. Half of me was mature, and the other half was immature.

I think hanging around adults or being a latchkey child forces a child's maturity. The child doesn't have time to be a whole child. A child needs to go through the evolution of childhood as a teenager becoming an adult. Being with peers at each stage helps development.

Sometimes I acted like a little girl as he acted like a little boy. I could snap out of it; Michael couldn't. My childhood was full of neglect. I was begging to grow up so I could make my decisions and be an adult. Michael was a kid; as an adult, he never grew up. He wanted to experience being a child, so he grew out of some of his shyness. He became more courageous offstage than he had been as a child.

Women who were sexually aggressive, demanding, and jealous scared him. He couldn't hang out with them. Michael feared he was going to be a victim of a fatal attraction. He feared that a desperate woman was going to lock him in a room and kill him. Michael wasn't afraid of them in public; he could run.

I thought he should have become a track star—that is how fast Michael ran. Michael dug his heels in stubbornly and did not make a move on them. They were trying to get pregnant so Michael could pay them millions. He loved feminine, nonaggressive women, and he liked to do the picking. They never gave him a chance; they wanted him to go to bed right away to fulfill their plan. The women got tired of pushing him and slept with his brothers or other men. Once they slept with his brothers or friends, he did not want anything to do with them.

He was the only man I knew who wasn't worried about a woman wanting him for his money. Michael viewed it as if they were using him to get to his brothers or the good-looking men who surrounded him.

He needed a patient, childlike female who was feminine. He needed someone who went along with him and would give in to him. He sang a song later titled "Give In to Me." He needed a woman who could wait and let him be the sexual aggressor when he felt comfortable, like the English royal court ladies-in-waiting with a chastity belt on. No sex before marriage. After the wedding, the king called upon the queen when he wanted her in his bedchamber. Until then she had to be beautiful and romantic, fun loving, with pride, because desperation is not sexy.

Michael wanted a virtuous woman. Not ever did he try to rob a lady of her virtues or make her prostitute herself for fame. Michael read the Bible, and he studied at the Jehovah's Witnesses church.

The women felt he wasn't going to make a move on them, so why should they wait? Or he had someone else, which he didn't. Girls didn't believe he was single; they couldn't wait. They took it like they needed to get laid and now. Michael had magnetism; females couldn't resist him. Michael treated everyone like a fan, and that made the ladies think Michael didn't have a romantic interest in them. An ordinary adult man would have taken them on the spot. Michael wasn't ordinary, even later on in his life. He tried to be normal.

Early on in Michael's life, his dates were out in public with his fans. Michael always put his fans first, and he never asked for privacy. If he wanted privacy, he could stay home. When Michael went out, fans and people were expected to approach him. Michael had high principles; he never exploited a woman.

I couldn't hang with a man like I did with Michael and acquired fame at the same time. They wanted me to go to bed with them and not get the fame and would destroy my career if I outshone them. Michael didn't worry about anyone exceeding him. The more successful you were, the more he wanted to be around you. If you weren't a success, you were a fan, and he enjoyed and loved his fans. His fans blocked non-fans from being around him.

Michael respected women; he was a big kid and a gentleman. His women didn't want that; they wanted to be taken, robbed of their virtues, and given instant intimacy. They wanted a caveman, and that wasn't Michael. He was a lover. He spoke beautifully; ugly words weren't in his vocabulary. His fans were first, and they didn't want anything from him—only to hear him sing or see him dance, which he loved to do.

It was energizing for him; the fans gave him energy. The more he gave his women, they more they wanted. They didn't give in to him, which scared him, and the fear drained his energy. That is why he stayed out in public and didn't keep the home fires burning. When he had his kids, that blocked the women and adult problems. He spent his time at home with the kids, and that energized him. He could be a kid with them as well as a birth father. He had money. That isn't a problem when children are small, for they are like your fans. They give you unconditional love along with endless laughter and harmony. Without the adult problems or stress, Michael had time to spend and raise his kids on his own.

When I had my child, I wanted to raise him and not dump him on anyone. I was a single parent like Michael, although I wasn't married. My baby's father wasn't responsible or ready for a kid, so I became a single parent. I did not want to share my son with an unstable man.

Elsa did give me some money, God bless her soul. I had nobody in the world to help me. It was my responsibility to support my child. I didn't want to be anything like my mother; I had to go it alone. I had my kid many years before Michael had his children. That disqualified me as a love interest. He'd never marry a woman who had a child out of wedlock. I knew we were friends. Unless he loved me as a man loves a wife, I wanted my son to be an adult before I married.

After I had delivered my baby, the men weren't the same people I was meeting before I had my baby. They needed all my time and attention; they were big kids.

During the decadent eighties, a wave of child abuse cases swept through the country. There was one particular instance in New York of a three-hundred-pound man who had a girlfriend with a two-year-old son. The child wasn't his, and he didn't stop crying. Maybe the child had gas pains or some kind of body pain. The mother should have taken the child to the doctor to see if the child was sick. Some babies cry because they wish to be hugged or be the center of attention. The boyfriend couldn't stand the child crying and went into a fit of rage and beat the two-year-old to death while the mother watched in fear of her life.

It shook me to the core of my being. In the newspaper, a photograph appeared of this huge man. I can only imagine what horror and pain that small child felt as that man was beating the life out of him. There were other similar cases, where the boyfriend, husband, or stepfather was abusing and even killing the kids. I took these cases seriously. I didn't think it only happened to other people. I didn't know where it stemmed from—anger, jealousy, stress? I received other warnings when I talked to other people, and they were telling me to protect my child.

When I hear several warnings or suggestions from other people, and they all are saying the same thing, I listen. The wealthy white woman is allowed to leave her kid with a nanny, and the black woman is frowned upon for doing so. My child came first. As a mother, I was supposed to protect my child.

Michael felt the same way about his kids when they arrived years later. As I raised my child, I never took my eyes off Michael. Going back to Studio 54, Michael was lucky spiritually before he became successful financially. Michael loved women. He liked to look beautiful, like the Egyptian pharaohs who wore makeup to enhance their beauty and to keep mosquitos from biting them on their eyelids. I wore red lips with black, wavy hair and black eyeliner. Michael loved it, and then he started wearing red lipstick, black eyeliner, and wavy black hair as well.

Michael had left Motown to go to the CBS label, and they wanted to change his image for the album *Going Places*. I had to go to an audition at Studio 54. Steve Rubell had his hands in everything. I went to the audition. Michael was there with Janet. She was a sweet little girl. She was talking to me, and I liked her. Michael kept picking at her—sibling rivalry—interrupting her to keep her from speaking to me. That was the first time I saw the gangster side of him. He wanted her to sit down and be quiet, not mingle or get attention.

"Leave that child alone, Michael," I yelled, and he stopped picking at her. The casting lady was from CBS records. I had to audition for her. Energy flowed through my body as the music started playing.

I danced and jumped high up in the air in front of the casting lady. She was smiling. I forgot Michael and Janet were there watching me. I got on the floor, and I danced like I never danced before. A couple of weeks before that, I'd had no energy, and I was severely depressed. Here I was back in the old days at the Apollo. This time I was not sitting in the audience; I was going to be onstage with Michael. That's what was going through my mind as I danced and put 100 percent of my energy into it.

"You got it—you got the job," she yelled over the music playing loudly.

Michael walked up to me. "Come early; we are going to rehearse before the show," he said in a calm voice. The show was the following night. Michael and Janet left to go back to their hotel, and I and the other girls who auditioned stayed.

We got fitted for our costumes; we were the Scarecrow ladies. CBS wanted to tie in *The Wiz* with his *Going Places* album. Michael had left Motown, and he was going places. Excitement overwhelmed me. I was living in Brooklyn, and I rode the D train to Fifty-Ninth Street and walked underground to Fifty-Fifth Street. I came out of that exit, and right around the corner was Studio 54.

Manhattan trains ran all night and faster after midnight. I didn't worry about staying out late at night without a car. The next day I got on the train and arrived at Studio 54 around four o'clock to get dressed in my costume with the other girls. Michael came with his brothers and their wives, along with Mrs. Jackson, Janet, and La Toya. Michael came down from the dressing room, and the family stayed upstairs.

There was a curtain partitioning the stage; it wasn't an elevated stage on the dance floor. I didn't think anything of it at the time. I was trying to focus on the dance steps. Michael and I were standing there.

"Let's do the bump," Michael said.

"Sure, I know how to do the bump," I replied. CBS wanted to show him with the girls around him, with each one of us dancing with him. We were his Scarecrow girls, the straw ladies. He was the Scarecrow in *The Wiz*. Getting a film and a deal with CBS was a big deal. It was his first major role in a movie as a character actor. It was around six, and the people start coming into Studio 54. These were all adult fans, no young girls: mainly photographers, people from CBS records, and TV, along with their guests. There were drinks at the bar, and hors d'oeuvres were served.

Michael's brothers came downstairs, and Jackie Jackson was saying to me, "Aren't you the girl who used to be in the back of the Apollo?"

"Yes, I was the one who used to sit in Mr. Jackson's car," I answered.

I didn't think he'd remembered me, yet he did. I had one foot in the past and one in the future. Michael and I did talk about his songs, which were beautiful, and when he sang to me, he sounded enchanting. Being entirely swept away and too wrapped up in Michael felt overwhelming. Something was exciting about Michael. He didn't do anything, nor did he say much. However this energy seemed like a live entity—like a force that surrounded us, went through us, and bound us together. It was alive even when he was perfectly quiet and still.

Michael said he was a vessel, and the energy was using him. The energy fed off me; it also energized me, and it did the same to the audience. It had a huge appetite and had to keep feeding. It didn't let Michael sleep; it couldn't feed when he was asleep. When he was on stage or in a crowd, this energy could drain. It energized the crowd in different ways. Some went into hysteria fits or whatever mode they went into when they weren't asleep. The energy from the fans, people, and crowds was its fuel.

When I left Michael and returned home, energy filled my body; I slept like I was in a high-wire stupor. I was up the next night, energized and ready to see Michael again. I couldn't sleep when electricity was flowing through the atmosphere with nonstop action.

Even the sick cancer kids in the hospital that Michael visited became energized; this energy had to create energy to feed. It was like a giant magnet pulling you toward Michael. There was an overwhelming, steady stream of energy, one in which you don't get tired and you can't sleep. This energy is what pushed Michael to be the greatest entertainer in history. The power came through Michael and spread like a blanket upon the crowd. It generated energy in people to feed itself.

Michael never did anything bad to anyone. Why couldn't he sleep? What was stressful about Michael's day to warrant him never being able to sleep? I know Michael never did a bad performance in his life. Studio 54 had a lot of people for this energy to feed off.

In New York, people were walking the streets on the subway. In California, he was alone at night in his room; people were in their cars and not walking the streets. Michael was not going out dancing around crowds of people. This energy had nothing to feed on except Michael. When Michael quietly sat down, the entity ran rampant. He couldn't control it, and in the end, the quest for sleep debilitated him. I figured it out: "to be or not to be, that is the question." Michael was in the "be" mode, and he let his energy work for him, filling the air with happiness and excitement.

Years later I read a quote by Bashar: "Everything is energy. That's all there is to it. Match the frequency of the reality you want and you cannot help but get that reality. It can be no other way. This is not philosophy. This is physics."

That night at Studio 54, I felt like a happy child playing and expending a level of energy. That is how Michael made me feel. I couldn't stop grinning or laughing. This night at Studio 54, something happened to me that had never happened before. I've been on many stages and around several performers. Nothing compares to being onstage with Michael. I was swept up in the powerful force of his energy, which was rhapsodic, enchanting, exuberant, and all in Michael. His energy enraptured me and the myriad of people who attended the show.

Michael and I, along with three other girls, entered the stage at Studio 54. I could see outlines of the crowd of people through the curtain that sectioned off the floor stage.

"Ladies and gentlemen, welcome to Studio 54 in honor of Michael Jackson's new album *Going Places* and his role in the film *The Wiz*. Here are Michael and the straw ladies," the female announcer said.

When the curtain opened, the music "Do What You Wanna" started playing. Michael and I danced the bump and then separately.

He danced with the other girls. Being onstage with Michael was electrifying. The audience gives energy to the performer, and it feels euphoric and becomes addictive. No wonder he loved to perform. Michael gave the audience 100 percent, and they gave it back to him. Michael danced with me.

"Go on, girl! Shake it, baby, shake it," he said, praising me. I had on L'eggs pantyhose. I didn't have any underwear on under the pantyhose. When I was bending over and bumping, Michael could see all my ass. The pantyhose were not sheer. They were a nude sun-tan color, with some thickness, but embarrassingly, not a lot. In some pictures, you could see the shadow of my vagina. They had to cut a lot of photos from the waist down. I should have had underwear made out of the same fabric.

When the music stopped, the dance was over. I was holding Michael's hand when we got finished dancing. All of a sudden, faces went into shock. Everyone's mouths dropped open, and their eyes popped out of their heads. Michael and I knew this was the moment when the crowd was going to go berserk. They were like the walking dead on speed. The crowd rushed toward Michael and me.

We turned around and ran, and the mob ran after us. I didn't let go of Michael's hand. Years later he wrote a song: "Whatever Happens." There weren't any security guards around; it was Michael and me running from the mob. We ran backstage, and the mob cornered us.

Earlier I had looked at the floor stage and said to myself that there was no reason to worry about these adults that we were entertaining. We were in New York, my hometown, and New Yorkers were the most civilized fans. Teenagers were not attending the event. No stage separated us from the audience. I should not have worried, as we were in Studio 54. Celebrities had entertained there before on a smaller stage. I became angry because the public didn't treat Michael as such. The audience transformed before our very eyes into a mob.

They saw that Michael was not a celebrity; he was the epitome of entertainment and music. The energy that circulated through the air became like a giant magnet, drawing the crowd to us at full speed. We couldn't run toward the group and exit Studio 54; they were blocking the door. Backstage there was no way out; we ran into a corner staircase that led to the basement door, which was locked. I was still holding Michael's hand, and he used my body as a shield. I went up the steps as he let go of my hand.

Michael stepped into the staircase and disappeared at the end of the banister pillar. I was forced to face the mob. My back and the mob were in Michael's view as he peeped out from the stairwell. The crowd saw Michael, and I was the only thing standing between Michael and the mob.

These were adults over twenty-one. Studio 54 sold liquor, this was New York, and I was bloody mad. The mob lost all self-control and attacked me to get to Michael. They were clawing at me, and I was trying to push them back, to no avail. I had flashbacks of Theresa and the girls in the gym who'd attacked me and the nineteen girls at the New Jersey camp who all punched me. I had seen angry mobs in Frankenstein movies and other horror films. The thought never crossed my mind that I could ever be a victim of a frenzied mob.

I didn't know any of these people in the crowd to reason with, and so holy terror fell upon me. I started fighting, hitting, kicking, and cursing. They were trying to pull my costume off; they pulled it up, so my ass blatantly showed.

I was flustered. "Get back. Leave Michael alone. Get your hands off me. What's the matter with you—are you crazy? Leave him alone," I yelled, along with other obscenities. In a fit of rage, I screamed at the top of my lungs. I started hitting, kicking them back. I looked back at Michael peeping out from the pillar on the staircase.

All the anger and depression I'd accumulated from my ex's harassment came out on that mob. They backed up and refused to move. They were still blocking the doorway. The crowd was determined to keep Michael and me trapped in the corner. Suddenly a black guy jumped in front of the mob and said, "Get back—let the man through." My anger fled, and I had the appearance of calmness upon my face.

He pretended to be security, although he wasn't. He was someone who had been in the audience. He spoke with authority, and they backed up and cleared the doorway. Michael clutched my hand, and we walked out, moving through the gauntlet of the mob.

"Come upstairs to the dressing room. I want you to meet my mom," Michael said.

Embarrassed that I'd uttered such harsh words in anger and shown such emotional rage, I looked at myself and discovered I was all messed up. I had to fix my costume; it hung off my shoulder. Michael and I went across the stage to the other side and upstairs to the dressing room.

"Let's stop in here; I need to fix myself up before I meet your mother," I said.

"OK," Michael replied.

We stopped in my dressing room, and I looked in the mirror. Michael sat down in the chair waiting for me. The other girls were in the dressing room. I had not realized that a photographer from *Time* magazine had accompanied Michael and me into the dressing room. He wanted to take pictures. Quickly, I made sure I looked good, though I couldn't fix my costume. So I sat on the left side, and the other girls gathered around Michael.

The photographer took the photo; it was in color. You can see it on my website with the other professional photos. After we had posed for pictures, it became crowded in the dressing room. Michael and I went out in the hallway, and he introduced me to Mrs. Jackson and La Toya. I had met Janet earlier at the audition. They all went into their dressing room, where the rest of the brothers were.

All the photographers and press were standing outside the room. One photographer said, "We are waiting for them to come out."

I opened the door, and Michael smiled at me. "Come on in," he said.

On that note, I turned around and invited the press into the dressing room. Michael's face went from a smile to an "Oh, the press." I was happy that the sight of me lit up his face. I wanted us to take all the pictures we could take. I knew we were making history, and my prediction was right. I was in the *Ebony* magazine issue dedicated to Michael. Once they started flashing their camera lights, Michael put a smile back on his face. I was glad I'd invited the press into the room; if they hadn't had access to take the pictures, I couldn't be writing about it now.

After the photographers left, we all went downstairs to mingle with the crowd. Mrs. Jackson, La Toya, and Janet left or stayed upstairs. When I went downstairs, as I was mingling around Studio 54, I saw Michael running to the left, then running to the right. A crowd of club patrons was chasing him around. I went out into the lobby, and Tito and his wife were standing there by the ashtray while he smoked a cigarette.

I was angry all over again. "Look at the people and how they are acting. Do they do this to Michael all the time?" I asked.

"Yep, all the time," Tito answered.

They were quite calm about it—business as usual. I didn't like the fact that the people attacked me like weird zombies who were trying to bite flesh off Michael and me.

My throat was sore the next day from screaming at the mob. They had scared me to death; I thought they were going to kill us for sure. I didn't mind autograph-seeking mobs or people who wanted to talk or take pictures, but don't mess with my clothes and appearance. Don't maul my skin or pull my hair and do bodily harm—that is a no-no. I was appalled to find out that Michael was a victim of this type of behavior regularly.

Michael took it like a champ and never said a word or tried to defend himself. Michael ran away. He could have been a track runner; that is how fast he ran. Later on, he eventually had to get bodyguards to walk around everywhere with him.

After that night, Steve Rubell went back to selecting only the well behaved and elite to be let into the club. The Jacksons left New York, and Michael stayed in Manhattan with me.

Diana Ross and Michael were finishing up *The Wiz*. They were working on a dream job. Michael had his nights free, and we'd meet at Studio 54. We'd dance for hours; nobody bothered him. He walked freely all around the club. Steve Rubell and his crowd disappeared into the basement, and Michael and I were left on the dance floor or at the bar together. VIPs were going in that cellar; I didn't see Truman or Halston. Liza was starring in the Broadway show *The Act*, and she came late after the show to party.

When Liza came, I'd leave Michael and go home and come back the next night. I had to get my beauty rest. Nevertheless on weekends, we'd dance all night.

Liza got sick with the flu and couldn't recover, so she went to Florida. Her doctors thought the warm weather in Florida could heal her faster than the cold weather of New York. Her show closed until she came back. Liza worked hard on *The Act*; I went to see the show, and it was fabulous.

Michael and I didn't make a commitment in writing or words spiritually; we knew when I came into the club, we were going to be together. Michael was so happy and free that he didn't have bodyguards, and he didn't have to worry about being chased all around the place by people. Michael could dance and have fun and listen to music. He could see what the public trends were with ease and comfort. If Michael wanted to sit on the side and watch everyone else, he could; if not, he got on the dance floor and danced.

Michael couldn't go anywhere else except the Apollo and relax without being mobbed. Studio 54 offered Michael sanctuary and peace; he could be Michael Jackson and at the same time blend in with all different types of people. We all had one thing in common: we loved music and dance. An instigator (I won't mention his name) was there one night with Michael. He was sitting with another guy from the music industry in between him and Bianca, Jack Haley, Liza, Halston, and Steve Rubell. The instigator and the other guy were Michael's guests. They all were sitting on Steve Rubell's couch for his VIP crowd on the club floor. They could watch everyone dancing while they enjoyed their drinks.

I arrived at the club and approached Halston and waved, and he yelled, "I love your hair." I had on my long, black, curly wig.

Michael was standing in front of everyone. I went over to him. He hugged me, and I hugged him back, and he said, "Do you know so-and-so?"

Before I could say anything, the instigator said, "Yeah, I know her. She used to be with the Five Stairsteps. What happened? You don't hang out with them no more?" Michael looked at me as if I were disloyal to him.

I replied, "I haven't seen the Five Stairsteps in years." I turned to Michael and said, "Yes, I used to hang out with the Five Stairsteps. That was before I met you."

The instigator sounded stupid in front of Michael. He had the nerve to disrespect Michael and me by confronting me in front of Michael. The instigator used to played drums. He dated and lived with Aloha, the Five Stairsteps' sister, who sang in the group. The instigator also traveled with the Five Stairsteps. I didn't go off on the instigator and tell Michael about him. He wanted to hurt Michael and me because he thought I was going to tell Michael about him. I didn't like the confrontation from somebody who knew about me from the past. I was already a successful model in my right.

I stayed happy and calm; I didn't want him to upset my applecart. I didn't pick up the gauntlet; I ignored him. I've heard the saying that everyone is with their camp, and you can't jump from one field to another. I attract people from all walks of life and from different groups who are fans of mine. I can't discriminate and restrict myself from all the benefits and opportunities in my life, because I am loyal to one camp. I can't show favoritism in business—it's unprofessional. That is why I am where I am, and he is still where he is in the past. I quit the past and progressed, and so did Michael.

That night Michael and I danced. He told Michael he would see him later.

It seemed to me that everyone Michael introduced me to other than his family members were negative people. All my associates were power players who were creative, successful, together people. Michael associated with instigators—treacherous and so dumb. They didn't want him to have any happiness or peace. If someone came to me and said Michael was hanging out with my rival, I'd ask, "When? Now or ten years ago?" Michael tolerated stupid people. As long as Michael made his music, they couldn't do anything to him except run all the right people away and replace them with the wrong people.

Later on, I asked Kirk Douglas what had been the key to his success for decades. "I surrounded myself with the right people," he answered. Kirk's statement confirmed what I was feeling about Michael and the people around him. Several other people were bringing bad people around him. They were up in my face telling how they were going to use me. I got upset and nipped them in the bud right away.

I complained to the people who introduced Michael to this con man in Studio 54. They were getting into the club by saying they were Michael's friends. I started bickering with Michael's unsophisticated associates. They'd say something in front of Michael that I didn't like it, and I'd snap at them. They didn't belong there with Michael and me.

That was one time I wish Steve Rubell could have taken them down into the basement and made them disappear. I told Michael to get rid of the wrong people around him. I noticed Michael liked to brag about the girls he was hanging with to the troublemakers. If she was a girl he liked or was getting close to, he'd bring the instigators around. Either the girl got mad and slept with the dudes, or she'd drop Michael. Either way, they'd break up, and then Michael was free to pursue his music. That's what he loved first.

Michael used these instigators to test a woman's loyalty to him. Nine times out of ten, the women would sleep with the instigators, and he would be hurt anyway. They were ill-mannered. They would say, "So-and-so asked me if he could have your phone number."

They didn't even know how to treat a woman, and the women would sleep with them. They were mad at Michael for allowing those troublemakers to be around them. That is why Michael sang the song "Who Is It?" He tried to find out who the girls he liked were sleeping with. All he had to do was ask. I doubt if they would have been truthful. The girls who honestly wanted him would have been honest.

Michael was honorable, impeccable, legitimate, and loyal. It wasn't that he wanted to show off for the instigators. Michael was shy, but at the same time, he wasn't ashamed of people, places, and things. Most men want to show off their women to other men. It was the kind of males he was around. I didn't mind being out and around his friends if they were real people. But these were treacherous, and stupid instigators put him on a path that brought about his downfall.

I didn't like the troublemakers who were around him, and they were not going to bring about my downfall. If Michael and I were married, those instigators would not have been allowed to step foot in my house. Michael and I weren't married, so I could only speak for me. I was the captain of my ship, however small it may be, and I didn't want them on it.

Michael didn't want to listen to wisdom; that wasn't wise of him not to listen to the voices people were saying the same things over about the kids his surroundings and appearance. When I hear a group of people saying the same thing, I become aware because enlightenment comes in many forms. I kept my eyes wide open instead of shut. Michael had so much love in his heart that he couldn't afford to associate with everyone. He began to think of himself as walking in Jesus's footsteps. He had great spiritual protection. Like God told Solomon, if you associate with strange women, you will be defeated. As I told Michael, if you keep associating with these unsavory individuals, you will be frustrated. Michael was godlike, although he didn't have the invincibility of a god. Jesus Christ was betrayed and crucified, and he was the Son of God sent to Earth to defeat the Roman gods. Jesus was a god; Michael wasn't a god.

Michael was sent to create music; that was his destiny. I think when we get so much fame and admiration, we acquire great courage. We forget that we have to have wisdom with our courage to make the right judgment. You can't afford to surround yourself with people, places, and things that cloud your judgment. Not being able to sleep clouded Michael's judgment. He was not to do things that interfered with or blocked his destiny. With his wealth, he could give to charity and not in a way that compromised his position. I may become queen, but I'm not a god. I'm not the closest thing you are going to get to a god. I am only human. I never dare to say or think that I am a god or godlike.

I respect all the gods, and they have blessed me. I became a tool, a vessel for the gods to use. Without my worship, faith, respect, and love, the gods ceased to exist. I need the gods, and the gods need me. When you make a deal with the gods, you have to keep it. The deal is your destiny; once you get on your ship, there is no getting off. Being in Michael's presence felt godlike. The energy he generated was like a powerful magnet.

We all are magnets. Michael's magnetism was so powerful, it was like an addictive drug that embraced my whole body. I got on the floor and danced with him. Ha-ha! Michael laughed as he does on the song "Get on the Floor." Michael and I danced all night. A month later he recorded the song. I know it was written about me. I was his muse. His voice, his songs, and his music were hypnotic. It was better than sex to me.

I've heard certain preachers say independence is a sin. I am independent in thought and action. Hallelujah! I was glad Michael went back to California. I assumed that Mr. Jackson was managing him and would block all the troublemakers from being around Michael.

I didn't see Mr. Jackson in New York, and it didn't occur to me that he no longer was managing Michael. I know Mr. Jackson. He'd kick those instigators who were hanging around Michael to the curb. Individuals around Michael didn't have the freedom to do whatever they wanted to do. When Mr. Jackson managed him, he didn't let anyone damage Michael's image. I never thought Michael would allow himself to marry a woman with children. As the years went on, he was forced to marry a woman with kids to protect his image.

Michael had good intentions, however his marriages failed. It takes a certain type of person to be in the music and film industry. Honesty and integrity are important. There is no compromise. Either you are going the same way, or you are not. When people in show business tell spouses about the direction they are set to go in, instead of saying, "Hell no, I won't go," they agree, as if they are for the person.

It takes a certain type of person to be in show business. If you are someone who needs sex and closeness, even when you travel with your mate, you will feel alone. The business demands so much focus that you can't divide the energy. You can find sex anywhere; love and compatibility are difficult to find.

If you are an entertainer who loves your freedom, don't marry someone who wants to stay home and keep the home fires burning— unless the person is OK with you not being there. You'll come back from a film or tour and find the person in bed with someone else. It would be a scandal you could have avoided. When the studios controlled everything in Hollywood, the actors and film crew worked at the studio and came home at night. It's easy to have a wife or husband when you have stability. After the studio system dissolved, actors traveled to locations, which is cheaper than shooting in a studio because you don't have to build anything. Entertainers went on tour, some with a spouse and some not.

When there was only one breadwinner, women stayed at home and waited for the husband to return. Now that women have their independence, they don't have to stay at home and wait. Few entertainers have remained married for forty years. Elizabeth Taylor married eight times because the men wanted her to be a housewife. She was a movie star. How could she be a housewife?

The same goes for a man. How can he be a househusband? If he's making a movie or on tour every two years, then yes, he can be home in the meantime. If he is someone who is always working in the public eye, then it's going to be difficult to keep a marriage—unless he or she is married to someone who is not self-serving. You can't be self-serving and be in the industry; it crushes all personal fulfillment.

TV and variety show entertainers are likely to have longer marriages. They are home more often and have weekends off after a long hiatus; there is a lot of private time. Movie stars and entertainers are workaholics; they are consistently working. You can be self-serving at different times if it does not conflict with your career and business.

You have to watch that your personal life doesn't overlap into your career. It becomes a problem when you deal with people who are not for your career and have individual needs that conflict with your job. If you need constant attention and a babysitter, sex, and other vices, you don't need to be in show business of any kind. You need to marry and be with your wife or husband all the time.

Show business is going to take you away from your spouse. If you can't stand on your own two feet, your marriage will crumble. I had several professors in show business, and they couldn't deal with it.

Now they teach so that they can go home and be with a spouse. Few people in show business can combine marriage and career.

As for the rest of us, we can't have it all at once; there will be periods of personal and non-personal fulfillment. For those of us who encounter the conflict in a career versus marriage, love affairs, friends, home, children, and family, look at what wins, and go with what wins. If the career wins, you have to let everything opposing it go. It's never going to work. I don't care how many times you try.

As long as you keep one foot out and one foot in and are not committed, you will have aggravation, heartache, and suffering. If the career is winning, it's going to continue to win. Society expects everyone to marry and have a traditional home, family, and married life. However there are those of us who will never fit into that compartment and need a freewheeling marriage. Marrying and putting on a facade is the worst thing that career people can do. Try as you will, you can't make it work. The public is going to find out sooner or later that your marriage is not working. It may not be amicable, bitter, or ugly. The worst is a divorce scandal, especially for successful people in the public eye.

Michael was committed to his career and determined to help other people's children. That conflicted with his job. If he waited until he had his kids, things could have been different. Once you are committed to your career, the universe will bring you the right people, places, and things. You have to be patient in the meantime. You as an individual have to be able to separate the wheat from the chaff.

The universe is going to test you to see if you know who you are. A high signal is when a romantic interest asks about needs. As a career person, you know you won't be there to fulfill his or her needs all the time. This person is a self-serving person, even if the person is with you everywhere you go. This person is not going to take a back seat to your career. He or she needs constant attention.

You are going to have to make a choice between the person and career. Some people fight to juggle the two until they can't struggle anymore. A casting director told me that a particular type of person is in the film and music industry. It can be grueling, tough, and painful, and it's not for everyone. Love is like a faucet; when you think it's on, it's turned off and gone.

CHAPTER 26

Michael and Everyone Else Are Talking

MICHAEL DIDN'T HAVE LONG, DEEP conversations with me about being his muse or inspiration. It was OK, because I used to have problems speaking; I had a speech impediment. I could write better than I could talk. When he sang and talked about his love songs, he was like an adult with such passion, emotions, and feeling. Not childlike at all, Michael carried himself as if he were on a job interview. As soon as he got offstage, he acted like a big kid with his brothers and sisters. Studio 54 didn't have children, and he carried himself very well on the dance floor. When Michael got back to Los Angeles, I started getting phone calls from people: Michael did this; Michael did that.

He hired Michael Peters to choreograph his dance moves for his albums. I knew Michael Peters, and I thought it was good for Michael to be working with him. If he could have stayed with the right people, he would still be alive, working and being with his fans. He continued to grow in his music, but so did the anxiety of having to deliver more than he could. Michael Peters choreographed his "Billie Jean" and "Thriller" hits. Michael Peters is gay, and I knew they wouldn't be tight as friends. Michael wasn't homophobic, so they could continue to work together.

Eddie Murphy started talking bad about Michael in his comedy act on stage. He didn't need to do that. He was an excellent comic without slandering Michael. Eddie Murphy was a big star in Hollywood, and other comics started talking about Michael. He and Michael became friends. MJ didn't like animosity. I'm sure he called Eddie to soothe any negative talk or jokes about him.

After Mr. Jackson was no longer Michael's manager and Frank Dileo became his manager, things got out of control. Dileo was a manipulator; he was making people think Michael wanted this or that, and Michael never knew anything about it. Dileo didn't let his left hand know what his right hand was doing. Michael was his left hand, and the instigators had a lot of influence in Michael's life. MJ was on TV asking for movie and TV projects; none appeared.

Dileo kept a lot of dissension going between Michael and Prince. Agitators were calling me about Prince. I didn't even know Prince. They knew I knew Michael, and that is why they were calling me. There was no competition; they were in two different markets. Dileo didn't want Michael's fans to buy Prince's records.

The comparison seeped into Hollywood on *Entertainment Tonight*. Andy Williams made a comparison between Prince and Michael. What did Andy Williams have to do with Michael Jackson and Prince?

Michael wanted to get rid of all the limitations that surrounded him. At the same time, he never wanted to grow up. Michael's business grew, and the little boy inside remained his persona. The child inside Michael yearned to get out, but as he got older, the child inside conflicted with his mature body. The more successful he became, the less control he had.

Dileo was the first player in sabotaging Michael. He was the man in the back ground pulling all the strings. All the advice he gave him was wrong. Michael complained about his business manager; he didn't tell Michael anything about his business when he asked him. Michael was too dependent on the subordinates in his camp; he wasn't given any accurate guidance. Dileo viewed Michael as an adult who should know. He was aware that Michael didn't know, and he took advantage of that lack of knowledge and Michael's young mind.

When Michael started hanging out with Emmanuel Lewis, people started talking, saying that Michael liked little boys. Michael wanted to address the rumors. Dileo said, "Oh, let them keep talking. Any publicity is good publicity, even bad publicity."

Dileo was feeding the papers bad publicity about Michael to give the public the impression Michael was a Wacko-Jacko pedophile. Michael and Emmanuel Lewis should have made a public announcement about their association. I learned that if rumors aren't true, then nip them in the bud right away. Let the public know. If you don't, it will snowball. Once that ball gets rolling downhill, it gets huge. When it crashes into a wall or hits rock bottom, it explodes.

I spoke to Dileo about some songs I had written, and I wanted Michael to look at them. Dileo was nasty. I can pick up on people's energy. I knew he wasn't any good and that he was going to be the damnation of Michael. Right after that, Michael fired him. Michael started talking, and he didn't sound good. He was saying he had more fans than anybody else, and the people in Hollywood were jealous of him, because they didn't have fans who loved them.

What he was saying was true, however the competitors who were listening perceived him as bragging in their faces about it. He tried to influence the people in Hollywood, and they didn't give a shit. Dileo knew that. Michael seemed off track and not himself to me. I was used to him being quiet and well mannered. Hollywood goes on recommendations, and Michael began to sound like the instigators. I wanted him to be with his fans who loved him, not up in the industry professionals' faces in Hollywood.

I called his lawyers and complained about Dileo. I predicted that Michael's destiny had derailed and he was headed for a fall. I cursed them all out about Dileo. Who did he think he was, and this is who I am, and I am glad that bastard got fired. You guys need to straighten up, because you are doing a shitty job with Michael and his image. I hung up the phone. I started getting harassing phone calls. They'd call and not say anything on the other end. I knew it was from Michael's people.

That next week, Michael hired Dileo back. It seemed like because I was glad he fired Dileo, he hired him back. I cared for Micheal, and I wasn't scared of the harassing phone calls. I didn't have the power to eliminate the instigators from his life although I knew they were going to destroy his career. Michael knew I didn't like the instigators around him. Users and abusers will get all the money they can get out of you and then move on to the next entertainer. Even if they don't like you, you are dependent upon them. They will set you up for a fall.

There are plenty or actors and singers they like. They will coach them before they talk to the press. They let Michael say and do whatever he wanted to in the media, knowing it could be used against him later on down the line. They were building a case against him. All these disrespectful devils were beneath him; they were nowhere near his level of success. I learned I had to be an adult, take control of my business, and be independent. That is the last thing Michael wanted—to be an adult and deal with all the adult responsibilities.

Maybe in the future, you will be able to change your adult body into a child's body through surgery. For those who have a child's soul in an adult body. Michael got persecuted for being a kid in Hollywood and the music industry. At the same time, Hollywood pushed youth without an adult supervisor, which is detrimental. Some wolves will prey on and devour a child. An adult with a childlike mind can exist and flourish in the creative realm. Outside of the realm of creativity, a child cannot survive without an adult or parent. Michael didn't take control over his business. Everyone is waiting for you to tell each person what to do and take control. Many stars and entertainers have not taken care of their financial activities, and their managers have run off with the money.

Mr. Jackson took care of everything when Michael was a kid. Then Diana Ross managed him for eleven years and took care of everything with Berry Gordy at Motown. Being an adult meant he had to take care of everything and stay on top of people.

With the massive success, there was no time to play. Michael created Neverland where he could be a kid and play with the kids at another Disneyland. Dileo and Michael's camp devised a campaign to make Mr. Jackson look bad and to keep him from managing Michael. Mr. Jackson would never allow Michael to be alone with the kids or have sleepovers without the parents being there. Everything had to be on camera for Michael's protection.

Some things you don't keep private; you let everyone see. I listened to his road manager talk. He had seen Michael go up to the room with a boy. He didn't say anything because it wasn't his place. Why not? He was thinking pedophile, so why didn't he tell Michael it didn't look appropriate and Michael was putting himself in a position to be accused? He was bringing suspicion on himself, and it didn't look right.

Michael's road manager was there to make sure that everything was safe and ran smoothly, even if Michael said nothing was going to happen. What if something does happen? Are you prepared to take that risk? Being the biggest star in the world doesn't make you invincible. You are vulnerable as a person, and image is everything. How people perceive you in your public and personal life can make or break you. Other people's children conflicted with Michael's career. Everyone heard the rumors, and they all encouraged Michael to continue to be around other people's children. I can see it was his escape from the pressures of success.

He was not a pedophile. He refused to grow up. Sex is intimate, and an adult Michael wasn't going to deal with intimacy. That is how I know he wasn't a pedophile. Pedophiles are sleeping with children, and they try to make the child an adult. First, they show them childish things to lure them in. Then they start showing them child-adult sexual pornography and sex toys. The child never goes back to being a child; the pedophile won't let that happen.

I heard Michael say he didn't want to be mature or grow old. He was terrified of growing old, and he thought it was ugly. It was hard for the public to understand how someone with that kind of success could be so childlike and never grow up. Michael was Peter Pan, and he wanted to play him in the movie. With all those accusations, that dream never came true.

The best plastic surgeons in the world are in Hollywood, in Beverly Hills on Bedford Drive. It must be magic that Michael remained the same person I knew from the sixties. He never hurt anyone. Michael wanted to get attention, and everything he did off the stage backfired. The press couldn't picture a grown man doing childish things. The adults around him assessed his mental state and preyed upon this. Elizabeth Taylor told him not to let the people destroy his love for children. She said he should continue to be with them. I would have advised him not to be alone with the kids and not bring suspicion upon himself. All actors are childlike. Elizabeth connected with him on that level. Michael wanted to be in Hollywood, and Elizabeth wanted to stay in the public eye. Michael bought her jewelry.

With all the accusations, the plan to be accepted in Hollywood didn't work. Elizabeth spoke highly of Michael on the one hand, and then she was telling him to be with the kids. Californians will kill you over their children and dogs. Michael kept going on TV and stating how people thought it was sexual. It was not sexual. He played music and gave them cookies and milk.

They didn't want him to babysit their children. The parents didn't like him, and they set him up. Michael was struggling, trying to help these kids, an effort that conflicted with his career and image. If only he could have been patient and waited until he had his children. He got hurt for whom he was trying to help.

He didn't understand that other people could sleep in the bed with kids and not get persecuted. He was not other people; as black people, we know that a light-skinned mulatto woman can be the biggest whore and no one will say anything. Let a brown-skinned woman do it, and she is labeled the scarlet Jezebel, the largest whore, because of her darker skin tone. It's not right; society says that is how it is. On the other hand, for a star, it's not about how it is; it's about how it looks.

Michael changed the music industry and brought whites and blacks together. He couldn't change everything. Change what you can change, and let someone else change the rest. Know your limitations. Dileo caused the rift between Michael and Sony. When anything goes down with the business, the manager gets it first, then the client, and then the lawyers.

There was a morals clause in the studio contracts for entertainers with studio deals. They had to behave in a straightforward, moral way back in the twenties when a lot of immoral acts got publicized. For actors, producers, directors, film crews, and singers, the clause was put into place if an entertainer with a studio deal acted in an immoral way or an inappropriate way that insinuated immorality.

In other words, if you get in a position to be set up, they will turn their back and take the public's side against the entertainer. With all the money and lawyers Michael had, why was he in the press talking about Sony? Why was he going to the Black Muslims and Al Sharpton, making a big case out of the fact they were not pushing his records in the United States? Dileo told Michael to take this route. Why? Because he wanted all the power over Michael. He didn't want to see Michael have peace and happiness or get what he wanted.

Dileo was in a position to help. He didn't help; he kept what he knew to himself. Michael had enough money to do an audit and to have his lawyers deal with Sony, not him. Because of the morals clause, Sony had a right to withhold his music.

Because of the accusation, Sony refused to distribute his music in the United States. Michael had enough money to sell and distribute his music. That was his chance to be independent. He could have made millions selling his music over seas. Fate didn't have it that way. Michael was talking more and more like a child. He'd say Jesus was around kids, or he'd say other rock musicians sleep in the bed with their children. Children don't have an identity; if so-and-so did it, I did it too. That is a child's philosophy. As an adult, you can't do what someone else does. You have to do what is right for you and your image. Adults have to know their limitations.

If you give one child a piece of candy, you have to give all of them a piece of candy. If someone gives my friend a scarf, he or she doesn't have to give me one, because I'm an adult. There were many signals from the universe that Michael and the parents didn't like one another.

Also, the rumors...people were talking. I know Michael and his camp heard the damaging accusations. Michael was up in the press, bragging about how the child likes to be with him more than their parents. They were jealous because he had money, success, the place, and the things to make their child's life a dream. The child came back to them living above their means. They wanted the money. They framed him and coached their kids to say he molested them.

In the end, a child is going to do whatever his or her parents say to do to extort money from Michael. Parents resented the fact that he could offer their kids more than they could provide. ("Ghosts") was a song Michael sang.

He sang and wrote songs that reflected what was happening in his life or someone else's life. He paid because his insurance company insisted he pay. Dileo and the insurance company wanted him to go on his tour and make money for them. The court case would delay the show. Being the big star Michael was, I wondered where his publicity and image consultants were. They could see his image damaged, and they heard the rumors. Why didn't they tell Michael to quit this kid crusade?

When he got on TV to explain why and what went on in private with these kids, the adults viewed it as sordid, and they wanted to hurt him—not for who he was, but because of who he was helping. He could have given a check to any child's charity and been looked upon as a hero. Why did he have to be hands-on, personally involved? Some people thought, oh, how great. Michael is fantastic with children. Others of the majority frowned upon it.

Michael's publicity staff, of all people, should have known it's not what it is that is fact; it's what people see, which can be far from the truth. The public believes what they see. Jesus said blessed are those who believe and don't see. As an entertainer or artist, you deal in illusions. Whatever illusion you create, people think what they see. It's like a TV series. If it's believable, it becomes real to the audience. Michael didn't wish to deal with the lawsuit. He was accused of a heinous sexual crime that only adults commit. Michael should have met this problem head-on where the world could see.

I wasn't there to advise him; I continued arguing and fighting with people on the street. Everyone thought he was guilty. All this time, everyone saw this rumor snowballing. No one cared as long as they were getting paid. They only started caring when the court case arrived, and their money was affected and delayed.

They didn't care about Michael. He needed to step up and care about himself. Damn the tour! He should have fought fiercely to protect his name and not pay a dime to his enemies. What is in a name? Does that depend on the name? I don't agree. You have to protect your name. It is all you have when everything else is gone. He did not take that path, and he regretted it.

Because Michael paid an out-of-court settlement, the studio looked at him as being guilty. Michael realized they didn't care about him. Michael sang the song "They Don't Care about Us." What is the worst thing that can happen? That is death; it's going to happen one way or another. There is no escape, so have courage and fight. You have to do things that are appropriate for your image.

If you don't, unsavory companions will change the perception of what you are doing and frame you. I have seen tapes where they say Michael had so many lawsuits. He wasn't out there. He didn't know half the time what was happening. Why were they suing Michael?

He never took control of his life or business, and nobody was allowed to see him that cared about him.

MJ didn't reach out and take action. If he didn't wish to go to court, his lawyers should have gone and fought for him, instead of settling out of court for false accusations. Most of the time, he was locked away, and when he did go out, the press was there. I never saw Michael insult, curse, hit, attack anyone, or defend himself from a fan. Michael was passive, and the universe doesn't reward passivity.

Michael should have secretly gone to the bank and transferred all his money to a new account that only he could withdraw from, and no one else could sign his checks. His accountant should have received funds from him every month to distribute payment to everyone, along with his bills.   Michael was supposed to have a copy of the receipts to show a list of paid bills and salaries. He was with all these troublemakers and manipulative associates; Dileo and some other person were managing him.

I heard Michael on tape talking on the phone, complaining about the business manager not even telling him how much money he had. Now, these were supposed to be private phone calls. The shady backstabbers and coattail riders he talked to or confessed to taped his calls. Also, his press people didn't advise him that being seen with young boys in private was not the best image for him. If the kids would've been his or a relative's, the public would have seen that as appropriate.

Michael was so sheltered. They told him the world sees everything sexual. Why didn't he listen? Because the enablers around him were telling him it was OK, so don't listen to what the public and the rumors are saying. If they see an entertainer with someone too many times, the first thing they think is they are having sex. If he was with a child who was not his, they were going to say it was sexual. It was the job of his publicist to make sure Michael he had the appropriate image.

His lawyers should have advised Michael that false accusations, trumped-up charges, could arise, so don't "keep it in the closet," which was one of Michael's songs ("In the Closet"). No matter how innocent it might have been, cameras should've been everywhere.

"Michael and the little boy had the flu, and they both spent the night in Michael's room with the door locked," the road manager said. "I believe they both had the flu, and they didn't sleep in the bed together. One slept on the cot on the floor, and the other slept in the bed. They both were knocked out, sleepy from the flu."

I knew Michael was lonely. He was introverted offstage and extroverted onstage. When we were out together, I was the lively one. I brought him out of his shell. Concerned acquaintances called me and told me Michael was lonely and needed someone to talk to, like a therapist. I didn't take it seriously. I said, "Ah, he'll grow out of it." As time went on and Michael insulated himself with the wrong crowd, I realized loneliness makes you do strange things.

Trying to be secretive about some things led to his demise. The secret was that he couldn't sleep. They talk about Michael being on drugs; why didn't the naysayers out him? If they'd outed him, I think once the fans knew about his drug use, Michael would have quit drugs. He did anything for his fans and to keep his face up for his fans. They were all sycophants who wanted to bring about his downfall through their stupidity and their bad advice.

Michael didn't take it seriously. Children don't take things seriously until it is too late. I couldn't be there to protect him, and I had a battle of my own I was involved in: a racist woman who lived next door was a drunk.

She cursed out my twelve-year-old son as we were moving into our apartment. She saw that he was a black boy, and she started cursing him out. The white neighbors came out of their apartments, yelling at her and saying my son was a kid and she shouldn't be cursing at him. That is a no-no for me.

A few days later, I got into an argument with her. When I went to work and left my twelve-year-old at home, she called the police and had my child taken away from me. She accused me of being an unfit parent. I was trying to make it and didn't want any help from anyone. It was my responsibility to take care of my child, and I did. I went to court and regained my child and cleared my name. Michael and I were both accused of something we were not doing.

I met my problems head-on. I wasn't about to surrender. I was not going to be passive; that was a path I did not take. I was never a neglectful mother. As a single parent, I had to work hard to provide for my child. I desired my child to be independent (with his disability, he's three years delayed mentally). He needed to be independent. I didn't abandon him. I came back that night. Three meals were prepared for him daily.

The site manager who was living upstairs told me she'd look out for my son. When the cops came, she panicked and hid in her closet and didn't answer her door. When I arrived home, I assessed the situation. I called the neighbor a bitch and went inside my house. I came to the conclusion that they all were cowards.

She attacked my son; she didn't attack me. I'd wipe the floor with her. I went to court and fought and won my case. I can't stand to be around cowardly, stupid, irresponsible people. Michael was an empathic sweetheart. He felt sorry for these people. They stabbed him in the back every chance they got. They kept the drama and mayhem going. Michael was the one left holding the bag.

Michael became dependent on these people and didn't have the strength to get rid of them. He didn't have an iron fist to control or dominate these people—people who bring misery, discontent, conflict, drama, and no happiness. It's my responsibility to monitor my environment and get away from those types of elements. I wasn't out of it. I had many arguments in Michael's defense.

In New York and Los Angeles, people said to me, "You love him. That is why you are defending him." The people were so quick to condemn him. Nobody in Michael's camp stood up and said that nothing happened. They all weren't in the room, and they didn't see what was going on or what happened. That made the public want to crucify him like they did Jesus Christ. I wish he could have taken control of his business and empire and stayed more with his fans. I knew if he stayed on his destiny ship, there was a woman for him— Peter Pan's Wendy—someone who could be childlike and share his fame.

Elizabeth Taylor was there, so he wasn't going to keep any women. No woman was going to be second fiddle to Elizabeth Taylor. He made a shrine to Elizabeth Taylor in his house; he'd also have to build a shrine to his wife.

I thought his family should have taken him out of the limelight and hidden him away in the Jackson compound. Elizabeth Taylor was the only one on the world stage with him. That's because he put Elizabeth before all his other friends. He put her up on a pedestal, and they all scattered long before the rain fell. Dileo stayed, and the lawyers had the contracts. The instigators stayed; they were never around Elizabeth. Nobody was going to take a back seat to Elizabeth Taylor. She protected her kids. You never saw her children in the press or out there in the street. You only saw Elizabeth.

I had to raise my son, and I didn't wish to dump my kid on anyone. I wanted him to know his mother and not have the same childhood I had. When he got grown, I wanted to be with Michael and dance with him again.

Michael left and lived out of the United States for a few years. He came back a year before he died. Michael belonged to his fans. The people who made demands on him weren't his fans. Fans didn't care about his nose or skin color; they loved him unconditionally. Fans never see you as ugly, only as beautiful. That is what I learned from Michael—what real fans are and what true happiness is. Michael had his kids, was twice divorced, and had no more accusations. Michael worked for what he attained all his life; no one gave him anything.

They didn't give him fame. He wasn't born rich. He got that through his hard work. Singing was comfortable for him. Dancing and performing was work. He appeared on TV with the announcement of the This Is It tour.

When my kid became grown, I was happy. I wanted to contact Michael. We could dance together and be happy again like we were when we were young. The entertainer didn't look happy to me anymore. He loved his work, excitement, and happy people. He was like a sponge; he needed to be around upbeat people.

That wasn't the case. Instead, Michael was around people who were the opposite of him—individuals who had severe psychological problems. These people drained his energy and his will to fight. Michael said people come out when the sun is shining. When it rains, they disappear. He failed to realize that there are sunshine people and there are rain people who only love it when it rains.

He was a joyful person, a kid, and he wasn't equipped to deal with rain people and the dark shit that surrounded them. It affected him and the success that he worked hard to attain. I learned that some paths you are not supposed to explore. Be careful about who you allow into your inner circle. Don't bring the beast home with you or enter its cave. Energy is contagious; good and bad energy affect you.

When we get lost, we can't control our environment. Michael got lost when fate took control, which never ends well. When I was pregnant, I went to the Catholic church every night and had an exorcism to expel the profanity from my mouth and to control my dark side. I know from the teachings that if you commit suicide, you go to hell.

Being the religious person he was, he could have never taken a life, not even his own. As far as his death goes, Michael was psychic, and he knew he was going to be killed or die. Michael didn't know how, and I don't think he thought it would be from drugs. He did propofol a couple of times. Michael was a happy-go-lucky guy. The drug was a dangerous pleasure for him to indulge in or partake. It stopped his mind from going for a few hours.

He should have gone on a boat for a weekend and slept in the middle of the ocean. The salt water makes you go to bed, and you sleep soundly. Michael should have gone to the Himalayas with the Tibetan monks and meditated for peace. With the ice and snow, fresh air, and pure water from the mountains, not even Michael would have been able to stay awake.

There were so many options. Why did he feel trapped in a fishbowl? That energy was devouring him with the help of his surroundings. He figured nothing was going to happen to him. Murray is the doctor who was administrating the drug. Nobody wanted to kill Michael; he was their cash cow. They knew all his wealth was going to his family, and they wouldn't be able to control the money anymore. They were in heaven when Michael was alive.

Murray was getting paid $100,000 a month for doing nothing. They did whatever they wanted, no questions asked. When you're not able to sleep, you start acting stupid. Michael was going on tour to make more money for them. Murray should have known better. He was the adult and the professional.

That propofol has to be given in a hospital with staff on watch duty and machines that accommodate the patient. How stupid was this? Murray knew the risk and left Michael to make a phone call to his girlfriend. Michael was going into cardiac arrest while Murray was on the phone making a lunch date. It's a perfect example of the stupid people Michael had around him.

Michael didn't realize they were a detriment to themselves and sometimes to others around them. They can cause a catastrophe, and that is what they did in Michael's life and business. It was one catastrophe after another. He never used his power to take control or to take advantage of women. I know he could never benefit from a child. Michael wasn't a coldhearted, mean, onerous person with no conscience. He was afraid of karma; if he did something wrong to anyone, it was going to come back to him.

Michael did childish, erratic things for attention and for jokes. He was a good person with a good heart and beautiful thoughts. He wasn't a wolf in sheep's clothing; Michael was a sheep with the courage to perform and use the gift that God gave him. He was charming to work with and to be around. The fans were great while we were onstage. He couldn't control what went on off the stage. That was the bodyguards' job. It is a shame, because Michael loved to mingle and hang out with most of the fans—not all, because of the wild behavior of some fans. It made Michael afraid and more withdrawn. He felt like he was a prisoner of his success. Michael made the best of it. He was endlessly pleasant.

Being accused of being a child molester by two parents he was helping killed Michael spiritually. It hurt him terribly to know that when people looked at him, that thought was in the back of their minds. Her was stigmatized and had to go on TV and beg for the public's sympathy. That is the first time Michael pleaded with anyone for anything. Michael perpetually acted like a king. His enemies delighted in seeing his pride taken away and in seeing him groveling for mercy. I learned to go with what is winning in my life, or I will be brought to my knees trying to defend what's losing in my life. Being mobbed by fans is one thing; being included with fans is another Michael was involved with his original fans from the Apollo theater. He was a family member to us and not an insulated pop idol.

Two days after Michael's TV appearance, I heard he was dead. I was in shock, and I thought back to when we were kids. He loved the pinball and Fascination games at the penny arcade. He loved the Disney stories and Peter Pan.

The public and the entertainment industry couldn't believe a man with massive success never grew up—that all he wanted to do was play and create. Michael's female lovers were demanding; he couldn't meet the requirements and be a child too. I also learned I have a limitation on what I can and cannot do. Because other people do it, that doesn't mean I can do it with impunity. I regret that I was not there and that Michael said somebody was going to kill him. Katherine, his mother, revealed this after Michael's death on TV.

I could have hidden him in my house. If the fans knew his mental state and fears or premonitions, we could have protected Michael. I had seen Jermaine three times before Michael's death in Beverly Hills, Brentwood, and at the Grove in Los Angeles. It seemed like Jermaine was trying to tell me something. I asked him each time how Michael was doing.

"He's doing fine," Jermaine answered.

Maybe Jermaine was ashamed to tell me how bad off Michael was, or he felt he was breaking a confidence, or he thought it was none of my business. Jermaine swears he didn't know how sick Michael was; when he saw Michael, he looked well. Jermaine claims Michael looked sober to him when he saw him in the daytime. Nobody around Michael told him to go and rest. No one said, "I will take care of everything. Don't worry. Go to sleep. Clear your mind. Everything is going to be fine."

After Michael's passing, I became depressed for two years. I gained weight. I had a touch of high cholesterol. My doctor ordered me to lose weight.

Michael's death hit me hard. It was so senseless; the circumstances under which it happened were preventable. What's done in the dark eventually comes to light one way or another. Propofol was Michael's dangerous secret, not little boys. That made me realize I needed to chart a new course, as I had done when Michael and I were young. He went his way, and I went mine, knowing we would meet again. All paths lead to the same road if it's meant to be.

I believe the universe is going to bring us together again. I had a dream the day before he died, in the dream, I was reading my dream book, and it read dangerous pleasures. I woke up from the nightmare, and I thought, I don't do anything hazardous for fun. Later on that day, I heard Michael died. Two nights after his death, Michael came to me in a dream, clear as day.

"You didn't belong to me," he said.

"Yes, I did. You didn't know it," I replied.

I know I will see him on the other side. I learned I couldn't go back physically; I have to go back mentally and remember all that has passed. I started as a fan with twenty other girls, and we never mobbed him. We included Michael as a family. Michael relaxed around us. When Michael withdrew from the fans, he became secretive, insulated, and unhappy. Everyone around him was not a fan.

Michael died with a broken heart, betrayed by people he loved and trusted. What was painful for Michael was that they were the people he tried to help the most. The people who were the least threatening—they were wolves in sheep's clothes. Mr. Jackson would have included the fans in Michael's life, and Michael still would be alive.

Mr. Jackson was aware of the enablers and the saboteurs who hung around Michael. Those were the troublemakers. For a top entertainer, everything comes through the manager and business manager/publicist. Sex, drugs, and rock 'n' roll. The rock stars' managers kept their business intact because the successful rock star stayed on top of their manager and took responsibility for their business.

I have been approached by agents to turn my residual checks over to them, and they'd pay me my money. No way, Jose. I will pay you with my money. You don't pay me with my own money. Once you turn all your money over to someone else, you have to trust that person. If someone runs away with your money or keeps it, there is nothing you can do because you gave it to that person. I will take responsibility for my wealth and write my checks.

One thing I can say about Mr. Jackson is that he never stole any money from Michael. He made sure Michael received every penny of his money. When Neverland became Michael's abode, instead of it being seen as a play land, adults assumed it to be a land of torture and pornography for kids. The worst thing Michael did was becoming too personally involved. Making appearances at Neverland was OK; he needed a private residence somewhere else.

That is the best thing for someone of his caliber. Also, he needed an island where he could escape and relax. You can take the boy out of the country, but you can't take the country out of the kid. You can look back in your mind once you reach a certain level of success. No matter how passionately you yearn for the past, you can't go back. You have to make accommodations for the present and future position.

Even if Michael had to have his bodyguards there with him and his fans, once or twice a month, he could have had a selection of fans spend time with him. Or he could have gotten on Twitter and Facebook to send out a love message. He couldn't talk individually to everyone; he'd be there all day. Michael could have drawn positive energy from that. I'd rather see Michael alive and the fans helping him to heal than to see him dead. I started with the fans, and I've come full circle. I am right back to the fans. Right after Michael's death.

I believe it wasn't Michael's destiny to die so soon. It was fate that killed him. The people, places, and things that surrounded him were all too convenient. Once you become passive with destiny, it devours you. He needed Mr. Jackson to block all that drama and enmity that was in his life. I also think he should have done a movie—*This Is It*—not the rehearsal, the actual show, instead of doing fifty shows. Although they were spaced out, the pressure on Michael, who hadn't performed in twelve years, was enormous.

Michael should have traveled around the world and promoted the film. The fans desired him to put material out on the market. Michael should have been in practice for six months to a year before the show, slowly building up his immune system and getting into the groove, flying away on weekends, relaxing, and pampering himself. With the kind of money and stardom he had, the sky had no limits.

His anxiety came from his environment and from being cooped up. Michael had time on his hands; he was worrying and felt unable to trust anyone. Eight weeks was too short a time to prepare for fifty shows. That in itself was enough to cause paranoia. You have the whole world waiting to see what you are going to do.

I had an epiphany; this is my second theory of what went wrong with Michael and his life. It's an ethereal, spiritual approach. I know it's far-fetched; I believe nothing is impossible.

"It is your responsibility to get your sleep," I have heard many employers say. What if there is an entity that is channeling through you and keeping you awake?

Michael was committed to this energy or thing. It drove him to be the biggest entertainer in history. He directed the energy, and it didn't let him sleep. Michael did whatever he could to find rest, however in spite of everything he had done, it eluded him. Sleep is priceless. It is our life force and regenerates us. Every living thing on this planet has to sleep. How Michael lost control of this energy, I don't know.

The entity could operate outside of Michael's body; it was always in his realm: the more people around, the more energy it found to feed on and fill its appetite. It was insatiable. When Michael didn't perform for twelve years, it devoured him. When the This Is It tour rehearsals started, Michael had to get a good night's sleep. The entity killed Michael, and it destroyed Murray also. When Michael finally found a medication that could knock him out the entity rather see him dead than get a good nights sleep. This energy that surrounded Michael was intelligent; it drew you in like a powerful giant horse-shoe magnet, and it put you in a stupor. It energized you so it could feed on you.

Maybe that is why everyone around him couldn't control this energy; the adults wanted to bring Michael down because the power robbed them of their will and sleep. Nobody was sleeping they all were wired; a lack of sleep affects adults in negative ways.

Michael didn't wish to perform after the age of fifty years, nor did he desire to be in Las Vegas doing a show every night.

"I don't want to be like James Brown, still performing after fifty," Michael kept saying. He did not wish to do the This Is It tour. He doubted his energy. Financial problems forced him to take this job.

When I was with Michael, I had to get away to sleep. The entity electrified me. I was so happy, in bliss, and couldn't sleep for six months. When I went home, I slept lightly, still charged with the energy I didn't have. It was like being in a twilight sleep; you are not sleeping. Your body doesn't regenerate, and you are on borrowed energy. If I don't sleep, I am going to die. I was sure Murray hadn't slept since he started working for Michael. He made mistakes. That's what happens when you don't rest. Murray wanted him to sleep. Michael was terrified of intimacy and getting old. This entity picked the perfect candidate in Michael.

The entity wasn't sexual. Michael never took advantage of anyone, even though the object took your will away from you when you were around Michael. He comforted fans, as you can see on YouTube.

I was with him. I know what I felt. The entity didn't like children because children went to sleep, and it couldn't keep them awake. Also, it couldn't feed off children thoroughly—maybe because they were still growing and their bodies were using their energy to grow and develop.

That is why it stirred up all the trouble between Michael and the kids. When the kids were at Neverland, and they slept in Michael's room or bed, the entity could not feed on him. Something with the kids were blocking the entity or leaving it unsatisfied. It liked adults because it could keep them awake.

Also, kids relaxed him, because they weren't irritable or evil from a lack of sleep. The invisible force got rid of the kids and anyone who wanted Michael to sleep. His first wife, Lisa Marie, suggested that Michael rested when she was with him, and his second wife, Debbie Rowe, was an anesthesiologist and could put him to sleep. The entity got rid of them both. Michael's death from sleep deprivation eventually would have happened. How long can the human body go without sleep? Insomnia affects one person; when it affects everyone around you, something is wrong.

The hospitals refused to take Michael in for a weekend and give him propofol. I viewed a picture of Michael before he died, totally drained. I had to take a second look, and I asked, "Is that Michael?" One of his fans said, "Yes, that's Michael." It seemed like the energy had entrapped him.

He didn't have the will to bail out or postpone the tour. I was trying to make sense out of a man who never hurt anyone—who grew up as an innocent soul. As a child, Michael went to sleep, and his brothers surrounded him. As an adult, he tried to induce sleep with drugs or alcohol; eventually, he was going to overdose, and that was only a quick fix. The bigger star you are, the more you need several safe houses to wind down, to be spiritually centered and at peace with oneself. Michael was at peace. It wasn't his conscience keeping him awake. I've been around many successful entertainers, and I have never felt that energy. That is what made me think long and hard about the answer.

If I work and build up a marketable name, it becomes a machine. Supply meets demand. I'm a human being, not a machine, and I'm never going to forget that. I will not let any entity take control of me. My conclusion is that anything that takes away your will or robs you of sleep is evil. The machine will go on long after I am dead.

While I'm here, sleep, pure water, and fresh air are the fountain of life. I have to take care of myself first before I can take care of everyone else. I devoted a Facebook page to Michael and invited his fans. They helped me get through the depression. His fans keep Michael and the energy alive. They send me beautiful clips of Michael and his music. I know they love him, and I thank them and appreciate them.

CHAPTER 27

Rejuvenating My
Life and Beauty

IN THE 1970S, DIANA VREELAND gave me the most valuable advice. We were at Joe Eula's party. Berry Berenson and I were talking to her. She said, "Drugs are dangerous. They take over, and drugs become the star. Drugs are no good; don't do drugs." Berry looked in my face as I was listening to the advice Diana was giving me. At the time, I didn't take it to heart. I didn't know the effects of drugs.

Diana Vreeland knew. She was around sixty years old, and she had seen what drugs do to a person of success and those who seek success in all aspects of life. While Michael had disappeared into success for those years, my life wasn't smooth sailing. I was living out of a suitcase during most of the seventies, jet-setting from one country to another.

During the eighties, I was on the battlefield of life; it wasn't like the old days. Everyone was dropping dead and fast from AIDS. It seemed like they contracted the disease, and in a few months, they were dead. I became pregnant, my last fling at freedom. Andy Warhol invited me to parties, and for seven months I went out every night. Andy Warhol gave me a hundred dollars every time he'd see me—which was a lot of occasions. Andy surprised me by being such a gentleman with me when I was pregnant. He would pull the chair out for me and order milk.

I didn't notice it at the time. I was used to men being men when you are a lady. Michael was a man and a gentleman. He was like Andy; you had to be a woman to see that. I showed my dark side to protect myself in an attack. Other than that, I acted like the utmost lady with Andy and Michael. The parties were perfume promotions or book promotion parties. They had a gift bag they gave to the guest, as well as the best food and drink, although I didn't drink any liquor or smoke while I was pregnant. Palmer's Cocoa Butter was a lifesaver to my stomach to prevent stretch marks.

Also, I took a lot of showers rather than warm oil baths. Then I'd moisturize with body butter and slide into bed. In New York, the apartment or house is dry; you get steam heat. You have to keep the face and body moisturized in the summer. It was humid, and hot/cool showers and baths with oils were good. The heat dries the skin and causes wrinkles.

Also, I drank lots of water and prune juice to clean out my system. I ate a lot of salads when I was pregnant. I didn't eat that much meat, and so by the seventh month, I was low on iron in my blood. The doctor put me on large, green iron pills that were almost as large as gum balls. I could wear some of my Stephen Burrows clothes that were loose. Maternity clothes were not for me; I had other dresses that fit. I wasn't that huge. I didn't blow up until the eighth month. That was in September, which wasn't that revealing. By then, I had a coat on, but because of my pregnant stomach, I couldn't fasten it. I had stopped going out.

I conceived in February. I had been going out nonstop. In March I was having lunch with Andy at the factory. My stomach blew up after I ate, and then it went back down. I didn't know I was pregnant.

I thought it was gas because I still had my menstruation. I was telling Andy, and he said, "That's funny. Jane Forth said the same thing. She had the same symptoms as you."

What a coincidence that two women close to him had the same type of pregnancy. Both of our babies were born in November. Scorpio boys. After I had the baby, I brought him to the factory for Andy to see him. Andy gave me some money. Then I ran into Andy in the winter on the street, and I let him hold my baby. Andy looked at him, and he gave me some money again.

"Your mother is crazy," Andy said, looking at my son.

I didn't say anything, and he gave me the baby back. I thanked him for the money and went to the bank. My bank is in downtown Manhattan. My baby and I visited the bank every day to get out of the house.

I ran into Andy walking the street several times. He was going to see advertisers promoting his business. Before I met Andy, I used to see him walking the streets downtown around Halston's store. I knew nothing about the art world. On Madison Avenue, men dressed in sophisticated business attire. I laughed to myself when I caught sight of Andy. He'd be walking on the other side of the street going about his business, and he stood out. He looked weird. I guess Michael looked funny to the public when he changed his look.

I had seen a lot of people on the street, and I never knew who would be in my destiny or what bonds I would form. My motto is to be kind to everyone, because you don't know who is going to come to your rescue. I met up with several other men from my past, and they saw me with my baby and said the same thing to my child: "Your mother is crazy." I put it all together and realized that these men had seen the devotion in my eyes for my baby and were jealous. I couldn't hang in the streets with them anymore; I was a mother now.

Elsa helped me, and then Andy died. It was sudden and a shock. Elsa was living in another country, and circumstances forced me to go it alone. I was glad, because it made me strong and independent. I wanted the respect of my child. I didn't want my child to be at the mercy of anyone like I was when growing up. I had to raise my child; nothing was going to get in the way of that.

It was a struggle and sometimes painful. I made up my mind to live with the pain. Being given superhuman energy, I thank the gods for allowing me to make it on my own. I wanted my child to say, "My mom was a good mom. She didn't dump me on someone else; she dealt with the responsibilities of being a mom. She met all problems head-on, and there were problems." It is a big responsibility being a parent.

I had a natural childbirth, no painkillers, and they say that makes a woman strong. I became a woman; I wasn't going to let anyone bring me down or destroy me. When you have a child, you have to learn to love yourself—if not for you, for the child's sake. The mother or father is God to a child or the closest thing the child is going to get to a god.

Even though I looked young, I acted like a little girl to be in a younger working group, because there was this age discrimination going on. They were hiring younger-looking women. When I was in my thirties and forties, everyone thought I was in my twenties. When I was in my forties, all my jobs were for twenty-year-olds. It was like I was an alien. I blended in with the younger crowd, like a foreigner. I looked like them, but at the same time, I wasn't one of them.

The younger group of girls was convinced I was their age. They wanted me to hang out with them after the film or job working hours. I didn't do it because I knew once I started talking about my past, that would give away my age. I'd be in a bar talking to a young guy and pouring out all my memories. Then he would realize I was twenty years older than he.

At twenty-eight, I stopped going out in the sun—lying in it and walking in it without being covered up. I noticed my skin getting sensitive to the sun. I had been in the sun all my life. Now the ozone layer was thinning, and ultraviolet rays were causing cancer. A lifeguard friend of mine got skin cancer on her thigh. She told me a spider bit her, and she had to go to the hospitable to get it cut out. I knew she was lying to me; it was cancer.

At the time, cancer had a stigma of AIDS. My life guard friend was the one who told me that her friend worked in a clinic and diagnosed a famous fashion designer with AIDS. That was after Perry Ellis and Willi Smith died. She said it was Halston, swearing to keep it a secret, knowing her friend could get fired for leaking confidential information.

Halston didn't want anybody to know until he was ready to reveal it. A wave of death swept through the fashion community. Gossipers were calling me from all over with information or telling me top secret info. I didn't ask. I kept a lot of confidences; people liked to vent to me or tell me what they found out or heard. They couldn't wait to call me and spread the news about Michael. It sounded like gossip and drama; that is how I know drama and gossip can kill you. I got it out of my life. It ages and stresses you out. Michael was in the news a lot; with his groundbreaking videos, the eighties were magnificent for him.

That is when Michael started changing his face. When he and I were in New York, I wore the red and black lipstick and jet-black, wavy hair. He loved the look, and when he went back to Los Angeles, he started implementing that look. Meanwhile, on the East Coast, I went to bed early and drank fresh water. I got interested in herbs and their healing.

One of my martial arts associates was a black belt in karate. He gave me some pure ginseng. It was like a drug; it made me alert and explorative. I discovered that pure ginseng is like a natural high. Painkillers and narcotics are so powerful today; if you take the drug or pill one time, you can die. I was in emotional and physical pain. I decided I was not going to let my pain destroy me. I was going to live with my pain.

I cleaned my face and body thoroughly with enemas and douches. When winter came, and it was fifteen below, I'd walk ten blocks and back. I'd take a shower to get the dirt off my body and then a hot oil bath. That ice air with the wind chill factor made it feel like ten below. The apartments were dry, with steam heat, and I had a humidifier. My baby was breaking out in bumps from the heat and couldn't breathe well. The humidifier makes the skin smoother, opens up the nasal cavity, and moisturizes the skin. Also, I used a face mask. Queen Helene face mask mud and mint julep is the best for me.

I used all of Queen Helene's products to fight wrinkles and sagging skin. For malar bags, I used Vicks VapoRub and put my face under steam or placed a hot washcloth on my face. Malar bags are the bags below your cheeks. Fluid from the sinuses collect in a bag under your eye, right over your cheekbones. The VapoRub will make your eyes watery. For bags under my eyes, I used Preparation H. I never slept with it, because there was a chance it would get into my eyes. That can cause blindness.

Make sure if you take hot oil baths that your heart is healthy, because you can have a heart attack from hot oil baths or Jacuzzis. In a Jacuzzi, the water is moving in a whirlpool circulation. In a hot oil bath, the water is still, and the heat climbs through the body. Make sure you can take the heat. If you can't, it's better to be safe than sorry.

I went swimming at the YWCA every day when my child became six years of age. Aquatic sports are easier on the muscles; it's good for old and young people and animals to exercise. Since the chlorine or salt water dries the skin and hair, extra moisturizing is important.

I also didn't drink alcohol for ten years, nor did I smoke cigarettes. I stopped smoking at twenty-eight—also no drugs. Drugs will age you and control your mood and take the vitamins out of your brain. If you take one drink and follow it with equal amounts of water, you are safe. Alcohol closes the blood vessels and dries the skin, so it causes wrinkles. Too much alcohol makes your features puffy, and your face begins to lose its shape. It has the same effect as sodium.

At twenty-eight, I was considered old. Brooke Shields was doing Calvin Klein ads and was with Michael. Years later, Michael said Brooke initiated their relationship and was the aggressor. She pursued him. Now I know why he brought Emmanuel Lewis on their date.

That started the rumor where everyone was saying Michael liked little boys. Why did he bring Emmanuel Lewis on a date with Brooke? That is when Michael should have stood up and said why: to keep a romance from happening between him and Brooke, who was only a good friend. The country was going bongos for young girls—young girls in tight jeans—and if you didn't fit into that mold, you didn't get hired. It seemed to be a crime to grow old. Michael even spoke about the fear of getting old and wrinkled, and he didn't want that to happen to him.

I wondered what the country was coming to, with America sweeping the old and the very young under the rug. The mothers' boyfriends were the ones abusing the child. Michael wanted to model his life after Peter Pan, and he never found his Wendy. Fans were modeling their life after Elvis or Scarface.

They persecuted Michael, an innocent man who wanted to be a child again. This abuse was sweeping across the country, and they wanted to make an example out of Michael. The authorities wanted to use him as a scapegoat. Enablers were telling him he was invincible, that he could project any image he wanted. Michael's album, later on, was titled *Invincible*. I protected my child from my boyfriends. I wasn't married to any of them, and I never slept with any of them in front of my son. I didn't believe in living together unless I was married. That was the sign of the times.

It was in the news every week that some child was molested or beaten to death by the mother's boyfriend. I didn't want to get married until my son was grown and could protect himself. That was my responsibility: to protect my child. I was happy to see Michael had his kids. He was an excellent father, and the accusations seemed to stop. The damage already had been done, and even though it hurt Michael spiritually, he became devoted to his kids.

We were similar parents. My child-rearing years were happy for me, a cleansing mentally and emotionally. I had to juggle my career and motherhood, and that is a challenge. God takes care of all fools and babies. When you don't misdirect your energy and focus on something, it will happen—be careful what you wish for, because it will come true. It's what comes along with your wish that you aren't prepared for or don't expect. I looked young, so I didn't get the respect of someone who had been around the block a couple of times. As I continued to expand my knowledge, people started saying to me, "You should start your own business."

When you hear several voices saying the same thing, listen. If you want to stay young, moisturize, eat, sleep well, and control the stress in your life. Stay out of the sun, take vitamins, and lower your sodium intake. Sodium puffs the skin, and then when it goes down, it causes wrinkles. I drink lots of water to keep my body hydrated. Whatever beverage I drink, I follow it with an equal glass of water. A thirty-two-ounce bottle of alkaline water ensures me that I'm getting hydrated. I still dance and keep active.

Being confident and busy when you're over fifty is very important. The worst thing to do is become inactive and not take care of yourself. Your legs are the first things that collapse, from the hips to your toes. Sitting, standing, or lying down for an extended period are not healthy for circulation. Change up your body positions. Have a different exercise every day.

Taking care of yourself is work. I accept that I will get old. My greatest fear is being homeless, alone, sick, and losing control of my body functions. I have a love for being healthy, ambitious, energetic, happy, creative, enthusiastic, positive, productive, spiritually and materially wealthy, creative, and for spreading joy and enlightenment. We all get tired and die, but until my day comes, I'm living in the now.

I have goals and things I have to do. I started my own business, using my ideas to create Agent Zero Productions LLC. Why didn't I do it sooner? I didn't have the ideas. In 1987, I got my visions. Some of my associates attained their success fast or over an extended period of time. They were right to start and achieve success when they did. In my case, time is on my side. As I look back, I see that for several people, if they didn't start when they did, they could have never made it. They had a small window in time. Their ship came in, and they had to get on it to fulfill their destiny.

Now it was truly my turn; everybody gets a turn. I attained my degree and education. Along with my psychic voice, I have the answers I didn't have before. I have an ailment. I do suffer from vertigo, due to a blood vessel pressing against my eardrum, and bright lights trigger this illness. I have been able to keep it under control.

I acquired vertigo from working around the clock, being stressed out, and not taking care of myself. If you've been taking care of yourself and you stop, you get sick. It was time for me to contribute to the world. I owe the world my talents; the world doesn't owe me. Everyone born into this world has a destiny and fate. There is a conflict between fate versus life. Everybody has a purpose, whether that person is a leader or follower—whether it's big or small.

The world is a stage, and everyone has a part to play: some good and some bad. We have choices and free will, and our choices determine our path. Everyone has conflict in life between two elements: career versus marriage, home, family, and friends, or perhaps family versus friends or marriage. It also could be love affairs versus shared resources and marriage.

Between the two conflicts, one of them wins, and that is how you know what your destiny is. A Catholic priest told me I have to look at my past and present to see my future. Whatever is conflicting in your past and present, look at what wins in the battle. That is how you can tell your future. I came out to Hollywood to be an actress. My teacher said it would take superhuman strength to be an actress. I enrolled in film school, and I graduated with my degree in cinema production.

Now I am a producer, director, writer, actor, and filmmaker. I wanted to know everything about film. It was a call to a destiny that beckoned me on. The gods have poured new life into me, and I am on my destiny ship, sailing across the sea of my life, and the stars are still shining.

They are my guiding light, leading me to new and exciting adventures. I'm looking forward to tomorrow. I will never forget yesterday. Those were the days, my friend. As time marched on, I realized nothing lasts forever, so I am going to enjoy every moment while I can. I discovered there is no freedom, only periods of rest. Whatever space you occupy over a period or you are comfortable with, you are held captive by that space, even if you are a drifter who goes from town to town, never able to settle down. If you run and hide in the hills, you are still not free. I didn't wish to come to terms with my life and get on my destiny ship.

I wanted to be free. I realized my actual life would always loom over me as if something were missing. I can run the other way, but there is no escape from life. I've learned that no matter where I run, I'm not free. I'm held captive by the space or responsibility that I am in, no matter how small it may be. I've come to terms with my life and destiny. I was never free of it; I have been resting and preparing. Now I know that once I get on my future ship, there is no getting off or turning back.

Before you get on your destiny ship, life is about doors opening and closing. There are cycles you can jump in and out of or see through to the end. It takes great courage to get on your destiny ship. Any fool can have power; greatness is unattainable for those who can't reach high and attain it. We all are born to live our best lives; for some of us, the effort is easier than others. I've accepted the fact that everyone who is born into the world makes an effort for something. No matter how small or large, it may be that is what makes us human. Every individual has a cross to bear. Power is addictive, and it doesn't discriminate.

If you misuse it, power will turn on you, and no one can save you from its retribution. In law, there is a motto about coming to the table with clean hands. If you have dirty hands, sooner or later you are going to get caught. The universe builds a case against you, and it's keeping track of those deeds for which you have to repent. The world gives some people more time than others to repent. Others are forced to repent after they have done the evil, whether spiritual or physical.

You are responsible for the energy you bring into the room. My objective in life is to stay on the HILL, which stands for Honorable, Impeccable, Legitimate, and Loyal. I was putting my dreams into action. What you put out, you get back. Fame is used to help people, whether it's selling a product and giving people work or bringing awareness to charities. It is not a self-serving life; it is a learning process and the opposite of a selfish life.

ABOUT THE AUTHOR

AMINA WARSUMA HAS BEEN A creative writer for many years. She started writing interviews for Andy Warhol's *Interview* magazine and the *Huffington Post* style blog. A former international top fashion model for ten years, she's lived all over the world and has been photographed for *Vogue, Harper's Bazaar,* and many other magazines. You can view photos of her on her website:

http://ablackmodelinparis.com/.
http://mediap5io.onlineview.it/FullScreenSlideShow.aspx?
gallery=4792093&mt=Photo

Amina graduated with an Associate degree in business from Monroe College in the Bronx, New York, her hometown. She graduated from Los Angeles City College, where she studied film, cinema production, and producing. Follow her on Twitter: https://twitter.com/aminawarsuma. She and her family now live in Los Angeles.

My Stars Are Still Shining
A Memoir
by
Amina Warsuma

I have felt throughout my life that people were my greatest asset as they suddenly appeared and disappeared in my life. I have wondered for years why I came in contact with wonderful and not-so-wonderful people. As I reflect back, there is a lesson I learned from each significant encounter and involvement. I've had four types of people in my life: the bully, the irresponsible freedom lover, the hypocrite, and the strong authority figure. One chapter closes, and another one opens in my life. Some things had a recurring theme, and I had to use my experience to deal with these repeating elements.

One thing that remained constant in my life was the authority figures, who taught me valuable lessons and inspired me. In this memoir, I write about my experience with the Five Stairsteps, the Delfonics, Michael Jackson, Andy Warhol, Truman Capote, Halston, Elsa Peretti, Calvin Klein, Stephen Burrows, Joe Eula, Maning Obregon, Antonio Lopez, Juan Ramos, Karl Lagerfeld, Diana Vreeland, Joel Schumacher, Giorgio di Sant' Angelo, Francesco Scavullo, Bill King, Charles Tracy, Liza Minnelli, Elizabeth Taylor, Josephine Baker, and much more.

Made in the USA
Middletown, DE
12 March 2020